D1098924

The Dynamics of Devolution

ALSO OF INTEREST FROM IMPRINT ACADEMIC

Robert Hazell (ed.), *The State and The Nations:*
The First Year of Devolution in the United Kingdom
ISBN 0907845800

Alan Trench (ed.), *The State of The Nations 2001:*
The Second Year of Devolution in the United Kingdom
ISBN 0907845193

Robert Hazell (ed.), *The State of The Nations 2003:*
The Third Year of Devolution in the United Kingdom
ISBN 0907845495

Alan Trench (ed.), *Has Devolution Made a Difference?*
The State of The Nations 2004
ISBN 0907845878

TOCs, reviews and sample chapters:

imprint-academic.com/state

The Dynamics of Devolution:
The State of the Nations
2005

Edited by Alan Trench

imprint-academic.com

Published in the UK by Imprint Academic
PO Box 200, Exeter EX5 5YX, UK

Published in the USA by Imprint Academic
Philosophy Documentation Center
PO Box 7147, Charlottesville, VA 22906-7147, USA

ISBN 1 84540 036 4

British Library Cataloguing in Publication Data
A catalogue record for this book is available from the
British Library and the US Library of Congress

Contents

PART II: UK-WIDE ISSUES

PART III: PUBLIC POLICY

List of Contributors

John Adams is Director of Research at IPPR North, the Newcastle office of the Institute for Public Policy Research. He was responsible for setting up and then launching ippr north in January 2004. Previously, John was a Special Adviser at the Welsh Office during the 1997 devolution referendum.

David Bell is Professor of Economics at the University of Stirling and co-director of the Scottish Economic Policy Network. He has carried out research as part of the Leverhulme Trust's programme on 'Nations and Regions: the dynamics of devolution', on the Barnett formula and was recently a member of the Care Development Group enquiry into Long-Term Care of the Elderly in Scotland.

Alex Christie is a research fellow with the Centre for Public Policy for Regions and the Fraser of Allander Institute at the University of Strathclyde. His research interests lie in the field of public finance and multi-level governance. He has written on the nature and future of the Scottish budget process and the future of territorial funding in the UK.

John Curtice is Deputy Director of the Centre for Research into Elections and Social Trends, and Professor of Politics at the University of Strathclyde. He has undertaken a particular interest in recent years in the impact of devolution on public opinion across the United Kingdom, most recently co-editing *Devolution – Scottish Answers to Scottish Questions?* (Edinburgh: Edinburgh University Press, 2003).

Scott Greer is Lecturer in Public Policy at the School of Public Policy, University College London, and was formerly Research Fellow at the Constitution Unit. He takes up a position in the School of Public Health at the University of Michigan, Ann Arbor, in 2005. His book *Territorial Politics and Health Policy: UK health policy in comparative perspective* was published by Manchester University Press in 2004.

Peter Hetherington is Regional Affairs Editor of *The Guardian* and a visiting professor at the Centre for Urban and Regional Development Studies.

Charlie Jeffery is Professor of Politics in the School of Social and Political Studies at the University of Edinburgh and Director of the Economic and Social Research Council's research programme on Devolution and Constitutional Change.

James Mitchell is Professor of Politics at Strathclyde University and headed the Scottish Devolution Monitoring team between 2001 and 2005. He is the author of numerous books and articles on Scottish and UK politics and devolution, most recently *Governing Scotland: The invention of administrative devolution* published by Palgrave in 2003.

John Osmond is Director of the Institute of Welsh Affairs, and has written widely on Welsh culture and politics. Recent edited volumes include *Second Term Challenge: Can the Welsh Assembly Government Hold its Course?* and *Welsh Politics Comes of Age: Responses to the Richard Commission,* published by the IWA in 2003 and 2005 respectively. A former journalist and television producer, he is a Fellow of the University of Wales Institute, Cardiff, and a Honorary Senior Research Fellow at the Constitution Unit, University College, London.

Peter Robinson has been Senior Economist at the ippr since October 1997. He leads the ippr teams dealing with economic and employment policy and public service reform. He is also a Research Associate at the Centre for Economic Performance at the LSE.

Mark Sandford is a Research Fellow at the Constitution Unit, University College London. He leads the Unit's research on regional government, and was co-author of the report *Unexplored Territory: Elected Regional Assemblies in England.* He has also researched aspects of strategy-making and civic engagement in the English regions and led a substantial project examining scrutiny processes at all levels of government. He is a sociologist by training, with a BSc from the University of Bristol and an MA from Goldsmiths College.

Alan Trench was a Senior Research Fellow at the Constitution Unit between 2001 and 2005, working on devolution and intergovernmental relations in the United Kingdom and comparative intergovernmental relations in federal systems. He remains an honorary Senior Research Fellow there. A solicitor by profession, he was specialist adviser to the House of Lords Select Committee on the Constitution for their inquiry into *Devolution: Inter-Institutional Relations in the United Kingdom* in 2001-03.

Rick Wilford is Professor of Politics at Queen's University, Belfast and co-leader with Robin Wilson of the Northern Ireland monitoring project team. He is the author of numerous articles and books on Northern Ireland politics and devolution.

Robin Wilson has been director of the think tank Democratic Dialogue since its foundation in 1995. Along with Prof. Rick Wilford of Queen's University, he is co-leader of the Northern Ireland team in the devolution monitoring project co-ordinated by the Constitution Unit, of which they are both honorary senior research fellows. He is a member of the board of the Institute of Governance at Queen's University and of the advisory council of the Dublin-based think tank TASC. He chairs the policy committee of the Northern Ireland Community Relations Council and is an adviser to the Council of Europe project on intercultural dialogue and conflict prevention.

Acronyms and Abbreviations

AM	Assembly Member [National Assembly for Wales]
BIC	British Irish Council
CoR	(EU) Committee of the Regions
DEFRA	Department for the Environment, Rural Affairs and Agriculture
DEL	Delegated Expenditure Limit (of a government department or devolved administration)
DfES	Department for Education and Skills
DG	Directorate-General (of the European Commission)
DH	UK Department of Health
DTLR	Department for Transport, Local Government and the Regions
DUP	Democratic Unionist Party
ECJ	European Court of Justice
ELWa	Education and Learning Wales
FCO	Foreign and Commonwealth Office
FEDS	Framework for Economic Development in Scotland
GLA	Greater London Assembly
IGR	Intergovernmental Relations
IMC	Independent Monitoring Commission
IRA	Irish Republican Army
MLA	Member of the Legislative Assembly [for Northern Ireland]
MP	Member of Parliament [Westminster]
MSP	Member of the Scottish Parliament
NESNO	North-East Says No campaign
NHS	National Health Service
NIO	Northern Ireland Office
NORPEC	Network of Regional Parliamentary European Committees
ODPM	Office of the Deputy Prime Minister
OMC	Open Method of Coordination
PUP	Popular Unionist Party

RAE	Research Assessment Exercise
RDA	Regional Development Agency
RED	Regional Emphasis Document
RSS	Regional Spatial Strategy
SDLP	Social Democratic and Labour Party
SF	Sinn Féin
SNP	Scottish National Party
SRA	Strategic Rail Authority
SSC	Sector Skills Council
SSDA	Sector Skills Development Agency
STV	Single Transferable Vote electoral system
TfL	Transport for London
UKRep	United Kingdom Permanent Representation to the European Union
UUP	Ulster Unionist Party
WAG	Welsh Assembly Government
WDA	Welsh Development Agency
WJEC	Welsh Joint Education Committee
WTD	European Working Time Directive

List of Figures and Tables

Chapter 8
FINANCE: PAYING THE PIPER, CALLING THE TUNE?

Chapter 9
DEVOLUTION AND THE EUROPEAN UNION:
TRAJECTORIES AND FUTURES

Chapter 11
REGIONAL ECONOMIC POLICIES IN A DEVOLVED UNITED KINGDOM

Chapter 12
CONCLUSION: THE FUTURE OF DEVOLUTION

Foreword

Robert Hazell

This is the fifth and final volume in the *State of the Nations* series, which began in 2000 with *The State and the Nations: The First Year of Devolution in the UK*. Since then we have produced each year a book summarising and reviewing the progress of devolution, and drawing on the fruits of a major five year research programme into the Dynamics of Devolution, funded by the Leverhulme Trust. The programme has linked the Constitution Unit with 25 research partners from 12 universities across the UK. It has been extraordinarily productive, with 11 books published or in preparation at the time of writing, as well as numerous journal articles and several Constitution Unit Briefings.

The backbone of the programme has been a series of quarterly monitoring reports written by teams of experts in Scotland, Wales, Northern Ireland and the English regions. The leaders of those teams each year have been the authors of the first part of the book, synthesising the reports compiled by their teams and highlighting the main devolution developments in their part of the UK. We should like in particular to thank them and all the members of their monitoring teams. In Scotland the team leader is James Mitchell, with David Bell, John Curtice, Neil McGarvey, Philip Schlesinger, Mark Shephard, Barry Winetrobe and Alex Wright. In Wales, John Osmond has led a team of Sarah Beasley, Alys Thomas, Gerald Taylor, Mark Lang, Denis Balsom, Suzanne Grazier and Jessica Mugaseth (and in previous years, Jane Jones, Adrian Kay, Martin Laffin and Nia Richardson). In Northern Ireland, Robin Wilson and Rick Wilford's team has been John Coakley, Lizanne Dowds, Greg McLaughlin, Elizabeth Meehan and Duncan Morrow (and in previous years Paul Gorecki, Aidan Gough and Michael Brennan). For the English regions, John Tomaney and Peter Hetherington have been supported by Emma Pinkney and Lynne Humphrey. And in a fifth series of reports on Devolution and the Centre, the Constitution Unit has chronicled the impact of devolution on Whitehall and Westminster in a series of reports written by Roger Masterman, Guy Lodge and Akash Paun, with support from Oonagh Gay, Meg Russell and Alan Trench.

The monitoring reports provide a unique contemporary record of the first five years of devolution. They comprise 96 reports and run to around 5000 pages. The quarterly reports can be viewed on the Constitution Unit's website (www.ucl.ac.uk/constitution-unit) on the Nations and Regions pages. They will shortly be available on CD-ROM. We hope to continue the monitoring programme for a further three years if sufficient funding can be made available by government departments and the ESRC.

From the start we have tried to record each year the main differences in public policy which result from devolution, and in 2003 and 2004 we included specific chapters by Scott Greer, Rachel Simeon and Helen Fawcett analysing the growing divergence in public policy. Each year we have also included a chapter by John Curtice recording the main changes in public attitudes to devolution and its consequences. The final chapter has always looked ahead, anticipating future developments, and this year the whole book is devoted to forecasting how devolution might evolve in the future.

Production of these books has involved a major team effort. Special thanks go to Alan Trench, who has edited three out of the five books in the series, and to Keith Sutherland and Sandra Good at Imprint Academic, who each year publish the books in record time. The Leverhulme Trust have supported our work throughout with their usual helpfulness and calm: our thanks there go to Barry Supple, Sir Richard Brook, Alison Cooper and Tony Clinch, and to their advisers Lord (Kenneth) Morgan and Professor Vernon Bogdanor. Charlie Jeffery has been a contributor, and as Director of the ESRC's Devolution research programme he has been a strong supporter of the monitoring reports and of the State of the Nations book series, together with that programme's research partners. Lastly I should thank all my colleagues in the Constitution Unit, most of whom have been involved in the production of these books over the years. Oonagh Gay, Scott Greer, Guy Lodge, Roger Masterman, Akash Paun, Mark Sandford, Meg Russell and Alan Trench have all written chapters, and we have been strongly supported by our administrators Rebecca Blackwell, Helen Daines, Matthew Butt and Gareth Lewes. To them and to all our partners and contributors in this enterprise, many, many thanks.

Robert Hazell
June 2005

Director, The Constitution Unit
School of Public Policy
University College London

Acknowledgements

As Robert Hazell notes in the preface, the production of each volume in the State of the Nations series has been a large team effort. For their help in producing this volume, I am grateful to the contributors and Robert Hazell, who have supported and cooperated with me hugely throughout the process. Particular thanks go to James Mitchell for facilitating a very useful meeting of the contributors at the University of Strathclyde. I am also grateful to past and present administrators at the Constitution Unit, especially Matthew Butt, Helen Daines, Iyan Adewuya and Hayden Thomas, for their help in making the arrangements that have led to the book run smoothly. Most of all, however, I am grateful to the three people who have made production of the book possible in practical terms: Keith Sutherland and Sandra Good at Imprint Academic, whose professional skill and speed continue to astound, and particularly Akash Paun at the Constitution Unit, who has borne the brunt of turning drafts of chapters into polished text. My deepest thanks go to all of them.

I should record that this book went to press in early June 2005. That means it covers events up to and including the UK General Election in May and its aftermath, but not subsequent events including notably the publication of the White Paper on devolution for Wales.

Alan Trench
4 June 2005

The Constitution Unit
School of Public Policy
University College London

1

Introduction: The Dynamics of Devolution

Alan Trench

The most famous single phrase about devolution is probably that of Ron Davies, late Secretary of State for Wales: 'Devolution is a process not an event'. This book will look at some of the ways in which devolution is and remains a process, and examine some of the respects in which devolution is dynamic, and some of those areas in which it has proved to be less dynamic than expected. It is therefore concerned with the future of devolution, and some of the ways in which devolution may develop over the coming ten or twenty years. It does not seek to make firm predictions, but instead to look at important topics to identify what are, or might be, important questions. The goal of the book is to spark thinking about two issues in particular: first, the extent to which devolution is a dynamic process, and to identify what those dynamics are, and second, to examine what those dynamics tell us about the nature of devolution.

There is a widespread assumption that devolution is dynamic. In the early phase of writing about devolution (say, between 1997 and 2002) scarcely an academic article or book appeared without quoting Ron Davies, although more recently its popularity has declined somewhat. The same applied to much journalism. What writers understood by Davies's remark varied a good deal and often had little to do with what he understood himself (he was commenting on the particular nature of the devolution arrangements for Wales, and how they would be 'filled out' over the coming months and years to produce a more comprehensive devolution settlement for Wales).[1] The more general use of the phrase appeared to reflect a view that it was necessary to see what actually happened to and with the new devolved institutions in order to see what devolution 'meant'. This would appear to relate to two distinct views. One was that formal change counted for little in itself and that its significance would only emerge when use was made of those and new patterns of political behaviour and new forms of policy and policy-making developed. In other words, this was largely a way of way of saying 'wait and

[1] R. Davies, *Devolution: A Process Not An Event, The Gregynog Papers*, 2 (2), (Cardiff: Institute of Welsh Affairs, 1999), especially pp. 9-12.

see'; only time will show what devolution means. The other was that devolution had some innate, usually separatist logic; once institutional change had happened, the floodgates would open, fissiparous forces would take over, and at the very least the United Kingdom would dramatically change in nature in short order. The more extreme versions of this view suggested that the UK would simply disintegrate. This view was shared by some strange bedfellows. One was John Major in arch-unionist mode:

> Labour says that devolution would promote the Union and give the Scots and Welsh more say over their own affairs. Whether it truly believes this I cannot say. I do know that devolution is more likely to break up the Union than promote it and that, in so far as it may offer the Scots and Welsh marginally more say over their own affairs in a few areas, this advantage is swamped by the disadvantages the advocates of devolution seek to hide. ... It would hurt people. It would take power away from individuals and mean higher taxes for Scots. It would eventually lead to the break-up of the United Kingdom.[2]

In this Major was following in the footsteps of Tam Dalyell, who led the charge against devolution in the 1970s.[3] Another was the Marxist nationalist Tom Nairn, who wrote of a 'rolling mutiny' caused not so much by the strength of nationalist forces as by the character of the UK state, and what he called its 'sovereignty-vacuum'.[4]

Such macro-scale visions of the dynamics of devolution were accompanied by other more focussed ones. Such accounts looked less at whether the United Kingdom has a future than at what exactly its foreseeable future might be. A notable example was a predecessor of this book as a product of the Constitution Unit, the collection of essays entitled *Constitutional Futures: a history of the next ten years* published in 1999.[5] The various contributors to *Constitutional Futures* assumed that constitutional change in general and devolution in particular were processes with an internal logic. Consequently, the institutional changes embodied in legislation mostly passed in 1998 (the Scotland, Northern Ireland and Government of Wales Acts, the Regional Development Agencies Act, the Human Rights Act, and also the Freedom of Information Act 2000 then still under discussion) would start a process that would lead to other changes to the fabric of the United Kingdom and its institutions in due course. One change would trigger others as a response: thus devolution of administration and legal powers would need to be matched in the financial sphere; Wales would seek greater autonomy to match the powers devolved to Scotland, possibly prompting further

---

[2] From John Major, 'Say no to this doomed enterprise', *The Times*, 30 August 1997.

[3] T. Dalyell, *Devolution: The end of Britain?* (London: Jonathan Cape, 1977).

[4] T. Nairn, *After Britain: New Labour and the return of Scotland* (London: Granta Books, 2000), p. 187, and see generally pp. 182-8.

[5] R. Hazell (ed.), *Constitutional Futures: A history of the next ten years* (Oxford: Oxford University Press, 1999).

demands for devolution from Scotland to maintain the previous differential; retaining a single integrated civil service, or separate territorial Secretaries of State in Whitehall, would be untenable. Some of these changes would require new legislation, but much would not. Once set running, however, the machine would go of its own motion.[6]

Part of this was based on the assumption that devolution's asymmetry was itself unstable and unsustainable in the longer term. Devolution was therefore seen as affecting the structure of the UK state as a whole, not the relations of particular parts with distinctive histories and identities with the whole. Consequently, the expectation was that the state as a whole would change, and become increasingly symmetrical. Thus some form of devolved institutions, albeit ones with differing powers and internal structures, would be created for each part of the UK. These would spread across the UK, creating a profoundly new structure for the state. Scotland might be in the vanguard of this, followed by Wales and with the English regions in the rear, but there would be a single train heading in one direction at more or less the same speed.

With hindsight many of these assumptions appear to have assumed greater dynamism, or propensity to change, than has in fact manifested itself. As a summary *Constitutional Futures* included a table setting out minimal and maximal forms scenarios for constitutional reform by 2009 (reproduced below).

While we are presently some four years short of that book's deadline, it does appear that come 2009 the UK will conform to the 'mini' rather than 'maxi' overall scenario set out there. In some respects it will not even reach the 'minimal' form. Thus we have a Scottish Parliament eschewing use of its tax-varying power, but no active Northern Ireland Assembly (and little sign that one will be restored in the near future); Regional Development Agencies and some regionalisation of central and local government in England, but no elected regional government and little interest in elected mayors outside London; few intergovernmental meetings of any sort, and limited reform of the House of Lords as a second chamber. Only when it comes to the removal of the Law Lords and the establishment of a supreme court does what has happened (or is clearly in the process of happening) approach the level of the 'maximal' scenario.

---

[6] The most concise and direct expression of this is in R. Hazell and B. O'Leary, 'A rolling programme of devolution: slippery slope or safeguard of the Union', in Hazell (ed.), 1999, but it can also be found in numerous other contributions to *Constitutional Futures*.

Figure 1.1: Minimal and Maximal Scenarios for Constitutional Reform[7]

Area	Minimal	Maximal
Devolution	Scottish Parliament with legislative power, not exercising its limited tax raising powers	Scottish Parliament exercising legislative and tax raising powers. Independent Scotland?
	Northern Ireland Assembly with legislative but no tax raising powers	Northern Ireland Assembly with legislative and tax raising powers
	Welsh Assembly with secondary legislation making powers only	Welsh Parliament with legislative and tax raising powers
	Regional Development Agencies in England appointed by central government	Elected Regional Assemblies in some English regions; Regional Chambers elsewhere
	Elected mayors in a few cities with limited powers	Strong elected mayors in the major cities
	Joint Ministerial Committee on Devolution meeting infrequently; fire fighting only	Joint Ministerial Committee as strong part of the devolution settlement
	Council of the Isles as token consultative body	Council of the Isles developing wider functions
Parliamentary reform	Limited reform of the House of Lords, involving removing the hereditary peers and re-balancing party numbers. House of Lords remains a nominated body	A predominantly or solely elected House of Lords representing the nations, regions and cities. Some changes to strengthen its functions and powers
	Referendum rejects electoral reform for the House of Commons	House of Commons elected by proportional representation
	Closed list PR for elections to the European Parliament, enabling voters only to choose between parties	Open list PR for EP elections, enabling voters to choose between individual candidates

[7] From R. Hazell, 'The shape of things to come: what will the UK Constitution look like in the early 21st Century?', in R. Hazell (ed.), *Constitutional Futures: A history of the next ten years* (Oxford: Oxford University Press, 1999), pp. 7-8.

A rights culture	ECHR as part of UK statute law but no Human Rights Commission to promote a new rights culture	ECHR as part of UK law, Human Rights Commission, domestic Bill of Rights either in preparation or already on the statute book
Openness	Restricted Freedom of Information regime, focused mainly on access to personal files	Liberal Freedom of Information Act enabling access to general government information
Judicial structure	Appellate Committee still sitting as members of the House of Lords. The Privy Council adapted to hear 'devolution' disputes	A new supreme court for the United Kingdom, separate from the House of Lords
Inter-governmental relations	Informal intergovernmental consultative processes based on Whitehall concordats	Formalised Council of British Isles with full time secretariat

It is not possible to say whether the doom-laden predictions of the John Major and Tam Dalyell school of thought will prove correct in the future; that is simply unknown and unknowable. But two things are clear. One is that these predictions have so far proven untrue. The British state has withstood the first wave of the changes triggered by devolution intact and indeed with minimal shock or adaptation. The UK Parliament, UK Government and its administrative arrangements, the UK parties and UK public attitudes all continue to function much as they did before devolution. The extent to which the system has not changed was charted by many of the contributors to this volume in *Has Devolution Made a Difference? The state of the nations 2004*.[8] As Guy Lodge, Meg Russell and Oonagh Gay showed, change at Westminster has been quite minimal, with the West Lothian Question remaining notable as a dog that politically has not barked, despite the constitutional anomalies that give rise to it. As Alan Trench showed, the UK Government has also adapted itself fairly easily, but by making limited and incremental changes even for matters that are profoundly affected by devolution.[9] Party organisation has similarly changed little, and remains in its essentials what it was before 1999.[10] On the institutional level, much has

[8] G. Lodge, M. Russell and O. Gay, 'The Impact of Devolution on Westminster: If Not Now, When?' and A. Trench 'The More Things Change, The More They Stay The Same: Intergovernmental Relations Four Years On', in A. Trench (ed.), *Has Devolution Made a Difference? The state of the nations 2004* (Exeter: Imprint Academic, 2004).

[9] See also ESRC Devolution & Constitutional Change programme Briefing No. 15, January 2005

[10] There has been little discussion of parties and devolution to date, but a notable exception is M. Laffin, E. Shaw and G. Taylor, 'The Political Parties and Devolution', in A. Trench (ed.), *Devolution and Power in the United Kingdom* (Manchester: Manchester University Press, forthcoming 2006).

been left to 'goodwill' and common approaches because of shared points of view, rather than restructuring institutions or establishing formal mechanisms for liaison or co-ordination. John Curtice showed how public attitudes in Scotland and England settled down soon shortly after devolution to a broadly-satisfied acceptance of the new status quo, with opinion in Wales keen on extending devolution to a more extensive form of devolution along Scottish lines.

The second thing that is clear about devolution so far is that the British state has proved itself to be more robust than had been predicted or believed. It has been able to absorb or contain changes that are far-reaching in their potential effect. A significant factor in this has been the willing participation of political forces across the UK. This has obviously included Labour politicians, dominating government across Great Britain, but it has included representatives of the other parties too. Support comes not just from long-term supporters of devolution like the Liberal Democrats. It also comes from nationalists who look to devolution as the first step to greater independence or autonomy for Scotland and Wales, and from Conservatives in Scotland and Wales to whom devolution has sent an electoral lifeline. That has created a very supportive political climate, but it is not the only factor. Favourable economic conditions, including generous increases in public spending which have worked their way through to the devolved administrations thanks to the Barnett formula is a second. A third has been the response of the civil service, in adapting to dramatic organisational change, developing or (in the case of Wales) building a capacity to develop policy, and undertaking the large amount of liaison and coordination needed to make an informal system of intergovernmental relations function.

This robustness may come as a shock to many, like Tom Nairn, who thought the British state fragile and at least on the verge of a terminal decline if not in its death throes. And it is not the first time that the British state has proved itself capable of responding to a major shock so effectively: in recent times it has similarly adapted to the impact of membership of the European Communities (as they were in 1973). Another possible example is the response of the UK to decolonisation in the twenty years or so after World War II, although that is more debatable. This suggests that the British state ought to be the subject of more research; that for too long assumptions have been made about its character which have neither been fully thought through nor tested empirically. Such an undertaking is beyond the scope of this book, however.

WHAT ARE THE DYNAMICS OF DEVOLUTION?

Devolution's dynamics take various forms. For convenience, this introduction (and the book more generally) will examine them as they relate to institutions, to parties, to policy and policy-making, and to society and public attitudes, themes which recur throughout the book. These are categories of convenience: they are not exclusive or definitive, and one could perfectly well examine devolution by reference to other dimensions. But they serve the purpose of illustrating the range of ways in which devolution has developed (and will continue to do so), and of pointing up the most important part of this dynamism – that what really counts is not any of these categories in itself, but how each relates to the others. It is in the interplay of its various factors that devolution's power to cause fundamental change lies.

Dynamics of Attitudes and Society

What has happened to public attitudes following devolution is complex. One generalisation is that the present arrangements are accepted as legitimate across the UK: public opinion in England (as well as Scotland and Wales) accepts asymmetric devolution, without demanding similar changes for England as well. Beyond that, the picture becomes complicated. In Chapter 6, John Curtice identifies a relationship between public attitudes toward constitutional arrangements in Scotland and Wales – a sense of mixed British and Scottish/Welsh identities translating into a preference for devolution, as opposed to independence or control from London. Despite a measure of disappointment with what devolution has actually delivered there is underlying support for the devolved institutions (and an ability to distinguish between the institutions and what they have done, or not done). In England, however, he finds no such relationship, noting that 'neither national nor regional identity seems to make much difference to people's views about how they should be governed' (p. 132). Instead there is general acceptance of what has happened for Scotland or Wales without demanding elected regional government or something similar. On this basis, he concludes that the present basis of devolution in public opinion is sound, and that (at least outside Wales) there is little demand for further change. This has to be read against James Mitchell's analysis of Scottish politics after devolution, and his suggestion that what Scots have come to understand as 'Britishness' relates not so much to a territorial state as to the welfare state. This implies that the Scottish attachment to Britishness that Curtice finds would prove to be fragile if the UK were to seek to undermine or significantly to restructure the welfare state.

Yet even this apparent satisfaction with the constitutional status quo takes us only so far. It is also clear that public attitudes in England have been sheltered, so far, from any reconsideration of what the UK is for or why it is there. A number of politicians are sensitive to these concerns, as recent speeches by Gordon Brown about 'Britishness' and David Blunkett about 'Englishness' show.[11] A form of national identity is used by both the UK Independence Party (and its offshoot Veritas) and the British National Party, and helped both to do well in the 2004 European Parliament elections. For UKIP and the BNP, 'Britishness' is clearly a proxy for 'Englishness'; their electoral bases are almost wholly in England, and both performed very poorly in Scotland and Wales.[12] The choice of election may have helped boost both parties' performances, with European Parliament elections being 'second-order' ones, encouraging protest votes, and also being to the only elected institution within the European Union (EU), thus serving as a convenient way for anti-EU objections to be manifested. There is no evidence, however, that this reaction is caused by or affects the UK state internally, and relations with Scotland, Wales or Northern Ireland. It is about the UK's place in Europe and a wider world, not the UK's own territorial politics.

Party Dynamics

The immediate consequence of devolution was to create new arenas for the political parties to compete electorally with one another. That has meant more than simply creating more spaces for Labour, Conservatives, Liberal Democrats, the Scottish National Party (SNP) and Plaid Cymru – to compete with each other. That can itself have very far-reaching implications, altering the way formal institutions operate, and creating meaningful territorial politics even in what had previously been a highly centralised state.[13] In the UK, devolution has also created new political environments (in Scotland and Wales) in which the political parties must operate. In these environments, Labour has meaningful competition from the left (notably from the SNP and Plaid Cymru), which affects its strategy quite profoundly. Labour in Wales (and to a lesser degree Scotland) is more 'old' than 'new' not just because of the inclinations of party membership or leadership but because that is where votes are, and it is from there that other parties can take votes Labour would otherwise be able to count on. This argument is further developed by Alan Trench in Chapter 7. However, the big question (examined by Charlie

---

[11] G. Brown, British Council Annual Lecture, 7 July 2004, available at: www.hm-treasury.gov.uk./newsroom_and_speeches/press/2004/press_63_04.cfm; D. Blunkett, 'A New England: an English identity within Britain' Speech to Institute for Public Policy Research, 14 March 2005, available at: www.ippr.org.uk/ecomm/files/a%20new%20england.pdf.

[12] In the 2004 European Parliament elections, UKIP and BNP combined polled an average of 22.85 per cent of the vote across England, 8.35 per cent in Scotland and 13.31 per cent in Wales.

[13] An intriguing recent discussion of this in comparative context can be found in E. L. Gibson (ed.), *Federalism and Democracy in Latin America* (Baltimore, Md: Johns Hopkins University Press, 2004), particularly the chapters on Brazil by Samuels and Mainwaring, Venezuela by Penfold-Becerra and Mexico by Ochoa-Reza.

Jeffery and Dan Hough in *The State of the Nations 2003*) is that of the extent to which such 'domestic' considerations drive electoral choice in the devolved parts of the UK.[14] They noted significant 'devolution bonuses' for the nationalist parties in devolved elections in Scotland and Wales, and suggested that we should not be surprised if devolved elections behave in different ways to Westminster ones, with the nationalist parties benefiting from attempts to 'build the nation', while voting in Westminster elections followed a more normal 'UK' pattern.

How have parties responded to the electoral challenge of devolution? In Wales Labour managed in 2003 to recover ground lost to Plaid Cymru in 1999, at least partly because Rhodri Morgan was able to claim that there was 'clear red water' between London and Cardiff. In other words, he improved his standing in the Welsh arena by separating Welsh Labour from the UK party. As a result he managed to gain 30 Assembly seats, a bare majority of one seat (given that the Presiding Officer was elected as a Plaid Cymru candidate and is neutral, and his deputy is a former Labour AM but now outside the party).[15] In Scotland Labour did not so change. It was fortunate that it did not face serious competition in 2003 from the SNP, but the effect was to strengthen the Liberal Democrats to a degree and fringe parties more so – not just organised groups like the Greens or the Scottish Socialist Party but also successful individual candidates like Dr Jean Turner opposing local hospital closures and John Swinburne representing pensioners. It might be going too far to say that the UK has four party systems after devolution, but that would not be a great exaggeration. If they are not different, they are at least differentiated.

Northern Ireland is of course different, if only because the UK parties do not contest elections there. Robin Wilson and Rick Wilford argue in Chapter 4 of this book (as they have long argued) that the electoral system chosen for the Assembly (the single transferable vote) has had a polarising effect. In a divided society, where there are two distinct communities each voting only for communal parties, the effect of the electoral system has been to encourage the votes of more extreme parties in each community and so to strengthen the parties least likely to agree with each other. This has been coupled with a rejection of the Belfast Agreement by the Democratic Unionist Party, by the IRA's failure to comply with the Agreement's express

[14] C. Jeffery and D. Hough, 'Elections in Multi-level Systems: Lessons for the UK from Abroad', in R. Hazell (ed.), *The State of the Nations 2003: The third year of devolution in the United Kingdom* (Exeter:

[15] In April 2005 Labour lost that majority, with the departure from the Party of Peter Law AM, long regarded as the group's most awkward member. Law was angered by the party's imposition of a women-only shortlist for the Westminster constituency of Blaenau Gwent (which he represented in the Assembly), and stood as an independent candidate in the May 2005 UK general election. Although he had already indicated his intention to quit the party group in the Assembly, his independent candidature led to his formal expulsion.

provisions about decommissioning and its spirit (actions justified by Sinn Féin), and so with the suspension of devolution and the peace process going into a deep freeze.

One characteristic of these differentiated party systems is that concerns about institutional issues arise to differing degrees and affect them in different ways. The status of the peace process and the institutions established under the Belfast Agreement is a prime concern (sometimes the only concern) of politics in Northern Ireland. The future of the devolved institutions in Wales is high on the political agenda there, with the determination of the Labour Party not to implement the recommendations of the Richard Commission creating a deep gulf between it and the opposition parties in the National Assembly. In Chapter 3 John Osmond argues that a grand coalition of all the non-Labour parties is a realistic prospect after the 2007 elections, as a way of obtaining power in Wales and putting pressure on London for legislative devolution. Some journalists have made suggestions about a similar coalition arising in the shorter term, after Labour became a minority administration following Peter Law's departure from the party.[16] There is something of an air of unreality about such arguments, given that the Welsh Conservatives are divided about devolution and the institution of the National Assembly and some remain deeply hostile to it. Even if Plaid Cymru were to seek a coalition with them (which would involve very considerable political risks), it is unclear if the Conservatives would cooperate. But the argument and the issues it raises are important as well as provocative. If devolution has changed attitudes toward politics in Wales – if the institutions have indeed acquired a momentum of their own – this should affect how all the parties approach politics there, and create at least an interest in holding a limited measure of power rather than being confined to opposition for the indefinite future. Moreover, such a coalition appears to offer the only way to seek to secure the implementation of the Richard Commission's recommendations, given the divisions in Welsh Labour and the support for devolution expressed by a majority of the Welsh population.[17]

Scotland has been largely immune from similar pressures, however. There, the party-political dynamics have been rather different, for two key reasons. First, Scottish Labour has (at least since the departure of Henry McLeish) been closer to UK Labour, and much less inclined to embark on policies that depart from UK ones. Second, since devolution the SNP has been in difficulties in staking out a distinctive position, although that may be changing following the re-election of Alex Salmond as leader in September 2004. The issue in Scotland has rather been a rejection of the dominant

---

[16] See for example M. Shipton, 'A nervous new year for Rhodri', *Western Mail*, 3 January 2005.
[17] See John Curtice, Chapter 6, this volume, Figure 6.1.

parties at the 2003 elections, with votes leaving Labour and SNP and heading to the Scottish Socialist Party and the Greens,

Policy Dynamics

One common indicator used to judge the significance of devolution, if not its success, is whether it leads to divergence in policy between the UK Government and the devolved administrations. Contributions to various *State of the Nations* volumes (as well as a growing literature elsewhere) have sought to make sense of this. In *The State of the Nations 2003* Scott Greer of the Constitution Unit explained the ways in which, even then, it was obvious that health policy was beginning significantly to diverge across the four parts of the United Kingdom.[18] Each part of the UK was clearly developing both substantive policy and approaches to the making of health policy that were distinctive. This sort of innovation has been much less marked in other areas. In *Has Devolution Made a Difference?* Helen Fawcett of the University of Strathclyde traced the creeping attempts of the Scottish Executive to develop its own policy on social exclusion, like health a field where Scotland has distinctive and pressing needs but unlike health an area where relatively few policy levers have been devolved.[19] She found that despite brave attempts the Scottish Executive had neither succeeded in establishing its own policy nor succeeded in influencing significant changes in UK-wide policy to deal with the particular problems found in Scotland.

This volume includes a consideration of policy relating to regional economic inequalities, by John Adams and Peter Robinson of the Institute for Public Policy Research. They find that devolution has had disappointingly little impact on regional economic performance across the UK. What is less clear from their analysis is why that is so. One possible answer is that the devolved administrations lack the means (whether in money or legal powers) to make such a policy work. However, similar problems persist in parts of the UK for which the UK Government is responsible, where the UK Government does have the necessary means. If the devolved administrations have performed 'poorly' by some external yardstick (and that begs the question of whether the yardstick is an appropriate one), they are not alone in doing so.

One conclusion does emerge from the work done as part of the devolution research, however. It is simple: powers matter. Mark Sandford reached a similar conclusion about the effectiveness of the Greater London Authority in *Has Devolution Made a Difference?*[20] New (devolved) institutions are

[18] S. Greer, 'Policy Divergence: Will It Change Something in Greenock?', in R. Hazell (ed.), *The State of the Nations 2003: The third year of devolution in the United Kingdom* (Exeter: Imprint Academic, 2003).

[19] H. Fawcett, 'The Making of Social Justice Policy in Scotland: Devolution and Social Exclusion', in Trench (ed.), 2004.

[20] M. Sandford, 'The Governance of London: Strategic Governance and Policy Divergence' in Trench (ed.), 2004.

able to make a difference where they have real powers. In such areas, they can make and deliver policies that respond to local needs and political demands. When they do not have such powers, they can achieve little. This point seems trite to the degree of being blindingly obvious, but it needs making. New Labour has become enamoured of 'strategic' policy in a range of areas, apparently believing that things will get better if someone publishes a document saying they should. It is now clear that scepticism about this approach was justified. If a problem is to be tackled, a government has to have the powers and money needed to tackle it. Documents identifying a good approach or policy which encourage others to act together to achieve those ends are not enough.

A second conclusion is that, for policy, what is important is the arena or setting in which policy is made. Different forces are at work in each part of the UK, and policy-making reflects how those forces work. This argument, sketched above, has been made most fully by Scott Greer in his book *Territorial Politics and Health Policy*.[21] The four different policy environments which devolution brought into being create quite different political interests and forces at work across the UK. Thus England is able to develop and implement a highly ideological policy. Scotland has come to rely on powerful and established professional groups. Northern Ireland remains mired in approaches that have not changed for many decades. Wales, lacking both the forces to resist change that are at work in Scotland or Northern Ireland and the powerful and effective health service management system present in England, has seen policy largely captured by another existing interest group (in this case, local government), and by a concern with public health. This has led to a lack of governmental concern (at least until 2004) in the issue of waiting lists which had dominated policy in England, and led to a ballooning of waiting lists and waiting times in Wales. This approach may reflect a particular characteristic of health policy, which is both extensively devolved to the four parts of the UK and a highly-developed policy area boasting a clear set of policy actors. That is much less the case for economic policy areas, where the actors are overwhelmingly concerned with the UK level rather than its constituent parts. While securing economic development is a major concern for the devolved administrations, the other interests in that field have only limited interest in the devolved territories and little presence there.

But if we are to regard the arenas in which policy is made as important, we have to think about how these might be changing. The influence of the European Union has been quite pervasive since devolution started. Chapters on intergovernmental relations in previous volumes of *The State of the Nations* have discussed institutional aspects of European Union policy-making, and

---

[21] Manchester: Manchester University Press, 2005.

the ways in which the devolved administrations have been able to influence this both through the UK Government's positions and through the Brussels institutions directly. Two chapters in this book address this issue more thoroughly than has been possible in the past. Charlie Jeffery looks in detail at these institutional issues. He notes the contrast between the UK's approach, which is informal but generally gives the devolved administrations a high level of involvement in forming the UK 'line', and that of other member states (notably Germany and Belgium) which tend to be much more formalistic but in fact appear to give less scope to the constituent units to influence policy. In those states, the rights of the constituent units may be more secure, but they are also less extensive. That raises, of course, the question of how matters will work in the UK when there start to be political differences between the devolved administrations and the UK Government – especially if the UK Government should become more Euro-sceptic than it presently is. Scott Greer addresses a different issue: what is the impact for the devolved administrations as (or if) the EU starts to enter an area of devolved competence where it has not hitherto been engaged? Many areas of devolved competence, notably agriculture and fisheries, and also criminal justice (for Scotland) are already within EU competence and have been regulated to varying degrees by the EU. Greer discusses the development of EU involvement in health policy, an area hitherto outside EU competence. This involvement could have far-reaching implications for the devolved administrations, stripping them of autonomy to make policy that they have only recently won and subjecting them to various forms of regulation which were not anticipated and which appear to have a limited recognition of how the UK, in contrast to continental countries, organises its services.[22] While Greer's analysis derives from health, the principles underlying what he says apply equally to other areas of growing EU activity. Education is the most likely candidate for this, but may not be the only one.

A further vital factor in policy divergence is finance. One virtue of the Treasury's grant-and-formula approach to funding the devolved administrations is that it has no direct control over their finance. The block grants can be allocated by each administration as it sees fit. Yet this is unlikely to be a sustainable approach in the longer term. As David Bell and Alex Christie show, the financial resources available to the devolved administrations bear no relation to their needs; the present system exposes the devolved administrations to the possible (if not actual) influence of the Treasury in London; and it means that the devolved administrations lack both fiscal autonomy and responsibility. These seriously question the viability of the present arrangements based around the Barnett formula. Alan Trench also examines

---

[22] Both Charlie Jeffery's and Scott Greer's chapters were written before the results of the referendums on the EU's constitutional treaty, in France and the Netherlands, on 29 May and 1 June 2005, were known.

the present system, more from a political point of view. This is no accident; finance is a key area of intergovernmental tension in all federal or decentralised systems, and in the UK is one of the key points at which the interests of the devolved administrations and the UK Government are likely to conflict.

None of this answers a bigger question about devolution – whether it is in fact appropriate to expect policy divergence to happen and to increase, as many seem to assume. There is a larger question of whether such divergence is in fact an appropriate measure of the success of devolution at all. It is perfectly proper to argue that the point of devolution is to recognise (both symbolically and practically) the distinctive character of parts of the UK. For that to happen, it is not necessary for those devolved institutions to pursue different courses of action (although it is likely that at least on occasion they will) and it is misleading to use policy divergence as the sole measure of devolution's success. What is also important is the existence of the devolved institutions and the recognition it gives to those nations or regions.[23] This position has at least one intriguing implication for Scotland: that devolution will succeed when Scotland adapts its already-distinctive policies so that they resemble those of England more, not less. That would demonstrate Scottish self-confidence, as the need consciously to do something different to England/UK would have vanished.[24] (The point applies much less to Wales or Northern Ireland because both territories have been so linked to the UK that they have many fewer existing differences from England to start with.)

Institutional Dynamics

Underlying the visions of the future set out in *Constitutional Futures* was the expectation that institutional change would have its own momentum. Once change had started, it would lead to consequential demands for other changes. To a startling degree this has not happened.

Northern Ireland has of course been an instance of stop-go devolution, with the UK Government assuming the power to suspend devolution and having done so four times, most notably since October 2002. As Robin Wilson and Rick Wilford show, that has reflected the nature of the peace process and the process of reviewing the framework of the Belfast Agreement.

The story has been rather different in Great Britain. The one appreciable revision to the 1998 devolution arrangements in Great Britain has been breaking the link between the number of Scottish MPs at Westminster and the number of MSPs at Holyrood, itself a decision taken after a protracted consultation exercise and much deliberation by the Secretary of State for

---

23 See A. Kay, 'Evaluating devolution in Wales', *Political Studies*, 51 (1): 51-66, (2003).
24 I am indebted to James Mitchell for this suggestion.

Scotland. In other respects the Scottish settlement has not been touched; it has proved adequate to the demands made on it, and while big questions remain about how Scottish and UK governments of different parties would deal with each other they have not needed any immediate answer. Underlying that, James Mitchell shows in Chapter 2, is a new issue in Scottish politics; how the underlying question for the future development of the Scottish institutions is not an institutional one, but that of how Scotland more generally comes to understand itself and its place in the world.

Similarly, expectations that devolution in the UK's Celtic fringes would lead to demands for devolution from the English regions have been proved false. Despite promises that there would be referendums on elected regional government in three northern regions, only one took place (in the North East, in November 2004), and that resulted in a crushing defeat for those supporting elected regional government. In Chapter 5 Mark Sandford and Peter Hetherington analyse the reasons for the defeat and its implications, and find an interesting parallel between that result and the defeat that devolution for Wales received in the 1979 referendum. Their argument about the continuing attractiveness of administrative regionalisation for central government is another element of the debate about regional government that has been overlooked so far, but which will loom large. In effect, the question for England to answer is not whether or not to have regional government, but whether there should an elected element in that regional government. For that reason alone, this is an issue that will return to the debate sooner or later.

The settlement for Wales has been under almost perpetual review since 1999, but the lack of enthusiasm with which Welsh Labour greeted the Richard Commission's report in the spring and summer of 2004 was startling. That report was a thoroughgoing expression of a view that the half-way house could not be left to continue. Wales needed an Assembly with proper legislative powers, along the Scottish model but with more limited powers (not including policing or criminal justice, or land and the civil law). Tax raising or varying powers were treated as optional. The executive should be formally and legally separated from the Assembly, the number of elected members increased from 60 to 80 and the electoral system changed to the single transferable vote. All this should take place over a lengthy timescale, with the Assembly not assuming its new powers until 2011 (after the next but one Assembly election, and two Westminster elections too), during which time the Assembly's powers should be gradually expanded by 'framework legislation' at Westminster.[25]

What was more startling than the report itself was the response of Rhodri Morgan, hitherto regarded as strongly supporting devolution and wanting to

---

[25] Commission on the Powers and Electoral Arrangements of the National Assembly for Wales, *Report of the Richard Commission* (Cardiff; National Assembly for Wales, 2004).

see it extended. Rather than embracing the report and seeking to secure its implementation as quickly as possible, he immediately declared that its recommendations regarding STV would not be pursued by the Assembly Government, then dropped the recommendation to increase the size of the Assembly, then suggested that what was necessary was not to grant the Assembly primary legislative powers but to increase its powers on a case-by-case basis through Westminster legislation and with enhanced powers to repeal existing legislation under what are known as 'Henry VIII' clauses. In unusually opaque language, he called this '13.2 plus, looking backwards as well as forwards' (box 13.2 being that part of the Richard Report outlining a version of this as an interim measure on the route to primary powers). This approach was adopted by the Welsh Labour Party at a special conference in September 2004, which also decided that what exactly this meant and how it should be delivered would be put in the hands of the Secretary of State for Wales.[26] Subsequently the UK Government announced that this would result in a White Paper, which was also foreshadowed in Labour's manifesto for the 2005 UK general election.[27] That White Paper was expected to appear in June 2005, shortly after this book went to press. The upshot has been that Peter Hain has become the chief arbiter of Wales's constitutional future – a curious outcome when the purpose of devolution was supposed to be to broaden participation in decision-making about Wales, not confine it to the person of the Secretary of State.

Rhodri Morgan's attitude appears to have been driven by a desire to improve his standing within the Welsh Labour Party. He has sought to appeal to party rather than to a broader constituency supportive of devolution but outside the Labour camp. He has preferred party unity to commitment either to his own long-standing principles or an attempt to make Labour more emphatically the party of devolution in Wales, and seek to win support from those presently voting for other parties or for none. He has therefore taken a significant gamble, not just with his own position but also that of the Labour Party. The extent to which he was ignoring the view of the general public in Wales was illustrated by an opinion poll carried out by NOP for ITV1 Wales in May-June 2004. This showed that 60 per cent of the public in Wales agreed that the Assembly should be given greater law-making powers, with majority support for that proposition from people intending to vote for Labour, the Liberal Democrats and Plaid Cymru (66 per cent, 62 per cent and 81 per cent respectively), and strong support from Conservative supporters too (45 per cent supported greater powers). Only 28 per cent of the public overall disagreed with the proposition, and even

---

[26] *Better Governance for Wales: A Welsh Labour policy document* (Cardiff; Wales Labour Party, 2004).

[27] *The Labour Party Manifesto 2005: Britain forward not back* (London: The Labour Party, 2005), p. 108.

among Tory voters that amounted to only 47 per cent of people.[28] This strong cross-party support for broader devolution could have been mobilised by Morgan to secure broader powers, through a referendum if need be. Such a strategy might have paid electoral dividends, by entrenching Labour as the party which delivered self-government for Wales, and so undermining (in particular) Plaid Cymru's claim to be 'the party of Wales'. By choosing to advance a narrower set of party interests, the First Minister ducked this challenge for a more comfortable but possibly, in the longer term, more dangerous approach.

The effect of Rhodri Morgan's choice is that decisions about Wales's constitutional future are not to be made in Wales, but principally in Whitehall and Westminster, by the Secretary of State. This is not a friendly setting, as interest in Wales there is limited, and there is considerable hostility toward the Assembly from a number of Welsh Labour MPs to whom Peter Hain looks for support. Securing time for new legislation and the passage of that legislation will not be straightforward, and the position taken by the First Minister both risks further dilution in the course of drafting a White Paper and translating that into legislation, and sacrifices that broader base of support for devolution within Wales.

This can be seen as an instance where party ties have proved remarkably strong. Their strength has been such that it has managed to overcome the many objections to the existing arrangements for Wales, and the problems presented by a complex and unstable Welsh settlement.

A similar story can be found in Whitehall and Westminster, where predictions of extensive change and restructuring have not been realised either. The lack of change in the central institutions of the UK state, including those established to accommodate devolution (such as the Joint Ministerial Committee), indicates a deep-seated resistance to institutional change. The cause of this appears to be the absence of immediate pressure for such changes – the fact that there is no crisis, so no urgent need to create new arrangements or alter existing arrangements. In such circumstances, neither a reactive civil service nor politicians with other matters on their mind wish to make more work for themselves – even if there are good reasons to make such changes in readiness for future challenges. The ability of the British state to withstand such a significant shock as devolution is itself something worth further consideration and investigation. Whether it will last, given the impact of an eventual change in government in Scotland or Wales as well as at Westminster, as well as the challenges of a changing domestic and European political environment, is perhaps the biggest of the questions devolution poses for the future.

---

[28] Reported by J. Osmond in the *May 2004 Wales Devolution Monitoring Report*, available at www.ucl.ac.uk/constitution-unit/nations/monitoring.php, p. 51.

THE PURPOSE OF THIS BOOK AND ITS CHAPTERS

This book as a whole does not seek to make predictions about the future. Rather, it seeks to raise questions about what the dynamics of devolution are, as they have been revealed by its first six years of practice. On that basis, each raises – often implicitly rather than explicitly – questions for the future. We are not offering so much a roadmap for the future as a way of indicating what the key decisions might be, and what answers to them will suggest. In doing this, the aim of the editor and the authors is to spark debate rather than reach conclusions. Where we do have conclusions to offer, we do so – but our aim is to provoke rather than to declaim solutions. Given this, the approach of the book is deliberately varied and eclectic, with chapters on a range of subjects which approach their subject-matter in a number of ways. Throughout the book, there is a heavy emphasis on the financial aspects of devolution – a deliberate choice, as this is the point at which the strains implicit in the present arrangements are most likely to manifest themselves, whether they are strictly speaking financial in nature or not.

The chapters in Part I combine the various thematic approaches more than the others, concerned as they are with particular nations or regions within the UK – Scotland, Wales, Northern Ireland and the English Regions. Part II addresses four UK-wide issues: public opinion and attitudes, intergovernmental relations, finance and the Barnett formula, and the impact of the EU. Part III turns to policy issues: health policy and the EU, and regional economic inequalities. The conclusion surveys briefly some of the implications of the 2005 UK general election, as well as trying to develop some more general arguments about the future development of devolution.

BIBLIOGRAPHY

Official Documents

Commission on the Powers and Electoral Arrangements of the National Assembly for Wales, *Report of the Richard Commission* (Cardiff; National Assembly for Wales, 2004).

Secondary Sources

Dalyell, T., *Devolution: The end of Britain?* (London: Jonathan Cape, 1977).
Davies, R., *Devolution: A process not an event, The Gregynog Papers*, 2 (2), (Cardiff: Institute of Welsh Affairs, 1999).
Fawcett, H., 'The Making of Social Justice Policy in Scotland: Devolution and Social Exclusion', in A. Trench (ed.), *Has Devolution Made a Difference? The state of the nations 2004* (Exeter: Imprint Academic, 2004).

Gibson, E. L. (ed.), *Federalism and Democracy in Latin America* (Baltimore, Md: Johns Hopkins University Press, 2004).

Greer, S., 'Policy Divergence: Will It Change Something in Greenock?', in R. Hazell (ed.), *The State of the Nations 2003: The third year of devolution in the United Kingdom* (Exeter: Imprint Academic, 2003).

Greer, S., *Territorial Politics and Health Policy* (Manchester: Manchester University Press, 2005).

Hazell, R. (ed.), *Constitutional Futures: A history of the next ten years* (Oxford: Oxford University Press, 1999).

Hazell, R., 'The shape of things to come: What will the UK Constitution look like in the early 21st Century?', in R. Hazell (ed.), *Constitutional Futures: A history of the next ten years* (Oxford: Oxford University Press, 1999).

Hazell, R. and B. O'Leary, 'A rolling programme of devolution: slippery slope or safeguard of the Union', in R. Hazell (ed.), *Constitutional Futures: A history of the next ten years* (Oxford: Oxford University Press, 1999).

Jeffery, C. and D. Hough, 'Elections in Multi-level Systems: Lessons for the UK from abroad', in R. Hazell (ed.), *The State of the Nations 2003: The third year of devolution in the United Kingdom* (Exeter: Imprint Academic, 2003).

Kay, A., 'Evaluating devolution in Wales', *Political Studies*, 51 (1): 51-66, (2003).

Labour Party, *The Labour Party Manifesto 2005: Britain forward not back* (London: The Labour Party, 2005).

Laffin, M., E. Shaw and G. Taylor, 'The Political Parties and Devolution', in A. Trench (ed.), *Devolution and Power in the United Kingdom* (Manchester: Manchester University Press, forthcoming 2006).

Lodge, G., M. Russell and O. Gay, 'The Impact of Devolution on Westminster: If Not Now, When?', in A. Trench (ed.), *Has Devolution Made a Difference? The state of the nations 2004* (Exeter: Imprint Academic, 2004).

Nairn, T., *After Britain: New Labour and the return of Scotland* (London: Granta Books, 2000)

Sandford, M., 'The Governance of London: Strategic Governance and Policy Divergence' in, A. Trench (ed.), *Has Devolution Made a Difference? The state of the nations 2004* (Exeter: Imprint Academic, 2004).

Trench, A., 'The More Things Change, The More They Stay The Same: Intergovernmental Relations Four Years On', in A. Trench (ed.), *Has Devolution Made a Difference? The state of the nations 2004* (Exeter: Imprint Academic, 2004).

Trench, A., *Central Government's Responses to Devolution*, ESRC Devolution & Constitutional Change programme, Briefing No. 15, January 2005, available at www.devolution.ac.uk/Briefing_papers.htm

Wales Labour Party, *Better Governance for Wales: A Welsh Labour policy document* (Cardiff; Wales Labour Party, 2004).

Part I

Nations and Regions

2

Scotland

Devolution Is Not Just For Christmas

James Mitchell

INTRODUCTION

As Michael Forsyth, the last Tory Secretary of State for Scotland, used to remind voters, devolution is not just for Christmas. Understanding how the Scottish Parliament came into being is the first step toward understanding what is likely to happen in the future; speculating on Scotland's constitutional future or imagining different scenarios will tell us little about future change. We must first describe and explain how devolution came about in the first place before we can hope to predict what is likely to happen in the future. In this chapter, the description and explanation of the present and recent past are offered as the best, perhaps the only, route towards understanding the future of Scottish devolution. However, we must tread warily. Polls and surveys provide a mere snapshot and are a very unreliable guide to the future. No-one would have predicted the establishment of the Scottish Parliament in the early to mid 1980s on the basis of polls which suggested that support for devolution remained where it had been since the first polls in the 1930s — wide but shallow. Similarly, predictions that an elected regional assembly in the North East of England would be supported at the referendum were based on flimsy evidence provided by polls which proved wildly off the mark.

In simple terms, devolution can be explained by the combination of a political base being mobilised in reaction to an 'Other'. The political base existed in the form of a widely-acknowledged distinct Scottish politics. This was both institutional and attitudinal, that is there were distinct public and political institutions as well as a distinct pattern of political behaviour or, at least, a perception that a distinct pattern of political behaviour existed, around distinct values and preferences in Scotland. Mobilisation was made possible because that which was distinct was perceived to be under threat. This mobilisation occurred because the Scottish base allied itself with a wider, progressive political movement. The 'Other' that threatened the Scottish base might best be described as Thatcherism. This Other was deemed to threaten both aspects of the Scottish base — Scottish institutions and policies — as well as directly challenging Scottish political preferences. Thatcherism, of course, is unlikely to return in its earlier form but we may well see again some of those features which provoked a Scottish backlash.

In the academic community, debate had long existed as to the precise nature of the Scottish base — whether:

- a Scottish political system existed as James Kellas insisted,[1]
- Scotland was a sub-system of the UK,[2]
- it consisted of a series of 'policy networks',[3]
- Scotland had an 'intermediate status within the UK' between political system and a region,[4] or
- it was a constituent of a union state.[5]

However, all who wrote about Scottish politics acknowledged the existence of some distinctive Scottish dimension. While there may have been disagreement on the degree of difference in policy terms, no-one doubted that much differed in these important respects in Scotland compared with the rest of the UK, including political behaviour and political institutions. Moore and Booth summed the consequences up well:

> For the centre this level of identity at the periphery is a double-edged sword. It can be used as a tool of management and control by the centre, but it also creates expectations in the periphery concerning control of decisions and provides some opportunity to express those expectations.[6]

What has also been noted is that many of these differences, especially public policy and institutional differences, accumulated incrementally over a long period of time despite common institutions such as Parliament at Westminster, a unified civil service and the activities of the main British-wide political parties and pressure groups. In addition to these political actors, other institutions played a significant part in unifying the state. The state with which Scots in the last half of the twentieth century identified was probably not so much the UK state, nor a potential Scottish state but the welfare state.[7] Both Scottish and British nationalisms existed increasingly as instrumental identities. The decline of traditional political bonds accentuated the need for

---

[1] J. Kellas, *The Scottish Political System*, fourth edition (Cambridge: Cambridge University Press, 1989).

[2] R. Rose, *Understanding the United Kingdom* (London: Longman, 1982), p. 52.

[3] M. Keating and A. Midwinter, *The Government of Scotland* (Edinburgh: Mainstream Press, 1983), pp. 3–4.

[4] C. Moore and S. Booth, *Managing Competition: Meso-corporatism, pluralism, and the negotiated order in Scotland* (Oxford: Clarendon Press, 1989), p. 147.

[5] J. Mitchell, *Governing Scotland* (Basingstoke: Palgrave, 2003).

[6] Moore and Booth, 1989, p. 148.

[7] J. Mitchell, 'Scotland in the union, 1945-95: the changing nature of the union state' in T.M. Devine and R.J. Finlay (eds.), *Scotland in the Twentieth Century* (Edinburgh: Edinburgh University Press, 1996), pp. 89-90.

the state to win the loyalty of its citizens, especially when a credible alternative existed.[8]

Significantly, this base did not simply take form in state institutions or institutions of civil society but was perceived to have an ideological dimension. Again, there may be debate as to the nature of that ideology — whether broad left, progressive, social democratic, radical or even socialist. What mattered, once more, was that the external threat provided sufficient common ground and a sense of ideological community. A peripheral identity combined with a class identity, two of the classic societal cleavages in electoral politics in Europe in the modern age identified by Lipset and Rokkan, to create an effective political force for political autonomy.[9]

Scholars have noted the importance of the 'Other' in nationalist mobilisation.[10] Mobilisation can occur even if that Other is imprecise, even partly fictional, so long as there is a perception that the Other threatens the base. The Other which brought about Scottish devolution can be personified, defined ideologically and geographically. It matters less whether this Other was believed to be Margaret Thatcher, Thatcherism or the value system of the south-east of England, London or England as a whole or some combination of these than that a perception existed of a threat. Benedict Anderson's famous 'imagined community' refers to the national community whereby 'in the minds of each lives the image of their community'.[11] But equally applicable is the imagined Other which may be as disparate and unconnected as the nation itself. The imagined threat to the Scottish imagined community may or may not have been imaginary but it had real consequences in mobilising the dormant cause of home rule.

In essence, Scottish home rule came about when what was perceived to be distinctive about Scottish politics was perceived to be under threat. Ironically, much of this Scottish base was British-made. Whether in the form of the policy-making institutions, the welfare state or the ideology of welfare and state intervention, what came to be seen as under threat had been a very British creation. Home rulers were mobilised in defence of very British institutions but saw their protection lying in distinctly Scottish terms. It is difficult to give precise form to that which was being defended, not least because different groups placed different emphases on different elements of Scottish distinctiveness but, broadly, it might be characterised as moderate leftist, statist and nationalist.

[8] See D. Kavanagh, 'Political Culture in Great Britain: The Decline of the Civic Culture', in G.A. Almond, and S. Verba (eds.), *Civic Culture Revisited* (Boston: Little Brown, 1980) for an early discussion of this phenomenon.

[9] S.M. Lipset and S. Rokkan (eds.), *Party Systems and Voter Alignments: Cross-national perspectives* (London: Collier-Macmillan, 1967).

[10] See, for discussion, A. Triandafyllidou, 'National identity and the "Other"', *Ethnic and Racial Studies*, 21(4), pp. 593–612 (1998).

[11] P. Anderson, *Imagined Communities* (London: Verso, 1991), p. 15.

Outsiders were as aware of it as were those intimately involved in Scottish politics. Following a visit to Scotland in 1984 as Shadow Education Secretary when he met various figures in Scottish higher education, Giles Radice recorded his thoughts in his diary, 'A note on Scotland. It is the first time I have been there for nearly twenty years. I find it very much a foreign country, with strong similarities with other northern social democratic lands, such as Sweden and Norway'.[12] This was a perception shared by many Scots who came to see devolution or independence as a means of defending Scottish social democracy. This understanding of Scotland in 1984 may appear fanciful or exaggerated but it was widely shared.

Neither a purely structural nor a purely agency explanation is therefore adequate. No similar demand for home rule arose elsewhere in the UK, even in areas which were objectively and subjectively more working-class or left-wing (though a weaker demand was articulated, partly on the back of Scottish demands, in Wales) — largely because there was no other community with a base as developed as Scotland's. Demand for Scottish home rule had long existed but despite the strength of the base previously, the absence of the perception of a threatening Other limited its appeal. Paul Scott, veteran Nationalist, in one of the most perceptive accounts of modern Scottish nationalism, noted a paradox. 'Scotland of the 80s had become more conscious of its distinctiveness and more anxious to preserve it against the pressure for global conformity; but, paradoxically, it had become markedly less distinctively Scottish in practice [than in his youth].'[13] Scott hints at an explanation for this paradox himself. The Scotland of Scott's pre-war youth was more distinctive but people were less aware of this then as it did not seem threatened. By the 1980s, Scotland may have become objectively less distinct as a result of a gradual process of assimilation. Although Scotland remained distinct in many respects, collectively it was more conscious of its distinctiveness and, crucially, highly conscious of threats to that distinctiveness.

When Scots voted on devolution in the 1997 referendum they did so primarily to prevent a repeat of Thatcherism and to allow greater autonomy.[14] A problem arises from this as devolution did not and does not involve the transfer of sufficient powers to prevent any London government from radically altering the welfare state if intent on doing so, which creates a capability-expectations gap.[15] Support for home rule was mobilised on a false prospectus. Nonetheless, preventing a repeat of Thatcherism and allowing

---

[12] G. Radice, *Diaries 1980–2001* (London: Weidenfeld and Nicolson, 2004), p. 112.

[13] P. Scott, *A Twentieth Century Life* (Glendaruel: Argyll Publishing, 2002), pp. 239–40.

[14] J. Mitchell and L. Bennie, 'Thatcherism and the Scottish Question' in C. Rallings *et al.* (eds.), *British Elections and Parties Yearbook, 1995* (London: Frank Cass, 1996), pp. 30–44; D. Denver, J. Mitchell, C. Pattie and C. Bochel, *Scotland Decides* (London: Frank Cass, 2000).

[15] See J. Mitchell, 'Scotland: Expectations, Policy Types and Devolution' in A. Trench (ed.), *Has Devolution Made a Difference?* (Exeter: Imprint Academic, 2004).

greater autonomy through devolution became interlinked in public perceptions. The 1997 devolution result was a vote to change institutions in order to
stay the same. There was also hope that devolution would deliver more —
more and better public services, jobs and so on, though this 'more' was,
again, fairly vague — and these expectations were built up especially when
it became necessary to win majority support in the referendum. The absence
of serious opposition, especially with the collapse of the Conservatives in
the 1997 UK general election, meant that the battle became very one-sided.
In normal political debate, each side can be expected to exaggerate its position and mutual exaggerations cancel each other out, but in the 1997 referendum the voice balancing the case for devolution was reduced to a whisper.
The expectations gap that already existed opened up further and has subsequently created problems. A more positive, public policy narrative based on
a better understanding of devolution's potential was required but has been
slow to emerge.

Of course, this broad generalisation hides a variety of undercurrents.
Amongst elites who supported constitutional change there was support for a
'new politics', ill-defined but variously including a more consensual style,
opening access to political power, less formality, and more fully reflecting
the diversity of Scottish society (especially a more significant role for
women). Those most closely associated with the Constitutional Convention,
whether participants, media or commentators, were particularly prone to use
the term loosely.[16] New politics lacked coherence but it had a simple point of
reference. Devolution would offer something different from traditional British politics focused on Westminster. It too was a reaction to the Other. Often,
the perception of Westminster was a caricature. Many devolutionary myths
have grown out of the Westminster caricature. One notable example is the
myth that the Scottish Parliament has developed a committee system worthy
of a modern parliament unlike that operating in the Commons. The Scottish
Parliament's committees have worked well but there has been a tendency
towards self-satisfied myth-making and an exaggeration of success which
has crowded out appreciation of failings.[17] This might be understandable if
there was a need to defend a vulnerable institution in its infancy but there is
little, if any, evidence that the Parliament requires this kind of defence. The
emphatic vote in its favour in the referendum and subsequent developments
suggest that Michael Forsyth's warning, as he saw it, has proved accurate.
Much of the new politics may have been worthy as ideal or aim but if treated
as a serious appreciation of how Westminster operates or how it compares
with the Scottish Parliament it has proved lamentable. Once more, the Other
which was to be avoided was unclear.

[16] See, for example, Scottish Constitutional Convention, *Scotland's Parliament, Scotland's Right*
(Edinburgh: SCC Rosebery House, 1995), p. 9.
[17] B. Winetrobe, *Realizing the Vision* (London: Constitution Unit, 2001).

However, mobilisation was not straightforward and some of the expectations of home rulers were far from realistic. In 1988, Kenyon Wright of the Scottish Constitutional Convention rhetorically asked his fellow home rulers what would happen if the demand for a Scottish Parliament was resisted: 'What if that other single voice we know so well responds by saying, "We say No and we are the state." Well, we say Yes and we are the People!'[18] All members of the Convention including all Scottish Labour MPs — Tam Dalyell apart — signed up to the Convention's document declaring popular, not Parliamentary sovereignty to be the basis of Scotland's constitutional claim. This was supposed to be the political manifestation of Wright's 'we are the people' chant. John Smith, Robin Cook, Gordon Brown, John Reid, Donald Dewar and George Robertson all agreed that Scots had a right to determine their own constitutional status. Four years later at the general election 'we are the people!' proved vapid. A UK general election resulted in a UK majority against devolution while another Scottish majority for home rule was returned which lacked authority compared to the UK majority. Talk of popular sovereignty had been cheap. The problem was that no authoritative Scottish voice other than Scottish MPs existed to challenge Parliamentary sovereignty. Scottish popular sovereignty proved useful rhetoric around which opinion could be mobilised for home rule but it lacked an authoritative means of expression. This is no longer the case after devolution. The Scottish Parliament may be seen as an alternative institutional expression of popular sovereignty. In the future, the institutional focus will change and, more importantly, there will be far greater legitimacy attached to the wishes of the Scottish Parliament which will be portrayed as the more 'Scottish', popular and democratic authority. Westminster will have more difficulty dismissing Scottish demands than it had pre-devolution.

DEVOLUTION:
FROM EXECUTIVE DEVOLUTION TO EXECUTIVE GOVERNMENT

Devolution changed Scottish politics in two respects: first, it enhanced the Scottish institutional base, and secondly, it created a perception that the centre is now more aware of Scottish sensitivities. Political institutions in Scotland are now more Scottish. But simultaneously, the Other is no longer seen as a threat. The very act of delivering devolution and the partnership between Edinburgh and London, a key theme of devolution in its earlier years to which we will return, has dimmed the sense of an antagonistic Other. Indeed, Paul Scott's paradox may work in reverse. It is conceivable that in time, despite evidence of a more Scottish polity, Scots may become less aware of this distinctiveness while Scotland becomes a contented part of

---

[18] Quoted in B. Taylor, *The Scottish Parliament* (Edinburgh: Polygon, 1999), p. 47.

the UK. It is not difficult to imagine a situation in which levels of satisfaction with existing or even more distinct arrangements will result in people taking their identity for granted and caring less about the Scottishness or Britishness of institutions, policies or themselves. But that will depend on the Other.

The enhanced Scottish base has involved one significant change. Contrary to much that has been written about devolution, devolved government has not created a new tier of government nor has it created a previously non-existent Scottish executive. Year Zero assumptions that there was no 'multi-level government' pre-devolution or that devolved government ushered in opportunities for distinctive policy-making which previously did not exist are all too common. These assumptions are not only historically inaccurate but lead to misconceptions about devolution and what is likely to happen in the future. The Scottish executive which existed throughout the union is now a Scottish Executive. The old Scottish Office that existed from 1885 was the mainstay of the pre-devolution Scottish executive. The capitalisation of Executive is justified by the democratic legitimacy provided first by the September 1997 referendum result and then by elections to the Scottish Parliament.

Increased legitimacy has had a number of consequences. The most evident has been the shift in media coverage of politics. Distinctly Scottish politics pre-devolution largely concerned the activities of the Scottish Office — latterly deemed to lack democratic legitimacy, local government, the politics of home rule and party political rivalry. One of the most significant changes — made more significant by the lack of comment on it — has been the removal of legitimacy as a distinct issue in Scottish politics. There is no talk now of a 'democratic deficit' or London's lack of a Scottish mandate to govern Scotland as was commonly heard in the 1980s and 1990s. The only residue from that period concerns the use of Sewel Motions. These motions, which allow Westminster to legislate on devolved matters with the consent of majority opinion in the Scottish Parliament, essentially Executive support, have given rise to criticisms which are weak echoes of the old argument regarding London's right to rule.[19]

Different views on Scotland's constitutional future continue to exist but debate now takes place against acceptance that current arrangements are legitimate. Many home rulers refer to devolution as the 'settled will' of the Scottish people thereby confusing the democratic legitimacy of the existing arrangements with a belief (or hope) that devolution has taken Scotland thus far and no further. Devolution settled only two aspects of the debate. First, the *status quo ante* is no longer an option. Secondly, the Scottish people now

[19] B. Winetrobe, 'Counter-Devolution? The Sewel Convention on Devolved Legislation at Westminster', *Scottish Law and Practice Quarterly*, 6: 286–92, (2001).

have a direct authoritative voice, if not necessarily the last say, in determining Scotland's constitutional status. It has not settled, and cannot settle, Scotland's constitutional status in perpetuity. In this sense at least, the devolution 'settlement' is a misnomer.

Media coverage of Scottish politics now has a much clearer institutional focus. The shift from covering the activities of Scottish MPs has been significant. Interest groups too have gravitated towards the Scottish Parliament, again lending it legitimacy. In these ways, politics has become more Scottish. We still cannot refer meaningfully to a Scottish political system but Scottish politics now exhibits more systemic features than before. In addition, the number of journalists covering Scottish politics has grown as indeed has the number of people employed by the political parties in their Scottish headquarters and as parliamentary assistants. The Scottish political village has grown considerably, it is more geographically concentrated in the capital and consists of a mélange of assorted journalists, commentators, politicians, and sundry 'hacks' who often mistake gossip for politics. In short, it is Westminster writ small. The key differences are that the focus is Scotland, the scale is smaller and the walls separating politicians and media are more often breached. It is difficult to imagine Prime Minister Blair being the guest of Newsnight's Jeremy Paxman over the New Year holiday though First Minister Jack McConnell and his family had been the guest of Kirsty Wark, Paxman's colleague, in her holiday home over New Year 2005. The scale of Scotland's political village requires greater care to avoid any whiff of impropriety precisely because the opportunities are greater.

The implications may not be apparent in these early days of devolution. Institutional stickiness means that even after formal institutional change has occurred, change in political behaviour has a habit of lagging behind. But that does not mean that political behaviour and outcomes will not eventually change. Labour's dominance of the House of Commons since 1997 combined with the existence of a Labour-Liberal Democrat coalition in Edinburgh has also muffled differences. But these are early days. The new institutions are encouraging a new form of politics but not necessarily in the sense ordinarily meant in pre- and early post-devolution politics. Nonetheless, just as the dominant view that Scotland would have a new form of politics gives way to a sober view that perhaps much remains as before, evidence is mounting that, in fact, there may indeed have been more to the notion of a new Scottish politics than was appreciated by even its most ardent advocates. The relationship between political institutions and political behaviour is complex and symbiotic. Changes in political institutions do not necessarily change patterns of behaviour, at least not overnight. Old habits die hard. But political behaviour is rational over the long-term and if institutional change creates new incentives to change behaviour then change can be expected. New voting patterns are already emerging and it is conceivable that more cooperation, when common ground is perceived to exist across the parties, will occur. The greater transparency, especially with greater freedom of information, combined with a larger number of political actors will, over time, encourage change.

PARTNERSHIP WITH THE OTHER

Westminster's establishment of the Scottish Parliament was a significant statement. Centres have a range of options available to them in responding to sub-state nationalism and demands for autonomy, from rejection, even outlawing, at the negative end of the spectrum through concessions to complete acceptance of demands. Devolution comes somewhere toward the positive end of this spectrum. The centre spoiled its efforts to be seen to respond to sub-state demands in its treatment of London and Wales by attempting to foist leaders on each. London's continued control over Scottish politics is subtle and, most notably, is accepted because it is deemed to be an unobtrusive partnership. But it will prove increasingly difficult to ensure that London's hand is hidden. Sewel Motions and London ministerial interference may have some rational basis in public policy terms but, unless much clearer principles inform London involvement, they may come to be seen as the Other's unwanted interference. Expediency has been the simple basis on which these motions have been used to date. Principles guiding their use have yet to be drawn up to ensure that these motions do not raise questions concerning their legitimacy. Measures designed to tackle underlying cultural norms are an obvious case when a debate within the Scottish Parliament would in itself be important, perhaps as important as any legislation. The French philosopher Joseph Joubert's comment that it is better to have a debate without settling the question than to settle the question without having a debate is apposite in such circumstances. The use of a Sewel Motion to allow Westminster to legislate for civil marriages exemplifies expediency over principle.

An emphasis on partnership for reasons of electoral expediency is unsustainable in Michael Forsyth's long term. Hints in the Scottish press in December 2004 that Labour intended to fight the 2005 UK general election on a theme that the return of the Conservatives would result in the break-up of Britain suggest that electoral expediency remains alive.[20] Some new idea of partnership that accommodates different partners operating in difficult economic circumstances will need to be developed. The current emphasis on electoral expediency leaves the impression that devolution cannot work without Labour being in power in London and Edinburgh. If this is the case,

[20] *Herald*, 19 December 2004.

devolution is bound to fail. If it is not to fail then a new understanding of partnership will be required before alternative party and economic configurations emerge. Old centralist expectations still exist which view divergence as dangerous. A more relaxed, pluralist attitude will need to develop to correspond with the formal institutions of devolution.

Devolution has only been one part of the changing perception in Scotland that London is now responsive to Scottish needs. Labour in government in London is perceived by Scots to be delivering. Scottish Labour has understandably stressed the partnership between the devolved and London governments in working in Scotland's interests. That has been made easy not just because Scotland's first party is in power in London but because such key London Labour figures as Gordon Brown and John Reid are Scottish MPs. Partnership as the key idea of Labour's new unionism has contributed to the short-term success of devolution.

It should, of course, be remembered that in supporting devolution, Scots did so, as we have seen, for primarily negative instrumental reasons. Devolution was to be a barrier to Thatcherism, which we might interpret in this context in simple terms as the imposition of unwanted policies on Scotland. There is little in the way of public policy coming out of London today to which Scots object strongly. This is not about which matters are devolved and which retained. The evidence suggests that such a constitutionalist perspective is not one shared by many voters. Purists may complain when MPs, even the Speaker, 'interfere' in devolved Scottish affairs but from the electorate's perspective it is more likely that this intervention is welcomed so long as it results in the desired policy end. Support for a Scottish Parliament, as we have seen, is instrumental rather than principled.

However, if London Labour's agenda, nudged along by electoral concerns in pivotal English constituencies, drifts ever rightwards, Scots must either support these changes, suggesting that British nationalism in Scotland is more primordial than previously thought, or else Scots will baulk at this trend and use the tools offered by devolution to open the ideological gap between Scotland and England. Labour's internal tensions, between Blair and Brown camps, thus potentially have a territorial dimension. This does not mean that London and Edinburgh must be on the same ideological trajectory but rather that if pressure builds up for Scotland and England to diverge then this has to be allowed. The danger, of course, is that a widening gap may in time undermine the integrity of the state. What is uncertain is the point, if any, at which this will occur. Fear of reaching such a tipping point appears to have led to an emphasis on a version of partnership that minimises any suggestion that Scotland might choose a radically different path. Based on past experience, there should be more concern that if the development of an ideological gap is frustrated, then issues of political legitimacy, laid to rest with devolution, will once more arise. The crucial difference with the Thatcher era is that when Scots next say 'We say Yes and we are the people' they will have a stronger, more legitimate Scottish voice: an institution created by Westminster with substantial political authority through which to articulate Scottish popular sovereignty.

Alternatively, devolution might be seen as a way of freeing London from responsibility for a range of public policy matters in Scotland. Ironically, this might be more likely if the Conservatives come to power in London. In part, the Tories are more likely to be hyper-sensitive to accusations that they are imposing policies on Scotland, especially as Labour is likely to redis-cover its Scottish nationalist roots when in opposition. An ideological gap or, at least, a perception of one is then likely, but if London adopts a relaxed attitude then devolution might develop in unexpected ways. Devolving responsibility need not involve the centre losing power but being freed from responsibilities and left to get on with other matters. The re-emergence of what Jim Bulpitt described as a dual state is then likely.[21] This may require London to provide the Scottish Parliament with greater financial autonomy in order to prevent the frustration of the development of difference. Under the current scheme of devolution, Barnett consequentials would make it difficult for the Scottish Parliament to avoid being carried along in the wake of radical changes to the welfare state. However, it is difficult to imagine London, regardless of party in power, conceding ground on economic management to the Scottish Parliament. It is, therefore, not inconceivable that the next stage in the process of devolution will occur when the Conservatives are returned to power in London.

Much, perhaps too much, attention has been paid to the divergence of public policy in the UK post-devolution. While some of the best work, nota-bly Greer's on health and Wincott's on child care and the early years policy, allows us to see the capacity of the devolved institutions by focussing on divergence with England, Greer referring to devolution as a divergence machine, this work does not seek to measure devolution in terms of diver-gence.[22] There are, however, assumptions, usually implicit, in much other commentary that devolution will but also should lead to divergence with England and when it does not, some commentators are either surprised, disappointed, or both. Scottish devolved institutions are expected by these commentators to build a nation through public policy.

This is a very limited view of devolution and its consequences. From a public policy perspective, divergence has two meanings: divergence with

[21] J. Bulpitt, *Territory and Power in the United Kingdom* (Manchester: Manchester University Press, 1983).

[22] S. L. Greer, *Territorial Politics and Health Policy* (Manchester: Manchester University Press, 2004), p. 221; D. Wincott, 'Reshaping Public Space? Devolution and policy change in British early childhood education and care', *Regional and Federal Studies* (forthcoming).

England and divergence with Scotland's past. Support for devolution had been mobilised around the defensive and more limited perspective of being different from England. One measurement of the maturity of devolution will be whether those involved, including commentators, expect devolution to lead to divergence from Scotland's past, where appropriate, regardless of what is happening in England. Indeed, paradoxically, a sign that devolution is working well may come when Scotland converges with England but diverges with its own past when there are good public policy reasons for doing so. The tendency to measure policy against what is happening in England is a limited and limiting perspective. Examples of divergence from England, championed as flagship policies, have not always proved happy experiences, as tuition fees and care for the elderly policies have demonstrated.

POWER LIMPING BEHIND RESPONSIBILITY

Commentators frequently noted the different purposes lying behind support for devolution. For some, devolution was a first step to independence; for others, it was a measure that would put paid to nationalist demands. Anti-devolutionists attempted to highlight this difference but had little impact pre-devolution. In large measure this was because the underlying logic of devolution was less to do with where devolution would take Scotland and more to do with what it would prevent. In the rhetoric of devolutionists in the 1980s and 1990s, devolution would 'stop Thatcher at the border'. Inevitably, since its inception, there has been much more interest in devolution's policy-making potential.

It is often asserted that the devolved institutions' policy-making capacity was decided by the Scottish Constitutional Convention. It suited the purposes of home rulers to create this myth in order to maximise support for devolution and avoid any suggestion that the policy was simply a modified version of Labour's policy. The Convention did play a significant part in shaping the nature of representation. Adopting a more proportional electoral system has, and will likely continue to have an impact on policy-making. However, to describe the devolution scheme as simply Labour's policy but with wider legitimacy and a different electoral system misses the central point that those matters which were devolved were drawn from the responsibilities of the Scottish Office. The logic of devolution was, therefore, the logic of matters which had been devolved incrementally over the course of a century-plus to the Scottish Office. In order to understand the public policy competencies of legislative devolution, therefore, the starting point is an understanding of the public policy purpose of administrative devolution.

There was no constitutional convention to deliberate rationally on which matters should come under the Scottish Parliament. Any logic in the Parliament's competencies was inherited from the Scottish Office. While issues of representation — related to devolution's democratic logic — were emphasised, issues of public policy were neglected in the discussions of devolution prior to its establishment. This is not to ignore the importance representation can have on the processing of policy and thereby on policy output, as will be discussed below.

Three themes that were evident in the development of administrative devolution have been replicated in legislative devolution. First, it had a symbolic function signifying the state's willingness to accept, even celebrate diversity. Secondly, it developed significant public policy functions. Thirdly, the Scottish Office was never intended to be a particularly innovative policy-making institution. The Scottish Office became a convenient repository for new and growing state functions rather than developing its own policy programme.[23] Some matters came under the Scottish Office while others did not less by conscious design or functional logic than historical accident.

The Scottish Office's functions not only developed incrementally but this development reflected wider public policy thinking. The Scottish Office became largely responsible for welfare matters and subsequently had some economic functions but ultimately the overall framework of policies was determined in London. That remains true of legislative devolution. The welfare and economic competencies and logic of devolution are those that were inherited at the point when the Scottish Parliament came into being.

As a part of Whitehall and with little expectation that it would be particularly innovative in public policy terms, the Scottish Office role was limited as compared with the expectations surrounding the Scottish Parliament. In an article on his experience as Labour's longest serving Scottish Secretary, Willie Ross accepted Lord Salisbury's comment that measured by the expectations of the Scottish people, the Scottish Secretaryship was 'Approaching the Archangelic'.[24] Power, as Ross lamented, limped lamely behind responsibility. That has proved to be even more true of devolution. Expectations that devolution should provide innovative, coherent policy-making have failed to take account of its origins. All of this has had consequences post-devolution. The most notable aspect of the historical basis of Scottish devolution is that its powers and responsibilities were not the outcome of deliberate design but historical accident. While there is a powerful democratic logic to devolution, it had multiple and distinct rather than coherent public policy logics, each historically-rooted and best understood as a series

[23] Mitchell, 2003.
[24] W. Ross, 'Approaching the Archangelic?', *Scottish Government Yearbook 1978* (Edinburgh: Paul Harris, 1978).

rather than part of some rational plan. The challenge has been to find a clear over-arching public policy purpose, a policy narrative that allows for innovation across responsibilities rather than compartmentalised, seriatim policy-making.

Under the leadership of three First Ministers, the Scottish Parliament has not clarified its public policy role. This is not to suggest that there have been no public policy developments but that public policy has developed without a clear overarching framework. In part, this reflects a weak core to the Scottish Executive. Henry McLeish's premiership can be seen to have been most significant, perhaps inadvertently, in developing a clear public policy narrative for devolution. A new understanding of McLeish's term has emerged, partly fed by the former First Minister's autobiography, that there was a clear public policy logic to his term in office but this was not so evident at the time.[25] Jack McConnell, First Minister since 2001, has added confusion by altering his administration's primary objectives in various speeches. Initially emphasising the delivery of public services in his early days as First Minister, McConnell then made amends by stressing his commitment to 'jobs' before correcting this and emphasising economic growth before declaring that 'tackling anti-social behaviour and fighting crime' had been the 'number one issue' in the 2003 elections.[26] These changes were effected within the first eighteen months of his premiership. The impression has been left of public policy driven by news headlines.

REPRESENTATION AND THE POLICY PROCESS

The most obvious public policy changes have been in the policy process. Policy is now the subject of more intense scrutiny and debate amongst Scotland's elected representatives, and the new Parliament offers a new access point for interest groups and others to influence policy. But, of course, the role of legislatures in policy-making is disputed. Two eminent public policy scholars once questioned whether the House of Commons contributed more to the policy process or the tourist trade.[27] Others have noted the legitimising role of Parliament at Westminster while acknowledging its limited role in everyday policy-making.[28] There can be little doubt concerning the importance the Parliament's existence has had on the legitimacy of policy-making. Additionally, the Scottish Parliament, theoretically, offers more scope for Parliamentary assertiveness in policy-making and, unlike the Commons

[25] H. McLeish, *Scotland First* (Edinburgh: Mainstream, 2004).

[26] J. McConnell, Speech to the Labour Party Conference in Bournemouth, www.scottishlabour.org.uk/fmbournemouthspeech (2003).

[27] A.G. Jordan and J. J. Richardson, *British Politics and Public Policy* (London: Allen & Unwin, 1987), p. 57.

[28] D. Judge, *The Parliamentary State* (London: Sage, 1993).

where Executive dominance is the norm, the Holyrood electoral system's consequences throw up opportunities rarely available in London.

It is, therefore, remarkable that Executive defeats have been so rare. Power lies in the coalition at least so long as the coalition acts coherently. Those few occasions when the Executive have been defeated have been the result of either some signal that the Executive is divided or because of significant local interests. Indeed, the doctrine of collective responsibility appears to have been redefined in a looser way in Edinburgh. Ministers have not been sacked or forced to resign after publicly disagreeing with Executive policy or even voting against the Executive. Members of the payroll vote have been allowed greater freedom than would be tolerated in London. This is the direct consequence of changes in formal institutions rather than any change in informal institutions. In other words, the electoral system rather than some vague notion of 'new politics' has been at work. Scottish Labour's decision to apply fairly rigorous loyalty tests pre-1999 on those who wished to become MSPs may have been attacked at the time as 'control freakery' but SNP leaders must occasionally wish they too had had more control of their MSPs. The liberal nature of pre-1999 SNP candidate selection has resulted in three SNP MSPs losing the whip since 1999.

Over time, as MSPs gain confidence and the role of 'senior' backbenchers, a term that has not yet been heard in the Parliament, begins to emerge, it is conceivable that the changes brought about through the electoral system will take root and future Executives will face more rebellions. MSPs who were ultra-loyal may not always remain so. Constituency interests, especially with the ever-present electoral threat witnessed recently in debates on hospital closures, suggest that we may not be far away from a more assertive Parliament in its relations with the Executive. Voting behaviour in the Commons suggests first, that once a member gets the taste for rebellion, that member is more likely to rebel repeatedly and secondly, that only a few rebels are required to cause an upset.

But the policy-making process is not simply about Parliament. Most policy-making is important but humdrum and it is not clear that devolution has had much impact here. In a speech to the Hansard Society, Parliament Minister Margaret Curran MSP remarked that the usual culprits still dominate policy consultations.[29] While strenuous efforts have been made to open up the system, including via the use of a public petitions committee and a civic forum, the success of such efforts remains fairly limited. In this sense, devolution appears more like an elaborate democratic veneer sitting atop long-established processes. Jordan and Stevenson thus conclude an essay on redemocratising Scotland sub-titled 'Towards the Politics of Disappointment?' as follows:

[29] Hansard Society's Scottish annual conference, Edinburgh, 29 November 2004.

> The discourse about consultation [and new politics] assumes that what has been
> wrong in the past is the failure to include the views of minorities. [We] instead
> assume that the major weakness was the lack of a political and parliamentary
> majority to reflect Scottish political views: the democratic deficit in Scotland.[30]

A real danger exists of unrealistic expectations overwhelming very real
progress.

TOWARDS A SCANDIC MODEL?

The period since 1999 has been favourable for the operation of devolution
for two reasons. The similar ideological outlook of governments in London
and Edinburgh has often been noted but more important has been the healthy
economic backdrop. Difficult economic times are likely to result in changes
in party support at one or both levels and create tensions. As has been
witnessed so often in the past, prosperity removes tensions and difficulties or
allows them to be hidden. It matters less that one part of the state benefits
more than another when all are benefiting, but it matters greatly that any part
suffers at all in difficult times. A genuine partnership has operated since
1999. But, devolution is not just for Christmas.

One part of the equation, a more pronounced Scottish base, has been
evident not only in the form of devolved institutions but also in media coverage of politics and led some, especially inside the SNP, to expect that this
would lead ineluctably to independence or at least to further devolution.
However, the second part of the equation was ignored in these expectations.
The perception that government at the centre is responsive to Scottish needs
and demands has helped devolution bed down. The centre remains crucial to
the course of Scottish politics including the prospect of further constitutional
reform. However, if perceptions change and the centre is once again deemed
unresponsive or insensitive, the enhanced Scottish base may create pressures
unprecedented in territorial politics.

On a return trip to Scotland today, Giles Radice would be less confident in
describing Scotland as a foreign country, one that merited the description of
a Scandic social democracy. Scotland has always been distinct; devolution
has added a democratic component to this distinctiveness but it still lacks a
clear direction. A social democratic narrative cannot yet be discerned
though, in a vague sense, that had been one of the reasons electors voted for
devolution. Ironically, Radice's comments seem more inappropriate today
after devolution than they did at the height of Thatcherism. Despite much of
the rhetoric and expectations surrounding devolution having a leftist tone

[30] G. Jordan and L. Stevenson, 'Redemocratizing Scotland: Towards the Politics of
Disappointment?', in A. Wright (ed.), *Scotland: The challenge of devolution* (Aldershot: Ashgate,
2000), p. 184.

and suggestions that it would enhance welfare provision and halt market-based public policy initiatives, Scotland has not been insulated from the dominant public policy agenda that marches onwards. However, though the march of the market may not have halted it moves at a slower pace north of the border. A gap is slowly opening up between Scotland and England and while this may not be caused by Scotland marching off in a different direction, the speed of change is nonetheless creating differences that would not have existed without devolution. Divergence is not so much the appropriate term as difference.

But developments appear unplanned. As yet no clear overall public policy rationale for devolution has emerged. In part this reflects tensions over the relative importance attached to economic growth and the provision of welfare services but it is mainly the result of devolution's origins. Intimations of a coherent public policy programme focusing on public health are discernible but fragmentary.

There remain a number of gaps in the structure of devolution. The capability-expectations gap, which was explored by the author in various papers pre-devolution and in last year's *State and the Nations* volume,[31] is returned to again this year. But there are others. One very basic gap is best summarised in the simple question: what is devolution for? Its democratic purpose is clear and the Scottish Parliament has fulfilled this admirably but what of its public policy purpose? Additionally, there is a gap in our understanding of partnership: how will partnership operate in different circumstances. This last leads us to one of the fundamental problems with devolution. To date, devolution has been articulated with little regard to future developments and changes in the political context in which it must operate. Devolution, after all, is not just for Christmas.

BIBLIOGRAPHY

Anderson, P., *Imagined Communities* (London: Verso, 1991).

Bulpitt, J., *Territory and Power in the United Kingdom* (Manchester: Manchester University Press, 1983).

Denver, D., J. Mitchell, C. Pattie and C. Bochel, *Scotland Decides* (London: Frank Cass, 2000).

Greer, S., 'Policy Divergence: Will it change anything in Greenock?' in Robert Hazell (ed.), *The State of the Nations 2003* (Exeter: Imprint Academic, 2003).

Greer, S.L., *Territorial Politics and Health Policy* (Manchester: Manchester University Press, 2004).

Hogwood, B., 'Whatever happened to regional government?', *Strathclyde Papers on Politics and Government*, 97, (1983).

---

[31] A. Trench (ed.), *Has Devolution Made a Difference?* (Exeter: Imprint Academic, 2004).

Jordan, A.G. and J.J. Richardson, *British Politics and Public Policy* (London: Allen & Unwin, 1987).

Judge, D., *The Parliamentary State* (London: Sage, 1993).

Jordan, G. and L. Stevenson, 'Redemocratizing Scotland: Towards the Politics of Disappointment?', in A. Wright (ed.), *Scotland: the Challenge of Devolution* (Aldershot: Ashgate, 2000).

Kavanagh, D., 'Political Culture in Great Britain: The Decline of the Civic Culture', in G.A. Almond and S. Verba (eds.), *Civic Culture Revisited* (Boston: Little Brown, 1980).

Keating, M. and A. Midwinter, *The Government of Scotland* (Edinburgh: Mainstream Press, 1983).

Lipset, S.M. and S. Rokkan (eds.), *Party Systems and Voter Alignments: Cross-national perspectives* (London: Collier-Macmillan, 1967).

McConnell, J., Speech to Labour Party Conference Bournemouth, (2003), www.scottishlabour.org.uk/fmbournemouthspeech.

McLeish, H., *Scotland First* (Edinburgh: Mainstream, 2004).

Mitchell, J., 'Scotland in the union, 1945–95: the changing nature of the union state' in T.M. Devine, and R.J. Finlay (eds.), *Scotland in the Twentieth Century* (Edinburgh: Edinburgh University Press, 1996).

Mitchell, J., *Governing Scotland* (Basingstoke: Palgrave, 2003).

Mitchell, J., 'Scotland: Expectations, Policy Types and Devolution' in A. Trench (ed.), *Has Devolution Made a Difference?* (Exeter: Imprint Academic, 2004).

Mitchell, J. and L. Bennie, 'Thatcherism and the Scottish Question' in C. Rallings, D. Farrell, D. Denver and D. Broughton (eds), *British Elections and Parties Yearbook, 1995* (London: Frank Cass, 1996), 30–44.

Mitchell, J., D. Denver, C. Pattie and H. Bochel, 'The Scottish Devolution Referendum', *Parliamentary Affairs*, 51: 166–81, (1998).

Moore, C. and S. Booth, *Managing Competition: Meso–corporatism, pluralism, and the negotiated order in Scotland* (Oxford: Clarendon Press, 1989).

Moravcsik, A., *The Choice for Europe: Social purpose and state power from Messina to Maastricht* (London: UCL Press, 1998).

Paterson, L., *The Autonomy of Modern Scotland* (Edinburgh: Edinburgh University Press, 1994).

Radice, G., *Diaries 1980–2001* (London: Weidenfeld and Nicolson, 2004).

Rose, R., *Understanding the United Kingdom* (London: Longman, 1982).

Ross, W., 'Approaching the Archangelic?', *Scottish Government Yearbook 1978* (Edinburgh: Paul Harris, 1978).

Scott, P., *A Twentieth Century Life* (Glendaruel: Argyll Publishing, 2002).

Scottish Constitutional Convention, *Scotland's Parliament, Scotland's Right* (Edinburgh: SCC Rosebery House, 1995).

Taylor, B., *The Scottish Parliament* (Edinburgh: Polygon, 1999).

Trench, A (ed.), *Has Devolution Made a Difference?* (Exeter: Imprint Academic, 2004).

Triandafyllidou, A., 'National identity and the "Other"', *Ethnic and Racial Studies*, 21 (4): 593–612, (1998).

Wincott, D., 'Reshaping Public Space? Devolution and policy change in British early childhood education and care', *Regional and Federal Studies* (forthcoming).

Winetrobe, B., *Realizing the Vision* (London: Constitution Unit, 2001).

Winetrobe, B., 'Counter–Devolution? The Sewel Convention on Devolved Legislation at Westminster', *Scottish Law and Practice Quarterly*, 6: 286–92 (2001).

3

Wales

Towards 2007[1]

John Osmond

The Richard Commission of 2004 set an agenda for the future development of Welsh politics that may well have unforeseen consequences. Certainly, given the history of Welsh devolution it was extraordinary that representatives nominated by each of the four parties could agree, not only on the Assembly becoming a legislative parliament, but that its members should be increased from 60 to 80 and elected by the single transferable vote proportional system. As Lord Richard himself declared, 'I didn't expect that the political representatives would be able to come to an agreed understanding. The reason they did was because they looked at the evidence.'[2]

In coming up with a coherent case for extending the Assembly's powers the Richard Commission report may well have the unintended consequence of altering the course of Welsh politics in more than just a constitutional sense. Due to its impact on the opposition parties, and especially leading Conservatives, the report had the immediate effect of throwing into sharp relief the realities of coalition politics in Wales. Put simply, these are:

1. Proportional voting for the Assembly makes coalition government more likely than not; and

2. If there is ever to be an Assembly Government other than one dominated by the Labour Party, then the other parties will need to cooperate.

And, indeed, altering the political governance of Wales so as to remove the Labour Party from its dominant position may prove to be a necessary precursor for full implementation of the Richard Commission's recommendations. If a democracy is to function its electorate needs to be able to effect a change of government. Welsh politics will come of age when the Welsh electorate have lived through the experience of changing their government.

---

[1] This Chapter was first published as the concluding essay in J. Osmond (ed.), *Welsh Politics Come of Age: Responses to the Richard Commission* (Cardiff: Institute of Welsh Affairs, January 2005).
[2] Speech at the ESRC/Institute of Welsh Affairs conference 'Responding to Richard', Cardiff, 23 April 2004.

Labour held on to power in the National Assembly as a result of winning just half the 60 seats in the May 2003 election.[3] Labour is unlikely to improve on this position at the 2007 election; rather, it is more likely to have fewer seats, an assertion that is explored below. In these circumstances, to continue in office Labour will have little recourse but to revisit the coalition with the Liberal Democrats that sustained it through much of the Assembly's first term. Whether the Liberal Democrats would oblige is a key question for any assessment of forthcoming political events.

More immediately, however, the question underlines the realities of coalition administration that now define the essential condition of Welsh politics. All the parties have been slow to come to terms with, or even understand, this reality. However, the process through which the Richard Commission made them examine the limitations of the Assembly's present operation, has also led them to address how, and under whose leadership, improvement might be brought about. As Plaid Cymru's former leader, Dafydd Wigley, asked: 'Do the pro-devolution forces in most — perhaps by now all — the parties of Wales, have the vision to cooperate to ensure that the historic opportunity provided by the Richard Commission report is not lost to Wales?'[4]

Speaking to a party gathering in Llandudno in September 2004, the Welsh Conservative leader in the Assembly, Nick Bourne, declared: 'Examining ways to increase cooperation with our opposition parties in the Assembly is vital both to hold Labour to account and to fight off continuous Labour government in Wales.'[5] Just over a week later, at the UK Conservative conference in Bournemouth, Bourne returned to the theme, acknowledging the difficulties but insisting that mutual antipathy to Labour made cooperation a necessary goal and a possibility:

> Cooperation with other parties has been largely born out of Labour arrogance. Policy differences are marked. We make an unlikely line-up. But in the face of one-party rule, it would be failing the people of Wales not to examine the potential for agreements and search for different ways ahead.[6]

To judge the likelihood of the opposition parties in the Assembly collaborating in the way suggested here it will be necessary to examine their internal pathologies. What are the chances of the 'unlikely line up' referred to by Nick Bourne finding common cause? Before that, however, we need to address two prior questions. How likely is it that the outcome of the 2007 elections will provide the opposition parties with a position where they can

---

[3] It is allowed to behave as though it is a majority administration because two opposition members, Lord Elis-Thomas, of Plaid Cymru, and John Marek, of Forward Wales, respectively occupy the positions of the Presiding Officer and Deputy Presiding Officer.

[4] D. Wigley, 'A charter for wreckers', *Institute of Welsh Affairs Agenda*, Autumn 2004.

[5] *Western Mail*, 26 September 2004.

[6] *Western Mail*, 4 October 2004.

cooperate in an alternative administration? Secondly, how likely are the opposition parties to be able to agree on the Richard Commission recommendations, a necessary requirement for them collaborating in government?

THE 2007 ASSEMBLY ELECTION

The 2003 election provided close to ideal conditions for Welsh Labour. They had delivered on the first term, had produced a strong and high-profile leader in Rhodri Morgan, and through him developed the 'clear red water' approach to policy delivery that gave the party a coherent message, at least in the short term.

In contrast the opposition parties were in disarray. The Welsh Conservatives were handicapped by the position and image of their party on the UK stage, while Plaid Cymru had a new, low-profile and untested leadership which failed to develop a sufficiently clear and contrasting position to Welsh Labour.

In these conditions Welsh Labour only managed to secure half the seats in the Assembly. Its position rested on a handful of votes in key marginal seats such as Llanelli and Conwy. This suggests that, in a different election year when less favourable conditions apply, Welsh Labour will find it extremely difficult to sustain this position. Six factors are likely to work to the party's disadvantage in the May 2007 election that were not present in 2003:

1. Welsh Labour will have been in power in Wales for two terms and many voters will be looking for a change.

2. At the UK level Labour will likely be mid-way through its third term with frustration and disillusion mounting.

3. The economic climate is unlikely to be as propitious — that is to say, in 2003 Labour benefited from a full term of stable growth, rising public expenditure and low interest rates. It will be difficult for this combination to be replicated in the period leading up to May 2007.

4. The boundary reconfiguration in north Wales, with a redistribution between Meirionnydd Nant Conwy, Caernarfon and Conwy is likely to work to Labour's disadvantage — that is to say, Conwy will be made more marginal in Plaid Cymru's favour.

5. In the 2005 UK general election Conservatives can expect to pick up a number of seats in Wales: Monmouth, Clwyd West and perhaps Cardiff North. As a result they will be well-placed to sustain the significant advance they made in the 2003 Assembly elections.[7]

---

[7] In the 2005 UK general election, the Conservatives did win three seats: Monmouth, Clwyd West and Preseli Pembrokeshire, but not Cardiff North (editor's note).

6.   The Welsh Liberal Democrats can be expected to at least sustain
      their overall share of the vote while Plaid Cymru has an opportunity
      to recover some of the losses it sustained in 2003.

For all these reasons the 2007 election is likely to result in Labour losing a
number of seats to both Plaid Cymru and the Welsh Conservatives: Llanelli,
Conwy and perhaps Carmarthen West to Plaid and Clwyd West and perhaps
Cardiff North to the Welsh Conservatives.

While winning first-past-the-post constituencies can produce losses on
the list, the overall result is likely to result in Labour falling back to between
26 and 29 seats, thereby losing its overall majority. In these circumstances
there will be an opportunity to create an alternative coalition government to
a Labour or Labour-Liberal Democrat formation.

WELSH LABOUR

Welsh Labour's response to the Richard Commission, published in August
2004, demonstrated why it will be an unlikely coalition partner in the event
of it failing to win a majority at the 2007 elections. Set up as a result of
Labour's coalition agreement with the Liberal Democrats in late 2000, the
Commission contained representatives from all four parties in the Assembly
as well as from a broader cross-section of Welsh society. As already stated,
the fact that it achieved broad agreement was a remarkable development in
Welsh politics. The First Minister Rhodri Morgan himself observed that it
reflected a maturing of civic society in Wales: 'All of us involved in political
life in Wales know just how contentious the remit provided to the Commission was capable of becoming.' [8]

The recommendations certainly proved contentious for the Welsh Labour
Party. Faced with implacable hostility from its backbench Westminster MPs
it was first forced to concede a referendum on any proposal for primary
powers, and then to delay reaching any definitive position until after the
2005 UK general election. Its document *Better Governance for Wales* was
only approved reluctantly at a special conference in Cardiff in September
2004. As the Wales Secretary of the Transport and General Workers Union
Jim Hancock, put it:

> This document offers one small step forward. It is not the major stride forward my
> union and many others had been hoping for. But we know that it is all we're going
> to achieve at this stage, with an election looming, without having a bloody war in
> the party.[9]

[8] National Assembly *Record of Proceedings*, 31 March 2004.
[9] Speech to Welsh Labour Special Conference, Cardiff, 11 September 2004.

However, the document was certainly not calculated to appeal to the Welsh Liberal Democrats, Labour's future potential coalition partner. At one point it refers to their 'federalist fantasies and constitutional wish lists', and at another declares, 'Unlike the Lib Dems, Labour does not believe the establishment of democratic devolution was the end in itself.'[10] For his part Welsh Liberal Democrat Assembly leader Mike German was uncompromising:

> My reading of this policy document is that the Labour Party in Wales is handing over to the UK Cabinet the power to do as it pleases about the future government of Wales after the next general election. This amounts to a shameful abdication of responsibility by a party that is offering no leadership to our nation and which is prepared to surrender to the so-called Northern Alliance of North Wales MPs who oppose devolution.[11]

The clear recommendations in the document have a direct appeal to Labour rather than the opposition parties, especially the Liberal Democrats. For example, it rejects without argument the Richard Commission's proposal to adopt the STV proportional representation system. On the other hand, it advocates a change to the voting system to prevent candidates from standing for election in both a constituency and on a regional list — a hostile move aimed at the opposition parties. It also rules out tax-varying powers and any reduction in the number of Welsh MPs at Westminster. Assuming it wins the 2005 General Election Labour will publish a White Paper that will set out two broad options for enhancing the legislative powers of the Assembly:

- Primary law making powers following a post-legislative referendum.
- Allowing the Assembly to amend or repeal existing legislation in those areas of policy for which it already has responsibility.

The option of widening the Assembly's secondary legislative powers had already been advocated by Rhodri Morgan as a compromise solution at the end of June. It is described in *Better Governance for Wales* in the following terms:

> One option would be to grant the Assembly enhanced Order-making powers to make new legal provision for Wales in defined fields within the responsibilities currently devolved to it, including a power to amend or repeal relevant earlier legislation in these fields. This would in effect apply the principle of framework legislation retrospectively. Parliament would continue to be the appropriate body to pass Wales-only primary legislation outside the areas covered by these Order-making powers (for example, the proposed Bill to create an older People's

---

[10] Welsh Labour Party, *Better Governance for Wales*, [response to the Richard Commission] (Cardiff: Welsh Labour Party, August 2004), paras. 41, 2 respectively.

[11] *The Western Mail*, 9 August 2004.

Commissioner for Wales) and Sewel-type measures on an England and Wales basis.[12] As with the ending of corporate body status, this option would require a Government of Wales (Amendment) Act. This sort of Order-making powers could be extended gradually over the devolved fields, or related to specific pieces of legislation.[13]

However, in the wake of Labour's conference Lord Richard said this compromise would have great difficulty in being accepted in Westminster:

> The House of Lords doesn't like 'Henry VIII' powers, which gives somebody the power to amend Acts of Parliament by delegated legislation, statutory instruments — people don't like that. I think you can pretend for the sake of unity in the party before the general election that this is going to be the permanent solution. I don't think it could be permanent and you could only pretend for so long.[14]

In a newspaper interview in late August, the Secretary of State Peter Hain, also appeared to rule out the approach. As he put it:

> In the next term (after the general election), a White Paper could consider options. But there may be only one option by the time the White Paper is put together. Rhodri's option, as he has made perfectly clear, has still to be 'bottomed out'.[15]

What we are left with is Welsh Labour broadly in favour of extending the Assembly's legislative powers, but keeping its options open, able to move in various directions depending on political circumstances and, in particular, views at Westminster. While this pragmatic approach is understandable in a governing party that is internally divided on the pace of change, it is not one calculated to appeal to the opposition parties in the Assembly. Developing a frame of mind and taking into account the compromises that have to be made in any approach to coalition politics does not come naturally to the Labour Party. Indeed, the opposite is the case.

WELSH LIBERAL DEMOCRATS

On the other hand, by virtue of their commitment to proportional representation, and also their experience of devolution — both in Wales and Scotland — Liberal Democrats are predisposed towards coalition politics. The

---

[12] As the document explains, 'The Sewel Convention' is named after Lord Sewel, a Labour Government Minister responsible for helping to take the Government of Scotland Bill through the House of Lords in 1998. Sewel Motions allow the UK Parliament to pass primary legislation in devolved areas on behalf of the Scottish Parliament. This is done at the request, or with the express consent, of the Scottish Parliament.'

[13] Welsh Labour Party, 2004, para 26.

[14] BBC Wales News online, 13 September 2004.

[15] *Western Mail*, 18 August 2004.

question for the argument being pursued here is what are the circumstances that would persuade them to participate in a coalition with Plaid Cymru and the Conservatives, rather than coalescing once more with the Welsh Labour Party. A number of considerations are likely to be influential in helping persuade the Liberal Democrats that they should make this choice.

In the first place, if such a choice was possible it would mean that in a definable sense Labour had lost the election. That is to say their number of seats would have fallen, and probably their overall vote as well. The greater the fall the stronger would be the impression that Labour had lost. In any event, in 2007 although Labour will probably still be the largest party in the Assembly its position is likely to be considerably weakened. Would the Liberal Democrats feel justified in giving the party a third successive term in office in these circumstances?

A second consideration is the Liberal Democrats' experience of their coalition with the Welsh Labour Party during the first term. The record is mixed. On the one hand, the partnership agreement that signalled the formation of the coalition between Labour and the Liberal Democrats in October 2000 contained a large number of Liberal Democrat policies. Also, Rhodri Morgan remained consistently loyal to Mike German during the year-long period when the Liberal Democrat leader had to temporarily step down from the Cabinet in order to defend himself against accusations (subsequently dismissed) about his conduct during a previous period when he worked for the examining body, the WJEC.

On the other hand, the most significant long-term commitment in the coalition agreement — to take the devolution process forward through the establishment of a Constitutional Commission — was ultimately reneged upon by the Labour Party. That is to say, it has now set its face against the unified recommendations of the Richard Commission. And, indeed, in relation to Liberal Democrat constitutional aspirations, Labour's most recent policy paper described them as 'federalist fantasies and constitutional wish lists.'[16] Linked to the second consideration is the reality that, unlike its counterpart in Scotland, Welsh Labour has also set its face against extending or improving the proportionality of the electoral system. It sidelined the report of the Sunderland Commission which recommended STV for local elections in Wales. And as for the National Assembly, the Welsh Labour Party is unequivocal:

> We reject the Richard Commission proposal for the use of the proportional representation system of Single Transferable Vote with a boundary reorganisation, and constituencies of four to six members.[17]

[16] Welsh Labour Party, 2004, para. 41.
[17] *Ibid.*, para. 7.

This rejection was baldly stated without any engagement with the arguments that the Richard Commission put forward. On the other hand Plaid Cymru favours the adoption of STV and there is no sign that the Welsh Conservatives will have any fundamental difficulty with its adoption.

There seems little reason why a package of measures cannot be agreed with the Liberal Democrats sufficient for them to claim that they will have at least as much influence upon a Plaid Cymru-led coalition as with one led by the Labour Party. The involvement of the Conservatives would be of assistance in a more general way, since it would ameliorate attacks that the Liberal Democrats were supporting a party whose ultimate aim is 'independence' or 'separation' of Wales from the rest of the UK. Rather, the position would be that they were engaged in a single term commitment, built around a limited but achievable set of objectives that more closely reflected the wishes of the people of Wales as expressed in the 2007 election.

WELSH CONSERVATIVES

The Welsh Conservatives have emerged as perhaps the most professional group of politicians within the National Assembly. It is certainly the case that as a party they have benefited most from devolution. In the first place, and as a result of the degree of proportionality allowed in elections for the Assembly, they have achieved representation. This compares with their experience in the 1997 UK election when they were removed from every Westminster constituency in Wales.

Under the leadership of Nick Bourne the Conservative Group in the Assembly resolved to take a constructive approach to their opposition role. Early on, some members of the group — in particular David Melding and Glyn Davies — decided that devolution offered Welsh Conservatives an opportunity to re-position their role in Welsh politics. First, they should become more 'Welsh' by adopting a positive approach to the Welsh language.

Secondly, they should embrace the devolution process through advocating legislative powers (albeit arguing that this would strengthen the unity of the United Kingdom by providing a stable constitutional settlement). These views were endorsed by such influential personalities outside the Assembly as Lord Roberts of Conwy and Lord Griffiths of Fforestfach, and to a lesser extent Jonathan Evans MEP.

Speaking to the Institute of Welsh Politics in Aberystwyth in 2002 Lord Griffiths argued that to have a future in Wales the Conservative Party must be seen as a Welsh party, not as an English party operating in Wales. He concluded that as a result Conservatives should fully engage with devolution. He linked this with an ideological commitment to subsidiarity, a principle — now enshrined in the European Constitution — that allows the greatest freedom of action to the individual and the community.[18] In another publication, written near the same time, Jonathan Evans MEP argued for a more autonomous organisation for the Welsh Conservative Party.[19]

However, it is David Melding AM who has developed the most cogent view of the future for Welsh brand of Conservatism based on a centre-right position that could offer a strong appeal to a significant segment of the Welsh electorate. For instance, reflecting on his experience campaigning in the 2001 UK general election in Wales he observed:

> It struck me when campaigning that what the people of Wales want is a light blue and genuinely Welsh Conservative Party. The spirit of one nation conservatism has attracted strong support in Wales in the past and could do so again. Given that there are now three left-of-centre parties in Wales, there is plenty of room for a moderate centre right party ... Perhaps our task is similar to that of the Anglican church in 1920. Seen by many as a church for English brewers and landowners, Anglicans were somehow not authentically Welsh. However, after the shock of disestablishment, the Church in Wales became a successful Welsh institution. While holding true to its Anglican identity and remaining in full communion with the Church in England, it managed its own affairs and prospered. The Welsh Conservative Party must undergo its own disestablishment so it can rebut all accusations of being an English party.[20]

Melding has also adopted a pragmatic attitude towards the potential for Welsh Conservatives participating in coalition politics. Acknowledging that proportional representation makes it difficult for any one of the parties in the Assembly to achieve an outright majority, he remarked in early 2003:

> We take the view that it is a question of thirds in our own Manifesto: a third that we must have in any deal, a third that would be highly desirable, and a third that could be jettisoned. The same I guess applies to the other parties. For my part I regard the Conservatives as a natural party of government not opposition. Our aim should be to reach a position of being strong enough numerically as a group to have these discussions on potential coalitions within eight years.[21]

These views were expressed ahead of the 2003 Assembly election when Welsh Conservatives were not expecting to do as well they did. In the event they increased their share of the poll from 16 to 20 per cent on the first vote, and their representation from nine to 11 seats. As a result they firmly established their position as a key potential coalition player. It therefore becomes

---

[18] Lord Griffiths of Fforestfach, 'A Conservative Agenda for Wales', Institute of Welsh Politics Annual Lecture, University of Wales Aberystwyth, November 2002.

[19] In J. Evans, *The Future of Welsh Conservatism* (Cardiff: Institute of Welsh Affairs, 2002).

[20] Quoted in J. Osmond and J. B. Jones, 'Conservatives', in J. Osmond (ed.), *The Birth of Welsh Democracy* (Cardiff: Institute of Welsh Affairs, 2003), p. 209.

[21] *Ibid.*, p. 208.

relevant to ask what might be the 'third' of their programme that they would insist upon? Leaving the constitutional question to one side it should not be too difficult to find elements that would be palatable to both Plaid Cymru and the Liberal Democrats. The May 2003 Welsh Conservative manifesto contained around 50 commitments, including the following:

- Establish an independent all-Wales health authority free of political inter-ference, with the Assembly restricting itself to setting strategic objectives for the NHS.
- Fully fund a children's hospital for Wales
- Abolish tuition fees for Welsh students
- Target resources for Welsh medium teaching at pre-school and primary levels.
- Limit increases for business rates to give a competitive edge to SMEs operating in Wales.
- Improve the A470 between north and south Wales.
- Establish a National Art Gallery for Wales.

Many of these commitments would be attractive, not only to other parties, but to voters. The key area where some negotiation and common understand-ing would need to be achieved would be in health. In any coalition they participated in, the Conservatives would need to hold at least one major port-folio, and health might be one they would advance. Here they would want the opportunity to bring what they would regard as an entrepreneurial and innovative approach to the public sector, perhaps along the lines that New Labour is attempting in England. Greater use of private sector investment and some variation upon Foundation Hospitals might be prime candidates. Undoubtedly there would be difficulties here for both Plaid Cymru and, to a lesser extent, for the Liberal Democrats.

However, there should be scope for developing a distinctive Welsh approach in this area that sustains the fundamental commitment to a free health service at the point of delivery and greater equality of provision across Wales, while allowing some innovative new approaches, especially with regard to reducing waiting times and lists. This has been a key area of failure of the Assembly Government in the first two terms, one which any third-term Government would have to have as a major policy priority.

Of course, Welsh Conservatives have a fundamental problem in that many of their grassroots activists, and certainly much of their core support, remain unreconciled, if not actively hostile to the devolution process. From a Welsh national point of view, an overwhelming benefit of Welsh Conservatives operating successfully within a coalition government would be to encourage their supporters to embrace the devolution project more wholeheartedly.

PLAID CYMRU

There is a paradox, and not a little irony, that the party that has found it most difficult to adjust to the coming of the National Assembly is Plaid Cymru. Some of the problems it faced were not of its own making. A major difficulty was the nature of the National Assembly within which it had to work. As a party Plaid was strongly identified with the 'devolution project' and this was reflected in its success at the 1999 election. On the other hand it had to operate within a flawed institution, the result of the compromises Ron Davies had to make with his own party in delivering it. Plaid Cymru's dilemmas have been analysed in the following terms:

> Was its priority to make the thing work or, conversely, to test the devolution settlement by creating difficulties for the minority Labour administration? Was it possible to conduct these two roles simultaneously? This debate within Plaid was also informed by an awareness of its role in a common drive to boost the public's fragile confidence in devolution, indicated by the wafer-thin referendum vote and a turn-out of just 46 per cent in the first elections. In some ways, Plaid had no choice. This was Wales's first democratically elected institution and, for all its limitations, the project was intrinsically linked with Plaid's longer-term goal of full national status within the European Union. Quite simply, Plaid could not afford for it to be labelled a failure. It had to work with the Labour administration, whilst simultaneously pressing the case for a more muscular Assembly to deliver the distinctive public policies it claimed Wales needed. This meant it had to perform as an effective opposition to Labour in Cardiff Bay, whilst studiously avoiding undermining the concept and legitimacy of the Assembly.[22]

Other issues the party faced during the first term revolved around personalities, and in particular the loss of Dafydd Wigley from the front rank of politics due to illness. At the same time, the party faced two, more fundamental and underlying structural problems which have been endemic since its foundation. These are: first, the difficulty it has had in coming to terms with its precise role as a political party, and secondly, a more subtle psychological failure to break free of the British context of political thought and behaviour. This last has been characterised by its symbiotic relationship with the Labour Party. Both issues need to be resolved if Plaid Cymru is to make itself fit for the new era of national political life in Wales.

However, a major problem for the party is that it has first to understand these dilemmas if they are to be addressed. It needs to appreciate that during the National Assembly's first term, and certainly as the May 2003 election approached, these two characteristics re-emerged to frustrate Plaid Cymru's efforts to project itself to the electorate, either clearly or convincingly. In terms of political strategy the party endeavoured to present itself as the

---

[22] L. McAllister, 'Plaid Cymru', in Osmond (ed.), 2003, pp. 211–12.

alternative party of government in the Assembly. Indeed, this had been the approach from the start. Perhaps Plaid Cymru was beguiled by its success in the 1999 election, in particular its apparent breakthrough in Labour's Valleys strongholds of Rhondda and Islwyn. However, the reality was, and continues to be, that no party in the Assembly can confidently plan on the basis of being a party of government on its own account, not even Labour. Instead, proportional representation requires that parties think in terms of coalition politics and plan their strategies and programmes accordingly. To do otherwise not only presents an ultimately unconvincing case to the electorate, but inevitably also leads to a sense of false consciousness or, perhaps more accurately a sense of denial, within the party itself.

This, then was Plaid Cymru's political failure during the first term. Indeed, it is one that continues since, as yet, there is no indication that the party is actively engaging with or debating the discipline that coalition politics would impose on its policies and strategy.

Plaid Cymru's second, related and more psychological problem in the first term was its failure to develop a distinctive enough policy profile to distinguish itself from the Labour Party. Instead, it remained enthralled and corralled within the same broad agenda, pushing leftwards at the edges to be sure, but failing to strike an innovative or loud enough note to mark out a distinctive position. The essential argument turned around the effectiveness of service delivery in the two key areas of the National Assembly's responsibility and budget, health and education. In both, the Labour-led Assembly Government itself recorded striking failures in the first term and the present Labour Assembly Government continues to do so.

In the Welsh health service, despite large increases in expenditure, waiting lists remained stubbornly long. Meanwhile across the border, in response to a concerted effort, English waiting lists were reduced substantially. This called into question the Assembly Government's competence and its sense of priorities. For, instead of focusing on this central problem it chose to embark upon a diversionary and questionable reorganisation of the health service structure, replacing the five health authorities with 22 local health boards.

In contesting this failing approach the Conservatives proved a more effective opposition during the first term. Plaid Cymru certainly opposed the thrust of the Assembly Government's line. However, it failed to articulate how it would deal with the waiting lists issue, a problem so immediately apparent to the Welsh electorate that its continuance is like a running sore that threatens to derail the whole devolution project itself.

In education the Assembly Government's record was more diffuse. Three broad areas of concern revealed themselves by the end of the first term:

1. The emergence of early years education as the key arena in which policy intervention could be most effective.

2.   A need to bring coherence to 14–18 education in terms of the shape of the curriculum and the distribution of its delivery between schools and colleges.

3.   The importance of developing innovative approaches in the higher education sector in at least three key areas: (a) to produce a more coherent student funding strategy; (b) to encourage more Welsh students to study at Welsh institutions; and (c) to develop higher education's economic role.

In some of these areas the first-term Labour-led Assembly Government showed signs of responding in a progressive way. With early years it began to put together an innovative approach. As far as higher education's role in developing the so-called knowledge economy was concerned, it produced some declaratory policy papers. However, in the 14–18 arena it got lost in the quagmire of the creation of Education and Learning Wales (ELWa) and in piloting a deeply flawed Welsh version of the baccalaureate qualification.

Yet, in the run-up to the May 2003 election there was little sign that Plaid Cymru had clearly identified these three priorities, and even less that it had come up with a coherent policy approach to address them. Instead, the party was left to argue a case that it should be relied upon to divert more resources and deliver health and education services in a way that would be broadly the same, but generally more effective than, Labour.

Consequently the way was left clear for Labour to articulate what sounded a more convincing case, and one that was certainly more elegant. This emerged in Rhodri Morgan's 'clear red water' intervention in November 2002. In it he drew attention to a philosophical distinctiveness between Welsh and New Labour:

> Our commitment to equality leads directly to a model of the relationship between the government and the individual as a citizen rather than as a consumer. Approaches which prioritise choice over equality of outcome rest, in the end, upon a market approach to public services, in which individual economic actors pursue their own best interests with little regard for wider considerations.[23]

Rhodri Morgan argued that a key theme in the first four years of the Assembly had been the creation of a new set of citizenship rights which, as far as possible, were free at the point of use, universal and unconditional. He then listed five examples where the Assembly Government had produced free services to provide individuals with an enhanced sense that they were stakeholders in society:

• Free school milk for the youngest children

[23] Speech to the National Centre for Public Policy, University of Wales, Swansea, 11 December 2002.

- A free nursery place for every three-year old
- Free prescriptions for young people in the age range 16 to 25
- Free entry to museums and galleries for all
- Free bus travel for pensioners and the disabled

Services that were reserved for the poor, he added, very quickly became poor services. Two further symbolic commitments appeared in Labour's May 2003 election manifesto. These were the abolition of prescription charges for all and the provision of free breakfasts for children in primary schools.

This philosophy and approach set itself against mainstream thinking on the need to adapt to the market and the global economy. It certainly sounded radical when compared with the Blairite New Labour project in England, though in terms of Welsh politics it was hardly original. New Labour is now in effect following a mainstream continental Christian Democracy programme, in contrast, to Rhodri Morgan's more traditional social democratic case. Of course, the fact that Labour is simultaneously articulating such divergent philosophical approaches suggests a split personality. At the end of the day which one will prevail? Despite Welsh Labour's attempt to carve out a distinctive position more amenable to the Welsh electorate, it is New Labour in London that holds the purse strings.

Not only that, but some of Rhodri Morgan's specific recommendations were highly dubious when subjected to the cold light of day. For example, more than 80 per cent of prescriptions are already free. It is doubtful whether extending them to the remaining 20 per cent, for people who can well afford to pay, is a wise use of resources.

However, Rhodri Morgan was allowed a free run to make his case through the six months leading up to the May 2003 election. Though vulnerable on key areas of delivery failure, specifically waiting lists in the health service, Plaid Cymru failed to mount an effective attack. On his 'clear red water' position Plaid Cymru could only limply say that he had stolen its policy, for example on free prescriptions.

So, to reiterate, during the first five years of Assembly politics Plaid Cymru failed on two fronts:

1. To sufficiently commit to a political as opposed to a protest role, and thereby develop a sufficiently robust strategy to address the realities of coalition politics; and

2. To develop innovative and credible policy positions sufficiently distinctive from those of the Welsh Labour Party.

It is not surprising that this has been the case since these two matters have run like threads through the party's history. This was made plain by Dr John Davies in his lecture to commemorate the 75th anniversary of Plaid Cymru, delivered at the Llanelli National Eisteddfod in 2000. Among the many themes he explored, two stand out for the propose of the analysis being explored here. The first was a continuing tension over whether Plaid should be more a political party or more a movement in defence of the language. Davies notes that this question came to a head during the campaign around the drowning of the Tryweryn Valley in Meirionnydd between 1956 and 1962. Despite a good deal of pressure the party, led by Gwynfor Evans, resisted the temptation to undertake a further symbolic act such as the burning of the bombing school in 1936. Saunders Lewis wrote in a letter to Gwynfor Evans in 1962, 'The Executive Committee of Plaid Cymru betrayed the cause of Tryweryn. I cannot forget that.'

However, as Davies records, the main reason the party undertook no direct action on behalf of Tryweryn was because of the attitude of its executive committee in Meirionnydd which at that time was the most winnable constituency in Wales. He quotes from a letter sent by the Meirionnydd constituency party to the national executive in 1961:

> It should be clearly borne in mind that the Party in Meirion was never in favour of acting outside the law. On the contrary; our considered opinion was that any such action would be a hindrance and a stumbling block to a growing political party ... Direct action, while not saving Tryweryn, would kill the nation's faith in, and support of the Party, even if such action stilled the consciences of a few.[24]

As Davies remarks, the key words here are 'a growing political party':

> By the 1960s, that is precisely what Plaid Cymru was determined to be ... It is possible to discern a fundamental shift in the thinking of party leaders in the late 1950s and the early 1960s, a shift which led them to decide to lead a political party rather than a protest group.[25]

The second of John Davies' themes that resonate for the argument being developed in this paper is Plaid Cymru's relationship with the Labour Party. This is the way the 'internal rhythms' of Labour and Plaid Cymru seem to march in step. That is to say, when Labour is doing well so often is Plaid Cymru; when Labour is facing vicissitudes and internal divisions, so often is Plaid. Plaid Cymru emerged as a serious political party in the 1960s, a time when Labour was in power for most of the decade. In the 1970s Labour's splits over Europe were matched by those in Plaid.

During the early 1980s Labour made a leftward lurch and spent much energy on internal divisions and disputes. In Plaid Cymru, the National Left (*Y Chwith Genedlaethol*) was established in 1980, a group that included elements of the hard left. Similar arguments divided Plaid Cymru members

---

[24] J. Davies, *Lecture Commemorating the 75th Anniversary of Plaid Cymru* (Cardiff: Plaid Cymru, 2000).
[25] *Ibid.*

to those that were being fought over in the Labour Party. By 1980 the National Left had a majority on the party's National Executive. Arguably, all of this is but a further expression of Wales's quasi-colonial relationship with, and dependency upon, England. That it should be played out within the ranks of Wales' national party is a reflection of how deep these roots of dependency go and, consequently, how difficult they are to eradicate.

Of course, by the 1990s the Labour Party had concluded that it could never hope to win power by moving further to the left. Whether it needed to move so far to the right under Blair is another matter. In any event, in his lecture John Davies notes that some in Plaid Cymru, notably Dafydd Elis Thomas, had earlier reached a similar conclusion.

In its early days he was closely associated with the National Left and, indeed, was President of the party for much of the time. However, by 1985 he was writing in *Radical Wales* of the 'gamble' of 1981, of the public's inability to grasp 'an excessively abstract' strategy and of the confusion which could arise if Plaid Cymru's image did not differ from that of the Labour Party'.[26]

The continuing presence of these tendencies within Plaid Cymru — struggles over its development as a political party and difficulties in discovering a distinctive policy position — were for a while concealed from view by the success of the 1999 Assembly election. Yet, hindsight now reveals that a good deal of this success was the result of a combination of unique circumstances. These included the fact that it was the first 'Welsh' election in which voters were prepared to respond to a Welsh approach. As a naturally 'Welsh' party Plaid Cymru benefited from that. On the other hand Labour failed to appreciate the importance of stressing such a profile and was also damaged by its internal divisions, especially the perceived imposition of Alun Michael as leader in the wake of the Ron Davies affair.[27]

However, the results of the May 2003 election and its aftermath have demonstrated that the party's twin dilemmas have still to be resolved in a way that can make Plaid Cymru fit for participating effectively in the politics of twenty-first century Wales. This is likely to prove extremely difficult for the party to address. The first requirement is for it to understand and acknowledge the challenge. Yet even the late Phil Williams, one of the most strategic thinkers Plaid Cymru has produced, did not identify the re-emergence of these underlying problems in the immediate aftermath of the election. He concluded that the result of the May 2003 election was in effect a return to normality. That is to say, the outcome was what the party had

[26] *Ibid.*
[27] See on this subject J. Osmond, 'A Constitutional Convention by Other Means', in R. Hazell (ed.) *The State and the Nations: The first year of devolution in the United Kingdom* (Exeter: Imprint Academic, 2000).

expected to achieve in 1999. That this is not the case has been persuasively argued by Richard Wyn Jones and Roger Scully:

> Our analysis suggests that the electoral defeat suffered by Plaid Cymru in May 2003 was not about Welsh politics returning to 'business as usual' following the 'aberration' of 1999. Labour's 2003 vote was little higher than four years previously, and Labour continues to attract much lower levels of support in Wales for National Assembly elections than Westminster ones. The more significant change was the collapse in support for Plaid Cymru. This defeat was not inevitable, but largely the consequence of three factors:
>
> 1. Plaid was hurt by the change in Labour leadership, and the efforts of Welsh Labour to rebrand itself and campaign more aggressively in the key seats. This was something largely outside the control of Plaid Cymru.
>
> 2. For much of the electorate Plaid's image was also damaged by the attacks from the Welsh Mirror and others. These attacks came from outside Plaid but the party might potentially have responded to them much more effectively than it did.
>
> 3. Finally, Plaid was damaged by the replacement of a popular leader, Dafydd Wigley, with a new party leader, Ieuan Wyn Jones, who was and is singularly lacking in electoral appeal. This was largely a self-inflicted wound for which Plaid Cymru had really only itself to blame.[28]

However, the analysis undertaken here demonstrates that far more than the personality of the leadership is at stake if Plaid Cymru is to turn its fortunes around. There has to be a fundamental reappraisal of the seriousness of the party as a *political* party in the sense of seeking a government rather than an opposition role.

Following on from this, the party needs to undertake a fundamental review of its policy commitments, to make them more fitting for the needs of contemporary Welsh society and the realities of coalition governance. The scale of the changes required can be gauged from the lack of ambition revealed by the late Phil Williams in his last assessment of the role of Plaid Cymru:

> Within the Party of Wales there is a recurring debate as to whether an essential pre-requisite for self-government is that Plaid Cymru replaces the Labour Party as the mainstream, dominant party in Wales. Alternatively, is it possible for a single-minded and uncompromising Plaid Cymru to create the conditions whereby other parties deliver self-government, albeit step-by-step and with some reluctance? Progress over the past forty years, and especially the establishment of the National Assembly, point to the latter strategy.[29]

---

[28] R. Wyn Jones and R. Scully, 'Must Plaid Lose?' *Institute of Welsh Affairs Agenda*, Summer 2004, p. 62.

[29] P. Williams, *The Psychology of Distance* (Cardiff: Institute of Welsh Affairs, 2003), p. 41.

The reference to the 'past forty years' is the critical qualification that should accompany this assessment. For the recurring debate Phil Williams described is one that looks back to the latter half of the 20th Century. At the beginning of the 21st Century Plaid Cymru faces a new debate: how seriously it takes its role as a political party in the life of Wales, and the strategy and policies that should flow from the answer it gives that question?

TOWARDS 2007

It has been argued here that the key question for the future of Welsh politics revolves around coalitions. If presented with the opportunity following the 2007 election, can Plaid Cymru, the Welsh Conservatives and the Welsh Liberal Democrats find common cause sufficient to form a coalition admin-istration with an agreed programme?

If this were to happen it would represent a decisive break with the past and, indeed, a seismic shift in Welsh politics. Arguably such a course is necessary both to advance the full agenda of the Richard Commission recommendations, and in the process to anchor devolution securely in the territory of Welsh politics. To assess the accuracy of this last judgement, consider the two crucial conditions that would have been fulfilled if that eventuality arose:

1.   In elections to the National Assembly the people of Wales would have exercised a real choice, not just between parties and candi-dates, but in producing an alternative government.

2.   The political parties participating in the new coalition government would have unambiguously accepted that the National Assembly should become an effective body along the lines recommended by the Richard Commission, and declared they would campaign for this in a referendum.

So, finally, how likely is this scenario? In electoral terms, as has been argued, the outcome of the 2007 election is more likely than not to deliver the conditions in which the opposition parties will be able to cooperate. How likely are they to seize the opportunity?

The first answer to this question is that in local politics across much of Wales they have already done so. As a result of the May 2003 elections coali-tions now rule in eight of the 22 Welsh councils, with informal coalitions in two others. Although Labour held on to its core Valley councils, it lost politi-cal control of a swathe of others across north and south Wales to administra-tions now run by combinations of the other parties. Swansea and Bridgend are now run by a coalition of Liberal Democrats, Conservatives and Inde-pendents. The Conservatives control the Vale of Glamorgan, with informal support from Plaid Cymru and the Independents. Cardiff is run by a minority Liberal Democrat administration, again with tacit support from the Conservatives and Plaid Cymru. In north Wales Conwy is the outstanding example of the pattern of anti-Labour coalitions, with the council being run by a combination of Independents, Conservatives, Plaid Cymru and Liberal Democrats. In much of Wales the main political message emanating from the local elections was: 'anything but Labour'.

A second answer revolves around the question of whether a coalition in the National Assembly could find enough common ground in policy terms. Enough should have been said in this chapter to suggest that this should not be too difficult. The health service might seem to offer most problems, but there should be enough common purpose in addressing the waiting lists issue to satisfy the demands of one four year term. Other areas where the parties might find a good deal in common include:

- Using the Assembly Government's large public expenditure programmes to promote private sector developments, especially in health, housing and education.
- Identifying a small number of community development zones in rural Wales to check the outward migration of young people and underpin the language and culture.
- Investing more aggressively in a renewable energy programme.
- Developing a more integrated and distinctive 14 to 19 education programme.
- Discovering a fresh approach to the problems of the south Wales Valleys, perhaps in the form of promoting a Development Corporation.
- Improving north-south communications.

Of course, a coalition along the lines speculated upon here will not emerge without political leadership. First the notion has to be floated and the parties convinced that it is necessary, desirable and possible. Secondly a figure has to emerge who has the capability and personality to make the case and reach out across the parties and to the wider electorate. In describing these required qualifications it should not be too difficult to identify potential candidates.

BIBLIOGRAPHY

Davies, J., *Lecture Commemorating the 75th Anniversary of Plaid Cymru* (Cardiff: Plaid Cymru, 2000).
Evans, J., *The Future of Welsh Conservatism* (Cardiff: Institute of Welsh Affairs, 2002).

Griffiths of Fforestfach, Lord, 'A Conservative Agenda for Wales', Institute of Welsh Politics Annual Lecture, University of Wales Aberystwyth, November 2002.

McAllister, L., 'Plaid Cymru', in J. Osmond (ed.) *The Birth of Welsh Democracy* (Cardiff: Institute of Welsh Affairs, 2003).

Osmond, J., 'A Constitutional Convention by Other Means', in R. Hazell (ed.) *The State and the Nations: The first year of devolution in the United Kingdom* (Exeter: Imprint Academic, 2000).

Osmond, J. (ed.), *Welsh Politics Come of Age: Responses to the Richard Commission* (Cardiff: Institute of Welsh Affairs, 2005).

Osmond, J. and J. B. Jones, 'Conservatives', in J. Osmond (ed.), *The Birth of Welsh Democracy* (Cardiff: Institute of Welsh Affairs, 2003).

Richard Commission, *Report of the Richard Commission*, at www.richardcommission.gov.uk/content/finalreport/report-e.pdf

Welsh Labour Party, *Better Governance for Wales*, [response to the Richard Commission] (Cardiff: Welsh Labour Party, August 2004).

Wigley, D., 'A charter for wreckers', *Agenda* (Cardiff: Institute of Welsh Affairs, Autumn 2004).

Williams, P., *The Psychology of Distance* (Cardiff: Institute of Welsh Affairs, 2003).

Wyn Jones, R. and R. Scully, 'Must Plaid Lose?', *Agenda* (Cardiff: Institute of Welsh Affairs, Summer 2004).

4

Northern Ireland

While You Take The High Road . . .

Rick Wilford and Robin Wilson[1]

INTRODUCTION: THE UNCIVIL PAST

'The dynamics of devolution' have a very different connotation in Northern Ireland than in the rest of the UK. Since October 2002, following revelations of an IRA spy ring, the power-sharing administration at Stormont has been in suspended animation, replaced by 'direct rule' from Westminster.[2] Standing back from the alarms and excursions of recent years, aside from the previous five-month interlude of power-sharing in 1974, this has been the default scenario for a generation.[3]

An even more *longue durée* look at modern Irish history shows just how fragile is the civic culture necessary for devolution to become embedded. It was not called that then, but 'direct rule' was how all of Ireland was governed under the Union with Great Britain until 1921, via the Lord Lieutenant and Chief Secretary at Dublin Castle. The 'ethnogenesis'[4] of mass politics in the 19th century saw political Protestantism and political Catholicism respectively dress themselves up in the incompatible sectarian colours of 'unionism' and 'nationalism'.[5] For the former, direct rule was fine, while for the latter the goal was 'repeal' of the union; neither felt able to coexist with the other in the same polity.[6]

---

[1] As with previous volumes arising from the devolution-monitoring project coordinated by the Constitution Unit, we are indebted to our colleagues in the research team generating the Northern Ireland reports (available at www.ucl.ac.uk/constitution-unit/nations/monitoring.php): John Coakley, Lizanne Dowds, Greg McLaughlin, Elizabeth Meehan and Duncan Morrow. We take total responsibility, however, for the contents of this chapter.

[2] See November 2002 Northern Ireland devolution monitoring report, at:
www.ucl.ac.uk/constitution-unit/monrep/ni/ni_november_2002.pdf

[3] P. Bew and G. Gillespie, *Northern Ireland: A chronology of the Troubles 1968–1999* (Dublin: Gill & Macmillan, 1999).

[4] P. Gibbon, *Origins of Ulster Unionism* (Manchester: Manchester University Press, 1975).

[5] D. H. Akenson, *Small Differences: Irish Catholics and Irish Protestants 1815–1922* (Dublin: Gill & Macmillan, 1988).

[6] 'as goat and ox may graze in the same field / and each gain something from proximity' — to take a phrase from Hewitt's 'The colony', in F. Ormsby (ed.), *The Collected Poems of John Hewitt* (Belfast: Blackstaff Press, 1991), p. 79.

For a generation of British politicians from the 1880s to the 1920s, Ireland persistently intruded, often to critical effect, on the Westminster stage. Despite unionist resistance, therefore, a growing section of the political class, and clearly a majority by the aftermath of the first world war, endorsed 'home rule'.[7]

Indeed, unionists were to have devolution, whether they wanted it or not. While nationalists chafed at the partition of the island under the Government of Ireland Act of 1920, a parliament was created in Belfast, whose modest minority protections were swiftly removed by the regionally dominant unionist bloc.[8] In the 1930s, this provincial (in both senses) political elite constructed for itself the grandiloquent building at Stormont. Half a century of one-party rule was shattered by the mainly-Catholic civil rights movement of the 1960s.[9]

But the reluctance of the British political class to re-engage — the then Home Secretary, James Callaghan, wrote inelegantly of being 'sucked into the Irish bog' — fatefully postponed the (re)introduction of direct rule.[10] The Stormont Parliament was not 'prorogued' until after a vertiginous explosion of violence in an atmosphere of constitutional insecurity — and only then to seek as quick a political exit as possible through a renewal of devolution, albeit now with power shared between unionists and 'constitutional' nationalists.[11] It failed on the rock of the north-south linkages the latter demanded, brought down by a decidedly unconstitutional 'loyalist' strike.[12]

It is one of the great 'what if?'s of modern Irish history that, around the time of the third home rule crisis in the run-up to war, an alternative approach was canvassed, that could have provided a *via media* — the notion of 'home rule all round'.[13] This would have been impossible for unionists to present as setting them apart from Britain and would have taken the wind from their political sails, thereby preventing partition.

Partition will not be easily reversed at this historical distance. But as the century came to a close, the Belfast Agreement of 1998 gave Northern Ireland the opportunity to lead the way in a renewed effort (albeit asymmetric) towards UK home rule all round and to rebuild the fabric of relationships

---

[7] R. Wilson, 'Imperialism in crisis: the "Irish dimension"', in M. Langan and B. Schwarz (eds.), *Crises in the British State 1880–1930* (London: Hutchinson, 1985).

[8] P. Buckland, *The Factory of Grievances: Devolved Government in Northern Ireland 1921–39* (Dublin: Gill & Macmillan, 1979).

[9] See the nuanced, revisionist account of the latter in R. English, *Armed Struggle: A history of the IRA* (London: Macmillan, 2003), 81–108.

[10] J. Callaghan, *A House Divided* (London: Collins, 1973), p. 15.

[11] P. Bew and H. Patterson, *The British State and the Ulster Crisis: From Wilson to Thatcher* (London: Verso, 1985).

[12] See the interview by one of the authors with the Northern Ireland Secretary of the time, the later Lord Whitelaw, in *Fortnight* 271 (March 1989).

[13] M. Burgess, 'The British federal tradition', in A. Duff (ed.), *Subsidiarity Within the EC* (London: Federal Trust, 1993).

with the rest of the island. While majority Protestant opinion had eventually turned against the 1974 arrangements, the new, 'inclusive' agreement was also to embrace the 'republican movement' of Sinn Féin and the IRA.

However, the inter-party disagreements which soon re-emerged, over the terms of inclusion of republicans, meant Scotland and Wales leapfrogged the region into the devolution of power. Protestant endorsement of the arrangements steadily haemorrhaged. Repeated, and eventually prolonged, suspension of the institutions inexorably followed.

THE AGREEMENT: WHAT HAS GONE WRONG?

Northern Ireland is, for the most part, now superficially free of obtrusive 'security' presences, the death toll from politically-motivated violence is vastly reduced from its early-1970s peak and unemployment has fallen in line with wider UK macroeconomic trends. On a more profound level, however, this is a society with pathological features.

First, in social terms, the decline in unemployment in Northern Ireland obscures the fact that *employment* remains lower than in any UK region except the North-East, owing to the high rate of economic inactivity.[14] Around three out of ten working-age adults play no role in the workforce. And an unprecedented large-scale survey has indicated that Northern Ireland is an even more unequal society than the Republic of Ireland or Great Britain, themselves outliers in this regard by European standards.[15] Given the predominance of sectarian over social solidarity, this is hardly surprising.

The region remains deeply divided along sectarian lines; indeed, those divisions are if anything deepening. Polarising electoral behaviour is the most obvious symptom: the more explicit hard-line 'ethno-nationalist' parties, the Democratic Unionist Party and Sinn Féin, moved clearly ahead of their more moderate, 'communal contender' counterparts, the Ulster Unionist Party and the Social Democratic and Labour Party, in the (twice-postponed) Assembly election of November 2003 and the election to the European Parliament in June 2004.[16]

On the ground, checkpoints may have gone, because police and soldiers are no longer threatened, but 'peace walls' have proliferated at interfaces marked by sectarian tension.[17] Data collected by the Northern Ireland Hous-

---

[14] National Statistics, *Regional Trends* (London: The Stationery Office, 2004), p. 72.

[15] P. Hillyard, G. Kelly, E. McLaughlin, D. Patsios and M. Tomlinson, *Bare Necessities: Poverty and social exclusion in Northern Ireland — key findings* (Belfast: Democratic Dialogue, 2003).

[16] This distinction *vis-à-vis* divided societies is made by the minority rights expert Asbjørn Eide, in A. Eide, *New Approaches to Minority Protection* (London: Minority Rights Group, 2003), p. 10.

[17] The Northern Ireland Office told BBC's *Newsnight* in early 2003 that it identified 37 of these barriers.

ing Executive show a dramatic rise in intimidation in recent years.[18] And the malaise of intolerance is finding further expression in domestic violence (nearly 17,000 incidents were recorded in the year 2003–04), and growing racist and homophobic harassment.[19]

At least the trend of declining public confidence about 'community relations' since the Belfast Agreement has begun to go into reverse.[20] This upturn, however, has come since the associated institutions which many hoped would lead the way in this regard were suspended, and with the most recent Northern Ireland Life and Times Survey data suggesting citizens have cast a colder eye on what difference devolution made as the experience has receded.[21]

Relatedly, paramilitarism has become entrenched, at the expense of the rule of law. At the height of the 'troubles', violence tended to be lethal and discrete; now it is less fatal, in terms of numbers, but diffuse. For many years this went officially unacknowledged, or was dismissed as internal 'housekeeping' as such activity mostly came within the permissive scope of the 'ceasefires' paramilitaries had declared. This had a corrosive effect, particularly on public confidence within the Protestant community, and, again after the suspension of the post-agreement institutions in October 2002, a tougher line was, at least formally, taken. The Joint Declaration issued by London and Dublin in May 2003 gave, in paragraph 13, a much more common-sense definition of paramilitary activity, which a new Independent Monitoring Commission was established inter alia to assess.[22]

In its first report, in April 2004, the IMC pointed out that paramilitary shootings and assaults had *increased* in the four years 1995–9 on the pre-ceasefire 1991–4 level and — even more remarkably — increased *again* post-agreement in 1999–2002. Such attacks, mainly because of the surge in 'loyalist' violence, were thus running in the latter period at nearly double the rate they were before the 'ceasefires' were announced![23] But — and this may explain the more benign perception emerging of the state of community

---

[18] We are grateful to Pete Shirlow, who has collated the data and highlighted this point.

[19] See on domestic violence: Police Service of Northern Ireland, *Community Safety Branch Statistics on Domestic Violence, Hate Crime and Youth Offences in Northern Ireland 2003/2004* (Belfast: PSNI, 2004); on racist harassment: P. Connolly and M. Keenan, *The Hidden Truth: Racist harassment in Northern Ireland* (Belfast: Northern Ireland Statistics and Research Agency, 2001); and on homophobic harassment: N. Jarman and A. Tennant, *An Acceptable Prejudice? Homophobic violence and harassment in Northern Ireland* (Belfast: Institute for Conflict Research, 2003).

[20] See the analysis by L. Dowds in the August 2004 Northern Ireland devolution monitoring report, at www.ucl.ac.uk/constitution-unit/monrep/ni/ni_august_2004.pdf

[21] See the analysis by L. Dowds in the May 2004 Northern Ireland devolution monitoring report, at www.ucl.ac.uk/constitution-unit/monrep/ni/ni_may_2004.pdf

[22] The *Joint Declaration* was finally released on 1 May 2003 after the two governments had failed to secure inter-party agreement to its terms. See www.nio.gov.uk/joint_declaration_between_the_british_and_irish_governments.pdf

[23] *First Report of the Independent Monitoring Commission*, HC 516 (London: The Stationery Office, 2004), p. 20, available at www.nio.gov.uk/pdf/imcreport.pdf

relations — in 2002–3 and 2003–4 the chief constable was able to report successive declines in the incidence of paramilitary violence.[24]

Moreover, a nexus has developed between paramilitarism and 'ordinary' crime, which has corroded the social fabric of working-class life, and has engendered a stratum of (to borrow Baldwin's phrase) 'hard-faced men who look as if they had done very well out of the war'. The IMC report spelled out how all the major paramilitary groups were enmeshed in racketeering of one sort or another. And the Organised Crime Task Force, launched by the Northern Ireland Office in 2000, reported shortly thereafter that it was aware of 235 criminal gangs operating in the region (population 1.7 million), of which more than 150 were linked to paramilitaries; counterfeiting alone, it said, was worth more than £150 million a year.[25] This represents a major vested interest in paramilitaries *not* complying with the end to their activities required by paragraph 13.

It was on this basis that the prominent cleric Mgr Denis Faul made front-page headlines in the mainly-Catholic *Irish News* in June 2004 by claiming in a homily: 'Things are worse than they were in 1968. Eight armed groups rule.' Coincidentally, the same day the new Presbyterian Moderator, Dr Ken Newell, told the General Assembly, meeting in Belfast, that the 'wave of hope' that had followed the agreement had given way to a 'trough of despair'. He said: 'Paramilitarism still burdens our communities with its interface tensions, internal feuding and rising criminality.'[26]

And it was paramilitary criminality — and SF's insouciance about the IRA version of it — which was to blow any short-to-medium-term restoration of devolution out of the water. First came the extraordinary heist of £26.5 million from the Northern Bank bang in the heart of Belfast City Centre in December 2004. The raid, attributed to the IRA publicly by the chief constable, Hugh Orde, and privately by the *Garda Síochána*, came within weeks of the latest failure by London and Dublin to 'choreograph' a resolution among the Northern Ireland parties (see below) — a failure which it quickly emerged had been in part due to the refusal of the IRA, once more, to renounce violence, including criminal activity. The episode indeed drew republican leaders to suggest that nothing the IRA did — including the notorious murder and 'disappearance' in 1972 of a mother of ten in west Belfast — could be deemed criminal at all.

This was followed by the brutal murder of Robert McCartney outside a Belfast bar in January 2005 with the site forensically cleaned and not a witness to be found, despite the bar having more than 70 people (including

---

[24] See table in 2003–4 report, at www.psni.police.uk/chief_constables_annual_report_2003–2004.pdf, p. 14.

[25] The Organised Crime Task Force 'Threat Assessment' is available at www.octf.gov.uk/Publications.cfm

[26] *Irish News* and *Irish Times*, 8 June 2004.

two former SF candidates) inside at the time. Clumsy attempts at witness intimidation were undone by the quiet insistence of the victim's family that witnesses should come forward to the police and the killers be brought to justice — attempts made worse by an IRA offer to deal with those it deemed responsible itself by shooting them.

How has this turn of events come about in the six years since the agreement, and after a decade of paramilitary 'ceasefires'? What has gone wrong?

Much of the focus of disillusionment has been the failure of the 'republican movement' and its 'loyalist' counterparts to fulfil their responsibilities under the Belfast Agreement to undergo 'total disarmament' by May 2000, working 'in good faith' with the Independent International Commission on Decommissioning set up to that end.[27] It is clear that this was a bad-faith commitment all round, with paramilitary spokespersons on both sides continuing since the agreement to indicate in public comments that they simply do not appreciate that paramilitarism is incompatible with democratic legitimacy.

The two main loyalist paramilitary groups, the Ulster Defence Association and the Ulster Volunteer Force, have not decommissioned a single weapon. The IRA, meanwhile, has through political pressure turned the process into one of putting an unquantified number of weapons in an undefined way 'beyond use', in a manner which may or may not be irreversible.[28] What should have been a means to build trust with the Protestant community has turned into its opposite.

The contrast with Macedonia, where power-sharing was reconfigured after the Ohrid Agreement of 2001, is stark: there, the political representatives of the ethnic-Albanian National Liberation Army share power, albeit shakily, with the Slav-Macedonian social democrats. But this was only possible because the NLA physically handed over a significant number of weapons, in the glare of TV cameras, to NATO at the conclusion of the conflict there.

But in one sense the argument over decommissioning in Northern Ireland, like other post-agreement rows over the flying of the Union flag above government departments, the reform of the old Royal Ulster Constabulary, or how to deal with the region's troubled past — even, on one occasion, whether republican Easter lilies could legitimately be displayed in the foyer of the Stormont Parliament — are all symptoms of a more profound difficulty. That is, that the Belfast Agreement was not a *settlement* of the Northern Ireland constitutional dispute; rather, as one of the politicians who negotiated it said, it was an 'agreement to disagree'.

---

[27] *The Agreement: Agreement reached in the multi-party negotiations* (Belfast and London: Northern Ireland Office, 1998), available at www.nio.gov.uk/issues/agreement.htm, p. 20.

[28] Speculative estimates have put the weapons thus far 'put beyond use' by the IRA at around 6 per cent of its arsenal.

Not only did the agreement restate the prior position, accepted by successive governments since its first enunciation in the Northern Ireland Constitution Act of 1973 — namely that Northern Ireland would remain part of the United Kingdom unless and until a majority opted for a united Ireland in a border poll — even though the institutions proposed for the region suggested it had a *sui generis* constitutional character. Furthermore, the provisions for 'parity of esteem' inscribed this fundamental divide between unionists and nationalists into the wiring of the institutions themselves.

And these two key, defining elements were themselves a product of the very division the agreement was intended to heal: unionists demanded the first, nationalists the second. Thus, on the divisive issues itemised above, unionists took the side of acting to embed the sovereignty of the UK in public symbolism, while nationalists argued for a neutral or bi-national alternative. On decommissioning, while unionists pressed for republicans to bow the knee to lawful authority, nationalists countered by pointing to the continuing (indeed greater) activities of loyalist paramilitaries.

This placed Northern Ireland at the centre of a much broader, indeed global, debate — concerning the form of democracy that is most appropriate for divided societies, particularly those emerging from a violent past.[29] (This is assuming that power-sharing is favoured over suppression or secession and that an international protectorate is eschewed.) The Belfast Agreement has, in its 'internal' or 'strand one' dimension, a 'consociationalist' character, embodying the conventional Lijphartian wisdom of grand-coalition government, mutual-veto arrangements, 'segmental autonomy' (that is, segregation) and proportionality in public employment (already largely secured).[30]

But that debate has tended to tilt towards an 'integrationist' alternative.[31] Consociationalism has been moving out of intellectual fashion, in large measure because its underpinning anthropological assumptions about 'plural societies' have become increasingly untenable. The associated view of ethnicity as fixed, singular and self-contained has given way to a recognition that individual identities are plastic, complex and relational. This implies a quite different constitutional prescription, focused on progressively achieving reconciliation through developing inter-ethnic relationships at all levels, including moderate political coalitions and more integrated social life.

Lijphart now concedes that the anthropology on which his theory relied is obsolete, yet claims, not very plausibly, that he can save the theory nonethe-

---

[29] See A. Reynolds (ed.), *The Architecture of Democracy: Constitutional design, conflict management and democracy* (Oxford: Oxford University Press, 2002).

[30] See A. Lijphart, *Democracy in Plural Societies* (New Haven, CT: Yale University Press, 1977).

[31] R. Wilson, *Northern Ireland: What's going wrong* (London: Constitution Unit, UCL and Belfast: Institute of Governance, Public Policy and Social Research, QUB, 2003).

less.[32] But even if one accepts the consociationalist policy toolkit for divided societies, the conditions that favour success, as Lijphart indicated, include the tempering of communal divisions by a multiple balance of power and cross-cutting cleavages, as well as traditions of elite accommodation and acceptance of the overarching legitimacy of the polity.[33]

The latter has never been conceded by republicans: 'Before the Good Friday Agreement, the six-county state was an undemocratic, illegitimate and failed political entity and after it, it remains so', according to the SF president, Gerry Adams.[34] Moreover, the efforts to render the republican movement more amenable in this regard have only served to ensure that the Protestant community, roughly equally divided on the agreement at its promulgation, is now largely alienated from it.[35] More generally, the infusion of the agreement with ethno-nationalist assumptions and the subsequent (and associated) marginalisation of civil society have reduced Northern Ireland's politico-cultural complexity to a polarised nationalist-unionist axis — and thereby undone the very power-sharing institutions the agreement established.

The evidence is that the strategy of 'implementing the agreement in full' has run its course, and that the danger is of a prolonged period of direct rule, perhaps ameliorated by enhanced local government. The experience of politics post-agreement would suggest that the high road of devolution, to an assembly with primary legislative powers and a power-sharing executive, will not be achieved without further 'constitutional engineering'. The position papers produced by the major parties for the review of the agreement that began in February 2004 illustrate the difficulties.

THE REVIEW OF THE AGREEMENT

Its pre-eminent election performance meant that the DUP was in a position to set unionist terms for a new agreement. In the run-up to the Assembly poll, the DUP published *Towards A New Agreement*, a summary critique of the 1998 accord, and made it clear that its aim was 'to win a majority of unionist seats ... to prevent the election of a First and Deputy First Minister and thereby force a renegotiation of the Belfast Agreement'.[36] Under the slogan 'It's time for a fair deal', the document made abundantly clear not only the DUP's refusal to countenance the inclusion of SF in government without

[32] A. Lijphart (2001), 'Constructivism and consociational theory', *Newsletter of the American Political Science Association Organized Section in Comparative Politics*, 12(1), pp. 11–13.

[33] Lijphart, 1977, p. 54.

[34] *Irish Times*, 12 March 1999.

[35] See the analysis by L. Dowds in the May 2004 Northern Ireland devolution monitoring report, at www.ucl.ac.uk/constitution-unit/monrep/ni/ni_may_2004.pdf

[36] See www.dup.org

compliance with the 'acts of completion' agenda set out in the Joint Declaration, but also its interim rejection of any negotiation with 'representatives of terrorism'. Any new agreement, it insisted, would have to command the support of both nationalists and unionists, and be a settlement within the Union.

It was not until early in 2004 that more concrete proposals were to emerge. In *Vision for Devolution*, published in February, the party set out what it considered to be three alternative means of establishing stable government:

- power-sharing via a voluntary coalition subject to collective responsibility;
- a corporate assembly model, with no overarching Executive, and key decisions taken by a reduced assembly on a weighted-majority basis; or
- a power-sharing, but reformed, executive as per the 1998 agreement — provided 'SF/IRA' engaged in the acts of completion and with an effective exclusion mechanism.

As we have made clear elsewhere, the option of a voluntary coalition is implicit in the 1998 agreement: there is no obligation upon parties to take their seats around the Executive table.[37] This is a matter of choice — one that all eligible parties, the DUP included, exercised when the first cabinet in waiting was nominated in November 1999. But the voluntary-coalition option has been serially rejected by the SDLP, wedded, like SF, to implementation in full of the original accord.

The second alternative, the corporate assembly model, would provide a committee-based system of devolved administration, akin to the original Welsh model, with decision-making authority vested in a 72-seat Assembly that would oversee a reduced number of government departments, the number of which would be similar to 'previous levels', i.e. no fewer than six. This option was the initially favoured position of the UUP when the negotiations that led to the 1998 agreement got under way; it was rejected *tout court* then by SF and the SDLP and when it was unveiled anew by the DUP in 2004.

The final option is common ground among all key parties, including London and Dublin. Given its provenance, however, it is significant since it demonstrates, as does the voluntary-coalition alternative, the readiness of the DUP, for the first time, to endorse power-sharing with nationalists and, in this case, republicans, signalling a step-change in the DUP's historic position. That said, besides the mechanisms for executive formation, the DUP sought to reduce the number of departments and MLAs (thereby favouring the larger parties), to dispense with the Civic Forum and to 'reform' the

---

[37] See, for instance, R. Wilford, 'Northern Ireland: resolving an ancient quarrel?' in M. O'Neill (ed.), *Devolution and British Politics* (Harlow: Pearson Longman, 2004), p. 43.

Equality Commission and the Human Rights Commission. Such proposals were consonant with that to create an efficiency commission, tasked to subject all existing 'strand one' institutions to a value-for-money audit, a process it also sought to apply to 'strand two' (north-south) institutions (see below).

The DUP's proposals for the strand two and three institutions (the latter 'east-west'), integral elements of the original design which it had boycotted from the first, were not published until the review was under way. Whereas the 1998 model provided for a referendum to be held on Northern Ireland's constitutional status only when the Secretary of State detected a mood for change, i.e. for unification with the Republic, and thereafter on a septennial basis, the DUP proposed that there be a moratorium on border polls for 30 years and that the authority to make the decision to hold a referendum should be transferred from the UK Government to the reformed assembly. Each provision would, in its view, create the constitutional certainty that is required to settle Northern Ireland's status for a generation and copper-fasten the 'consent principle' underwritten by the 1998 agreement. With those undertakings in place the opportunity would then purportedly exist for 'stability and positive relations between Northern Ireland and the Republic of Ireland', which 'could transform inter-party and community relationships in Northern Ireland'.

In place of the British-Irish Council the DUP proposed a new all-islands council and a parallel parliamentary body. The former's task was to address the totality of relationships within the British Isles, including those between London and Dublin, thereby displacing the free-standing British-Irish Inter-governmental Conference created in 1998. The proposed council would be served by a new secretariat, based in Northern Ireland, charged to co-ordinate and support all plenary, bilateral and multilateral meetings of its members.

In relation to north-south matters, the DUP accepts that there should be a mutually beneficial and practical set of arrangements — provided that they are in the interests of Northern Ireland, that they are fully accountable to the proposed assembly and that they respect the constitutional status of Northern Ireland, i.e. they are not presented or understood as a means of promoting Irish unity. Accepting that north-south relationships will be institutionalised marks another significant development, although the DUP argues that their shape and form should be subjected to a time-limited efficiency audit. Any such arrangements would only be effected, however, if there were prior agreement on the internal governance of Northern Ireland and the north–south bodies would cease to operate in the event of the suspension of devolution.

This is important because the small print of the DUP plan, under the first or third models, includes the potential of a vote of confidence in the Northern Ireland Executive being called at any time; were this not to secure at least a 70 per cent Assembly majority the administration would fall. As the DUP already enjoys 30 per cent plus support in the (suspended) Assembly, this seems geared to ensuring it has a veto in any power-sharing government.

Each of the DUP's options contemplates power-sharing with nationalists and/or republicans; as the party's former social development minister Nigel Dodds put it, 'both nationalist parties have a place in Executive Government in their grasp if they are prepared to act'.[38] But the breadth and depth of the agenda it set out militated against any progress. In effect, it was a version of 'nothing can be agreed until everything is agreed', especially since it made clear that any agreement over north-south bodies was reliant upon prior acceptance of any of its alternatives for the internal governance of Northern Ireland, preferably — and certainly in the short run — the proposed voluntary coalition predicated on the exclusion of SF.

The SDLP's position was clear: to quote from its initial submission to the review, 'we will not renegotiate the Agreement'. Beyond the blunt defence of the 1998 model, it sought a strategic coalition of all pro-agreement parties, 'based on the need for [its] full and faithful implementation', and offered no substantive proposals for altering its institutional architecture. Instead, it proposed to defer consideration of the working arrangements of the existing institutions until they were again up and running. It did, however, propose extending north-south cooperation and improving the 'efficacy' of the BIC and opposed any dilution of the human rights and equality agendas; in effect, it wanted the speedy implementation of the agreement and the undertakings set out in the Joint Declaration and during the Weston Park negotiations of 2001, including the total disarmament of all paramilitary organisations.[39]

The party's position at the outset of the review was very much the *status quo ante*, as detected by the Alliance Party. In a short reaction to the proposals one of its MLAs-elect, Seamus Close, was scathing. Describing them as 'a recipe for continued deadlock', he remarked: 'It does not seem to have dawned on the SDLP that there are serious problems with the working of the Agreement, and with the new post-election context it is impossible for the current structures to operate.'[40] By contrast, Alliance's deputy leader, Eileen Bell, also re-elected to the virtual Assembly, issued a warm response to the DUP's proposals, describing as 'welcome' the movement towards weighted-majority voting, endorsing the proposal for a voluntary power-

[38] See DUP press release, '10 Reasons to Support "Devolution Now"', 11 February 2004.

[39] See the August 2001 Northern Ireland devolution monitoring report, at www.ucl.ac.uk/constitution-unit/monrep/ni/niaug01.pdf

[40] www.allianceparty.org, 21 January 2004.

sharing coalition but doubting the viability of the corporate assembly model.[41]

For its part, Alliance had been working on the review since September 2003 and its position paper, the first in the fray, proved the most substantial. It contained a total of 37 reform proposals, including support for a voluntary coalition endorsed by a weighted-majority vote in the Assembly, abandonment of the designation requirement provided for in the original agreement in favour of weighted-majority voting, an efficiency review of the number of devolved departments, a reduction in the number of MLAs, increased scope for north-south cooperation based on practical benefits for both jurisdictions, and a stipulation that the constitutional futures available be widened beyond those of simply maintaining the Union or Irish unification. It was a radical agenda and, perhaps, too ambitious given the already difficult, if not impossible, task of forging some sort of consensus, though the DUP's deputy leader, Peter Robinson, welcomed its recognition that 'the old Agreement has failed'.[42]

Alliance's advocacy of a shift away from rigid consociationalist thinking was, the DUP excepted, a lone voice. The SDLP's vision of inclusive government — including the retention of the d'Hondt proportionality rule for executive formation as opposed to a negotiated, voluntary coalition — was, predictably, the position of SF. Like the SDLP, it remained wedded to the 1998 agreement; in the words of the party president, Gerry Adams, the purpose of the review was 'to identify how best to deliver [its] full implementation'.[43] This stance was reiterated by Mr Adams in his remarks at the start of the review; its purpose was, he stated, 'about improving the delivery of the Agreement', which 'continues to enjoy the substantial support of the majority of the people' — a view based upon the election of 74 ostensibly pro-agreement candidates to the 108–member Assembly.[44]

SF released its substantive proposals a week before the review began, and repeated its view that that its purpose was 'to identify how best to deliver the full implementation of the Agreement'.[45] To that end it sought its re-endorsement by all parties, guarantees of inclusivity, including within devolved institutions, repeal of the UK's suspension legislation, expansion of all-Ireland cooperation and the north-south implementation bodies,[46]

---

[41] www.allianceparty.org, 6 February 2004.

[42] www.dup.org, 9 January 2004.

[43] www.sinnfein.ie, 28 January 2004.

[44] www.sinnfein.ie, 3 February 2004. This figure was arrived at by aggregating the MLAs elected for SF, the UUP, the SDLP, Alliance, the PUP and the Independent, Kieran Deeny. The inclusion of all 24 UUP MLAs was generous, even disingenuous, given that they included some devout agreement sceptics.

[45] www.sinnfein.ie, 28 January 2004.

[46] The full range of bodies was outlined in a SF press release: www.sinnfein.ie, 12 February 2004.

'demilitarisation' by the UK, abolition of the IMC and full implementation of the 'equality agenda'.[47]

The UUP approached the review with but a single agenda item — that the 'acts of completion' required of the IRA were finally and transparently executed. However, a little over a fortnight after the review began, a republican, Bobby Tohill, was the victim of an attempted abduction involving the IRA, according to the chief constable. This prompted the UUP leader, David Trimble, to call — vainly, as might have been predicted — for the exclusion of SF from the review. Consequently, Mr Trimble announced that his party would take no further part. Thus, just as the negotiations that led to the agreement itself had become multi- rather than all-party talks (with the departures of the DUP and the UKUP upon SF's inclusion), so too with the review.

Part-way through the review process, the SDLP did unveil a second set of proposals, designed as much as anything to inject regional accountability into direct rule.[48] It proposed to restore the original institutional architecture of the agreement but, instead of ministers, the two governments were urged to nominate 10 administrators, drawn from the trade unions, business and the voluntary sector, to lead the departments, two of whom would also co-chair the Office of the First Minister and Deputy First Minister. The nominees would be approved by a cross-community vote in the reconvened Assembly, and would represent Northern Ireland's interests in the north-south and east-west bodies and seek advice from and consult the re-established Civic Forum.

Restoring the original template, but with technocrats in executive roles, would have the virtue of enabling a regional administration to function alongside the review. It also provided the opportunity for systematic scrutiny of devolved issues which, under direct rule, was relegated to the margins of Westminster. But the proposals found no friends among the other parties and they fell from view.

The two parties which had invested so much in the agreement, the UUP and the SDLP, were in effect cast into minor roles, underlined in the former's case by the boycott decision, although the party maintained contact with both governments. Reeling from its swingeing electoral defeat in November 2003, and with a repeat performance at the European Parliament election, the UUP recognised that any momentum would turn even more on the DUP/SF axis.

After the Euro-election, the two governments engaged in separate and joint meetings with party leaders in London, Dublin and Belfast. Afterwards,

[47] Later, SF also proposed the creation of three new government departments: equality; policing and justice; and children and young people: www.sinnfein.ie, 16 February 2004.

[48] The proposals, 'Getting the Agreement Moving: Ending Suspension', are available on the SDLP's website, www.sdlp.ie

the two premiers announced further talks in September. This was, finally it was suggested, to be the last chance for devolution to be restored.

Mr Blair insisted: 'I think there is a recognition that it is time to come to the point of decision and make up our minds one way or another so that at the end of this negotiation we either have, and let us hope we do, a concluded agreement that allows everyone to move forward together, or alternatively, we are going to have to search for a different way forward.' Mr Ahern concurred:

> We will use the summer period to prepare ourselves and be ready to come to this final move ... We have fairly well exhausted discussion. The question is whether we can come to a final understanding on these issues. We are not there now, but we have to be in September; otherwise we will have to think again.[49]

But, as so often in Northern Ireland, this apparent deadline proved to be moveable the nearer it approached. With the DUP stressing it was in no particular hurry to come to an agreement, the Northern Ireland Secretary, Paul Murphy, said he was 'not going to put a date' on when the parties would 'resolve the big issues'.[50]

The talks, at Leeds Castle in Kent, duly came and went. Chaired by the Prime Minister and the Taoiseach, they once again saw warm words from SF meet cold practicality from unionists, now led by the DUP. This time there was an added ingredient, however, with threats from the UUP and SDLP that they might refuse to take part in any new, 'inclusive' government negotiated by their ethnic rivals.[51]

Despite the failure of their May 2003 Joint Declaration to turn the trick — notably over that paragraph 13 on the ending of paramilitarism — the two premiers tried again to put together what was now being touted as a take-it-or-leave-it document to shoehorn the DUP and SF into agreement. Implicit was a threat — which was unfortunately transparently hollow — that these proposals might be presented over the heads of the intransigent parties to the long-suffering Northern Ireland public.

And when Messrs Blair and Ahern came to that icon of post-agreement Belfast, the Waterfront Hall, on 8 December, it was to present proposals to which no one else had signed up.[52] As ever talking things up to the point of disingenuousness, the prime minister said there was only one issue outstanding. Notably, however, Mr Ahern referred to a few.[53]

49 Downing Street press release, 25 June 2004.
50 *Belfast Telegraph*, 24 August 2004.
51 *Irish Times*, 20 September 2004.
52 available   at   www.nio.gov.uk/proposals_by_the_british_and_irish_governments_for_a_ comprehensive_agreement.pdf
53 *Irish Times*, 9 December 2004.

What was well advertised, and had been since Leeds Castle, was a row between the DUP and SF as to whether any further IRA putting of weapons 'beyond use' — whatever that now meant — would be photographed. The republican movement said this was 'humiliation'; in Biblical mode, Mr Paisley said the IRA had to wear 'sackcloth and ashes'.[54]

But the respected security editor of the Dublin-based *Irish Independent*, Tom Brady, revealed that Mr Ahern's more sanguine view was correct.[55] The IRA, he wrote, had not yet:

- discussed an inventory of its weapons with the decommissioning commission,
- finalised arrangements on how and when it proposed to dispose of its arsenal,
- agreed a timescale on SF's commitment to the new policing arrangements, or
- declared that it would not endanger anyone's personal safety.

The next day the IRA corroborated this claim. Bizarrely, the two governments' proposals included a proposed statement that they presumed the IRA would make. A statement duly emerged from the pseudonymous 'P. O'Neill' which differed in important respects. While it included a reference to 'IRA volunteers' doing nothing to endanger the new agreement — if such the proposals had become — it notably omitted, once again, any commitment to renounce violence.

Were the proposals otherwise workable? Key procedural changes were envisaged, not least in selecting the First and Deputy First Ministers. Whereas under the terms of the 1998 agreement these were jointly elected by 'parallel consent' of the unionist and nationalist Assembly blocs, under the 2004 model they would be nominated, along with the ten other ministers, by means of d'Hondt and all would then be subject to the same procedure. Given the outcome of the 2003 Assembly election, and assuming that each of the four major parties would be prepared to nominate Executive members, the process would yield seven unionist and five nationalist ministers, including a DUP nominee for First Minister and an SF nominee for Deputy First Minister. This procedure would free the DUP's nominee from having to stand alone on a joint platform with SF's nominee, thereby sparing the former from any embarrassment.

Could a DUP First Minister and an SF Deputy First Minister achieve a *modus operandi*? Possibly — but there is a risk that such an administration would resemble an especially 'hard' rather than 'soft' form of consociational governance. This loveless marriage of political opposites would function

---

[54] *News Letter*, 1 December 2004.
[55] *Irish Independent*, 9 December 2004.

only by elevating the 'segmental autonomy' aspect of consociationalism, whereby the First Minister was preoccupied with defending and extending the perceived interests of unionists and the Deputy First Minister those of nationalists: in short, Northern Ireland could be subject to a de facto Balkanisation. True, there are safeguards built into the devolved legislative and policy processes, not least equality and rights proofing, but consociationalism's maxim that high fences make for good neighbours might be realised with renewed vigour, in a context wherein unionists in general already believe that they have been the material and symbolic 'losers' following the 1998 agreement while nationalists have emerged as the clear 'winners'.

That scenario suggests that Northern Ireland may be even more mired in ethno-nationalism for the foreseeable future. This would place a special responsibility on the shoulders of the UUP and the SDLP to act as ameliorating influences, but whether they would do so in government or in opposition is not yet clear: before the 'deal' failed neither party had made the strategic decision to participate in a new Executive rather than take up its seats on the opposition benches. If each chose the latter option and they were able to act in concert on key issues, then a new form of party competition could emerge and the basis for a genuinely voluntary coalition could be forged.

THE ONLY SHOW IN TOWN

There are, of course, thinkable constitutional alternatives to devolution for Northern Ireland, including joint London-Dublin authority or even independence, but though they may be intellectually engaging they lack political feasibility. In the meantime, there is the safety net of direct rule. But disquiet within the political classes, not least at Westminster, suggests that it cannot be sustained without some means of softening its blunt character, especially in relation to the handling of Northern Ireland legislation and the scrutiny of the NIO and formerly devolved matters.

Treating the region as an undifferentiated part of the UK was a popular option among unionists in the late 1980s, recoiling against the involvement of the Republic in the governance of Northern Ireland via the Anglo-Irish Agreement of 1985. Just as 'home rule all round' in the 1910s might have trumped unionist resistance to home rule for Ireland, however, so today devolution to Scotland and Wales makes the idea of Northern Ireland as some kind of colonial satrapy — with, for instance, a British-based Westminster health minister forced to react to any dropped bedpan in Tullycarnet — increasingly absurd.

Meantime, as a senior Catholic civil servant predicted privately in the run-up to the agreement, devolution has posed a question for Northern

Ireland's minority citizens: do they want to sacrifice newfound regional power in favour of a centralised Irish state? The answer they have largely arrived at, publicly in the case of the position adopted by Mark Durkan since assuming leadership of the SDLP in 2001, privately in the case of a senior republican source — is that they would want to see the Assembly survive in a formally 'united' Ireland. In the SDLP's case, to that is added a commitment that the institutions of the agreement, and in particular its minority-rights safeguards, should be sustained in the eventuality of a formal change of 'sovereignty' over the region. In any event, since the 2003 Northern Ireland Life and Times survey showed a 55–24 split between, respectively, those supporting the region's continuing membership of the UK and those favouring unification with the Irish Republic, among committed respondents, that option remains a long way off.[56]

Devolution remains, therefore, the only political show in town. Yet, that is not to shy away from the need for reform of the current model, which the review of the agreement flunked. The 1998 agreement is not, and ought not, to be regarded as unimpeachable Holy Grail. Whatever the outcome of the latest round of political negotiations, and irrespective of the travails of the Belfast Agreement, London and Dublin — and, hopefully, political actors in Northern Ireland — will be forced to return to devolution, allied to a political accommodation that guarantees equality of citizenship.

THE PARTY SYSTEM

The factor that sustained the faltering and interrupted momentum of the review was the shared understanding that all the key players wish to see the end of devolution; where they part company is over the means. Beyond that evident difficulty is the mutually-exclusive perception of the 1998 agreement: pro-agreement unionists understood it to copper-fasten the Union for the indefinite future, whereas their anti-agreement counterparts, and nationalists and republicans, saw it (respectively) as the threat and the opportunity to effect unification. Thus, the prospect that the 1998 model could yield a win-win outcome was heavily mortgaged, notwithstanding the consent principle underpinning it.

Between 1998 and 2004 there were five elections, including the European parliamentary contest in June 2004. Over that period, SF's share of the total vote — albeit on varying turnouts and employing both preferential and plurality systems — rose from 17.6 per cent in May 1998 to 26.3 per cent and the DUP's from 18 per cent to 32 per cent. At the 2004 European election, the DUP's share of the unionist (DUP + UUP) vote was 65.8 per cent, and SF's share of the nationalist (SF + SDLP) vote 62.3 per cent. SF overhauled

[56] Data at www.ark.ac.uk/nilt/2003/Political_Attitudes/NIRELAND.html

its nationalist competitor for the first time at the 2001 Westminster election and has remained in prime place ever since; the DUP overtook the UUP at the second Assembly election in 2003. The change since the first Assembly election in 1998 is significant: at that poll the DUP secured 45.9 per cent of the unionist vote and SF 44.5 per cent of the nationalist vote. Buoyed by its increased vote share, the DUP confidently predicted that it would make further substantial gains in both the 2005 local government election and the Westminster election, relishing the prospect that it could capture all the parliamentary seats held by the UUP — including the prize of Upper Bann, the seat of the party leader, David Trimble.[57]

Having lost its totem seat in the European Parliament, formerly held by John Hume, the SDLP seemed likely to suffer further losses in future local and Westminster contests. From topping the poll in 1998 for the first time in a region-wide election, it witnessed a halving of its total vote from 177,963 at the first Assembly election to 87,559 in June 2004. The UUP has also experienced a marked decline, although the pattern is less linear than that for the SDLP. A low point (indeed its then worst ever electoral performance) was in 1998, with a poll of 172,225. It recovered in 2001 at the local and Westminster elections, but fell again in 2003 to 156,931 and in 2004 to its lowest ever aggregate of 91,164 at the European election. From the 2001 Westminster election, albeit on a significantly higher turnout than in 2004, it saw its total fall by more than 125,000 votes.

The respective fortunes of the major parties suggest a trend. Yet the increases in vote shares for the DUP and SF may be less a matter of unionist and nationalist voter realignment than a tactical desertion from their competitors, especially within the Protestant community. The seemingly irresistible rise of SF may have persuaded unionist voters that their best form of defence was electoral attack, i.e. supporting the DUP. Whatever the motives, though, the nature of party competition has changed and has created a context within which the now predominant parties can, to coin a phrase, stick to their guns and thereby create a condition of political immobilism.

Even this was called into question by the unravelling of SF organisationally following the Northern Bank raid and the murder of Robert McCartney. Each action gravely discredited the party as well as the IRA, and the aftermath of the McCartney murder — with heavy-handed threats from Martin McGuinness and the collapse of Gerry Adams' St Patrick's day visit to the US, with no senior US politician being willing to see him — left the party looking increasingly discredited and adrift.

It will only be if some means is found to re-devolve power that politics in Northern Ireland will get beyond the stage of sterile constitutional wrangling to a debate about party performance and day-to-day policy issues. It may yet

---

[57] See DUP press release, 'DUP upgrade Westminster target list' (16 June 2004), at www.dup.org

be the case that broadening the options for Northern Ireland's constitutional status at a referendum beyond the pro-Union / pro-unification choice is the only means of unravelling the Gordian knot. Whether the existing party structure is compatible with that is another difficult question, particularly as the second Assembly election in Northern Ireland handed power to the explicit ethno-nationalists.

Northern Ireland is in that sense suffering a similar stagnation to Bosnia-Herzegovina, where the eclipse of the non-nationalistic parties in the latest elections has made shared governance ineffective and ensured significant decisions are taken elsewhere. In Bosnia this is the Office of the High Representative of the international community, Paddy Ashdown; in Northern Ireland's case it is Westminster, albeit with Dublin input.

RETURN OF THE 'DEMOCRATIC DEFICIT'

Between 1998 and 2004, Northern Ireland had four secretaries of state and several reshuffles of junior ministers, including during the review. The relatively quick turnover of the ministerial team has not, however, led to policy discontinuity in the realm of high politics, nor have the four suspensions that occurred between February 2000 and October 2002: each was designed to protect the agreement, although the first was a unilateral decision by the UK Government, while the others were supported by Dublin.

The relative ease with which the suspensions were imposed is testament to the sovereignty of the Westminster Parliament, much to the irritation of both the SDLP and SF, each of which called for the repeal of the 2000 suspension legislation in the review. Indeed, the 2003 Joint Declaration and the December 2004 document indicated the preparedness of London to relinquish this power as part of the 'deal' to restore devolution, contingent upon 'acts of completion' by the IRA.

At Westminster, the six-monthly renewal of direct rule has by no means passed unremarked, because of mounting disquiet about the inadequacy of procedures for dealing with Northern Ireland business. Such disquiet is not new, but the political hiatus, allied with an active ministerial team in the Northern Ireland Office, has sharpened its focus. This activism in relation to formerly devolved matters was in large part caused by the legislative legacy of the outgoing administration; a raft of primary legislation and policy decisions was in the pipeline when the fourth suspension was introduced on 15 October 2002.

The then Secretary of State, John Reid, gave notice of intent during his statement to the House of Commons to the effect that the NIO would not 'duck the difficult issues' bequeathed by the devolved ministers. He also announced that his ministerial team would increase by two — a signal of activist intent and, for that matter, of an unacknowledged apprehension that the period of suspension was likely to prove a long one.[58]

It fell to his successor, Paul Murphy, appointed on 24 October 2002, to pick up the legislative and policy baton, which he did with some vigour. On 19 November 2002 he indicated the government's intention to bring forward the legislative programme as a 'clear sign of our commitment to the good governance of Northern Ireland'. He added: 'We will continue, for as long as necessary, the good work started by the Executive and the Assembly to ensure the people of Northern Ireland are not disadvantaged.'[59]

Such activism also extended to some of the thornier issues left in abeyance, including setting the budget, reform of the rating system, the future of 'community-relations' policy, the introduction of water charges, the ending of the '11+' (or transfer test) and the review of public administration. While some of these issues — not least the budget — could not be left to languish on departmental shelves, it was clear that there was a determination that the expanded ministerial team would be active, even proactive, in pushing the legislative and policy agenda. But squeezing Northern Ireland's formerly devolved business into the parliamentary agenda meant, *inter alia*, resorting to the order-in-council procedure to deal with the legislative programme, much to the dissatisfaction of members of all parties, in the Commons and the Lords, and not just those from within the region.

There is now a settled view at Westminster that the scrutiny of legislation and policy relating to Northern Ireland leaves much to be desired, such that should direct rule continue indefinitely new means would have to be found of improving the quality of scrutiny afforded to formerly devolved matters.[60] But, while the UK Government remains committed to the restoration of devolution, it is reluctant to effect any changes that could be construed as qualifying that commitment. Nevertheless, some MPs have adapted to the changed circumstances by seeking reforms to the legislative process, while the Northern Ireland Affairs Committee has, for the first time, established a dedicated sub-committee to scrutinise formerly devolved matters.

Such an initiative is, though, improvised and remedial: it does not cure the underlying condition whereby, under direct rule, Northern Ireland business is dealt with in a summary way. Prolonged direct rule, if it does come to pass, will require invasive parliamentary surgery, not mere procedural first aid.

---

[58] HC Deb, 15 October 2002, col 193.

[59] See NIO press release, 19 November 2002.

[60] The proposal voiced by both the DUP and the UUP to enable the Northern Ireland Grand Committee to hold at least some of its sessions in the region has been vetoed serially by the SDLP. See for example the remarks by Mr Trimble at the Committee's session on 17 June 2004. The proposal would, if acted upon, have the virtue of lending some immediacy and proximity to the Committee's deliberations by enabling regional interests ease of access to attend and observe the proceedings — as well as injecting some life into the mothballed chambers at Parliament Buildings.

CONCLUSION: THE WIDER PICTURE

From the 2003 Northern Ireland Life and Times survey, the population seems broadly neutral about continued direct rule. Asked whether they would be 'sorry', 'pleased' or 'wouldn't mind either way' if the Assembly was to be abolished and direct rule maintained indefinitely, whilst only 7 per cent said they would be pleased, 50 per cent chose the last option, as against 37 per cent for the first. Just 11 per cent of Protestant respondents said they would be pleased, but 56 per cent were ambivalent, as were 41 per cent of Catholics, although a bare majority of the latter (50 per cent) expressed regret at the prospect. However, majorities in both communities (69 per cent of Catholics and 54 per cent of Protestants) believed that the devolved Assembly had achieved either a lot or a little and either agreed or strongly agreed that any future form of government had to be founded on power-sharing — a view held by 92 per cent of Catholics and 78 per cent of Protestants. Moreover, an overwhelming majority of Protestants (90 per cent) and a commanding majority of Catholics (60 per cent) rejected the proposition that parties linked to paramilitary groups should be included in any future form of devolved government.

As to the details of any new agreement, while a plurality of the Catholic population (41 per cent) took the view that the 1998 agreement is 'basically right and needs to be implemented in full' — a view held by just 10 per cent of Protestants — a significant minority (36 per cent) agreed that, whilst basically right, 'its specifics need to be renegotiated', which was also the view of a plurality (33 per cent) of Protestants, albeit that 24 per cent believed it to be 'basically wrong and needs to be renegotiated' and 16 per cent that it 'is basically wrong and should be abandoned'.[61]

There does, then, seem to be some space for the fashioning of a new political dispensation but it is narrow and, among Protestants, highly contested. Whether the major parties can negotiate what space exists to yield a renascent form of devolution remains to be seen.

One way to reduce the 'democratic deficit' and Westminster overload regarding Northern Ireland affairs would be by introducing a significantly more powerful system of local government. The Review of Public Administration, established by the devolved executive to review sub-regional government, identified five potential options, ranging from the most centralised to the most localised.[62] Opinion in the review team and beyond (for example, in the Northern Ireland Local Government Association) has favoured the model built around strong local government, which would imply a much smaller number of councils than the current 26 — the relevant

---

[61] Data available at www.ark.ac.uk/nilt/2003/Political_Attitudes/index.html

[62] These were set out in an October 2003 consultation document by the review team, *The Review of Public Administration*, available at www.rpani.gov.uk/consult.pdf

NIO minister, Ian Pearson, signalled he would support between five and eight,[63] though NILGA opposed such a sharp cull.

This would still require councils to share the enhanced powers they had but the hope might be that greater pragmatism would be exhibited than is evidenced in the 'high' politics of the region's political/paramilitary elite. In the absence of regional devolution, however, this would remain a *faute de mieux* solution, and it could even lead over time to a de facto cantonisation of Northern Ireland into increasingly monocultural authorities.

Regardless of developments at Stormont or their absence, the unfolding of UK devolution will keep the Barnett formula in the spotlight. Northern Ireland's position is exposed in this regard, with by far the highest per capita public expenditure of any UK region/nation on the one hand and diminishing goodwill, due to the prolonged stalling of the devolution project, on the other. While there will be some kind of 'PEACE 3' EU programme for the region, it is highly unlikely that the Treasury will act as in the past to ease Northern Ireland's fiscal position, such as by the Chancellor's Initiative of 1998 or the Reinvestment and Reform Initiative of 2002.

On the contrary, recent signs have been towards a tightening of the Treasury's purse strings. The Chief Secretary to the Treasury, Paul Boateng, floated the idea of regionalised pay arrangements during a 2004 visit to Northern Ireland — lower house prices in the region plus the capture of the public educational system by the middle class means that a professional lifestyle is much more affordable than in most parts of the UK. And a leaked letter from the Northern Ireland Secretary, Paul Murphy, to Mr Boateng indicated that the latter had sought the privatisation of water, not just the introduction of charging.[64]

On a wider canvas, short of welcome political or unwelcome violent events, Northern Ireland can no longer expect to command significant media, and so public political, attention. The Assembly election was widely seen in the international media as a victory for the 'hard-line' parties and a setback for the 'peace process',[65] a verdict which the result of the Euro-election compounded. Tony Blair's ambition to settle Northern Ireland's polity in the run-up to a general election foundered; the region remains in the 'pending' tray.

---

[63] See the August 2004 Northern Ireland devolution monitoring report, available at www.ucl.ac.uk/constitution-unit/monrep/ni/ni_august_2004.pdf

[64] *Belfast Telegraph*, 20 August 2004.

[65] L. Fawcett and R.Wilson, 'The media election: coverage of the November 2003 Northern Ireland Assembly poll' (Belfast: Democratic Dialogue, 2004), p. 55, available at: www.democraticdialogue.org/documents/Mediacover_000.pdf

APPENDIX: ELECTION RESULTS IN NORTHERN IRELAND

Table 4.1: Assembly Election Results 1998 and 2003

Party	1998 First preference votes			2003 First preference votes		
	N	%	Seats	N	%	Seats
DUP	145917	18.03	20	177944	25.71	30
UUP	172225	21.28	28	156931	22.68	27
SDLP	177963	21.99	24	117547	16.99	18
SF	142858	17.65	18	162758	23.52	24
Alliance	52636	6.50	6	25372	3.67	6
UKUP	36541	4.52	5	5700	0.82	1
PUP	20634	2.55	2	8032	1.16	1
Ind	N/A	N/A	N/A	6158	0.88	1
NIWC	13019	1.61	2	5785	0.83	0
Others	47452	5.8	3	25801	3.7	0
Total	824391		108	692028		108
Turnout		69.95			63.98	

Table 4.2:
Summary of 1999 and 2004 European Parliamentary Elections (NI)

	DUP	UUP	SDLP	SF	Others
Votes (N) 2004	175761	91164	87559	144541	50252
Votes (%) 2004	31.9	16.6	15.9	26.3	9.1
Seats (N) 2004	1	1	0	1	0
Votes (N) 1999	192762	119507	190731	117643	58166
Votes (%) 1999	28.4	17.6	28.1	17.3	8.4
Seats (N) 1999	1	1	1	0	0
Turnout (2004): 51.7% Turnout (1999): 57.8%					

ADDENDUM:
THE 2005 ELECTION RESULTS IN NORTHERN IRELAND

The outcomes of the elections on 5 May represented a triumph for the DUP, an almost unmitigated disaster for the UUP, relief for the SDLP and a steadying in the votes and vote share for Sinn Féin. The DUP entered the Westminster election with six MPs — given Jeffrey Donaldson's defection from the UUP in January 2004 — and emerged with nine, strictly speaking a net gain of four seats. The UUP retained only one of the five seats it was defending, North Down, in the person of Lady Sylvia Hermon. Its chief casualty was the party's leader, David Trimble. He lost his Upper Bann seat to the DUP's David Simpson, who overturned a UUP majority of more than 2000 votes, winning comfortably with a majority of more than 5000 votes. Within 48 hours of the count, Mr Trimble resigned his leadership; thus the DUP had succeeded in Northern Ireland in decapitating — and amputating — its major unionist opponent.

Within the unionist electorate, the ascendancy of the DUP is inescapable. It took 66 per cent of the combined DUP-UUP vote at the parliamentary elections and 62 per cent at the concurrent district council elections. European Parliamentary elections aside, these results represented the best ever electoral performances by the DUP and, correspondingly, in terms of votes and vote share, the UUP's worst. The decline in the latter's fortunes is dramatic: since 1997 its support has more than halved whilst that of the DUP has doubled (see Table 4.3).

The emphatic nature of the DUP's performance was not matched by its chief ethnic rival, SF. While SF did gain one seat from the SDLP, Newry and Armagh, formerly held by Seamus Mallon, the former deputy leader of the party and Deputy First Minister who stood down at the election, the SDLP gained South Belfast from the UUP because of a split in the unionist vote. Thus, the SDLP returns to Westminster with three MPs, retaining South Down and, against an all-out challenge from SF, the Foyle seat, formerly held by John Hume and defended in 2005 by his successor as party leader, Mark Durkan. Mr Durkan saw the SDLP majority cut to 6000 or so votes, compared with more than 11000 in 2001, but it was a signal victory and one that did not rely on tactical votes from unionists determined to defeat SF's candidate, Mitchel McLaughlin.

Table 4.3: Votes (N) and Vote Share (%): 1997–2005

Election	DUP		UUP		SDLP		SF	
	N	%	N	%	N	%	N	%
1997 Westminster	107348	13.6	258349	32.7	190814	24.1	126921	16.1
1997 Local Government	99651	15.8	175036	27.9	130387	22.6	106934	16.9
1998 Assembly	145917	18.0	172225	21.3	177963	21.9	142858	17.6
2001 Westminster	181999	22.5	216839	26.8	169865	20.9	175392	21.7
2001 Local Government	169477	21.4	181336	22.9	153424	19.4	163269	20.6
2003 Assembly	177944	25.4	156931	22.7	117547	16.9	162758	23.5
2005 Westminster	241856	33.7	127314	17.7	125626	17.5	174530	24.3
2005 Local Government	208278	29.6	126317	18.0	121991	17.4	163205	23.2

In terms of overall vote share, SF has consolidated its lead over the SDLP first achieved in 2001, extending it to around six per cent or so. However, its share of the combined SF-SDLP vote at the Westminster and council elections remained at around 58 per cent, the same proportion it achieved at the 2003 Assembly election. One inference one can draw is that its vote share within the nationalist electorate may have stabilised, and that its advance may have been checked. This, though, is to fashion a hostage to fortune. Had, for instance, Derry-born Martin McGuinness contested Foyle instead of defending his Mid-Ulster seat, the party might have ousted the SDLP — and that may well be the case at the next general election.

The results confront the new Secretary of State, Peter Hain — the fifth since the election of 'new' Labour in 1997 — and his almost new ministerial team at the NIO with a knotty set of problems. Confirmation of the electoral dominance of the DUP and SF creates an inauspicious context for the restoration of devolution: opposites may attract in matters of the heart, but in political terms such a union seems implausible, at least in Northern Ireland. That said, there are pragmatists within the DUP who, if we are to lend credence to the proposition that there was a near deal last December, seemed to be in the driving seat, prepared to effect a political marriage (albeit loveless) with SF. The absence of a pre-nuptial photograph — although other issues did emerge as the prospective deal unravelled — appeared to be all that stood in the way of the creation of a new Executive and the restoration of the other devolved political institutions.

Be that as it may, the alteration in the political landscape, the Northern Bank robbery, the murder of Robert McCartney and the post-election publication of the latest report from the IMC confirming, in particular, the continuing involvement of the IRA in paramilitary and criminal activities, have together set back the prospective return of self-government. The onus now rests upon the republican movement to begin the process of restoring or, rather, introducing trust into the troubled political discourse of Northern Ireland. At the outset of the election campaign, Gerry Adams publicly exhorted the IRA to pursue its goal of Irish unification by 'purely political and democratic activity'. At the time of writing we still await the IRA's response: whether it will prove to be not only necessary but sufficient to restore momentum to the 'peace process' remains to be seen.

BIBLIOGRAPHY

Official Documents

Independent Monitoring Commission, First Report, HC 516 (London: The Stationery Office, 2004), available at www.nio.gov.uk/pdf/imcreport.pdf
National Statistics, *Regional Trends* (London: The Stationery Office, 2004).
Northern Ireland Office, *The Agreement: Agreement reached in the multi-party negotiations* (Belfast and London: Northern Ireland Office, 1998), available at www.nio.gov.uk/issues/agreement.htm
Northern Ireland Office, *Joint Declaration by the British and Irish Governments* (Belfast and London: Northern Ireland Office, 2003), available at www.nio. gov.uk/joint_declaration_between_the_british_and_irish_governments.pdf
Organised Crime Task Force 'Threat Assessment', available at www.octf. gov.uk/Publications.cfm
Police Service of Northern Ireland, *Annual Report of the Chief Constable 2003/2004*, (2004), available at www.psni.police.uk/chief_constables_annual_report_2003–2004.pdf
Police Service of Northern Ireland, *Community Safety Branch Statistics on Domestic Violence, Hate Crime and Youth Offences in Northern Ireland 2003/2004* (Belfast: PSNI, 2004).
Review of Public Administration, *The Review of Public Administration in Northern Ireland Consultation Document*, (2003), available at www.rpani. gov.uk/consult.pdf

Secondary Sources

Akenson, D. H., *Small Differences: Irish Catholics and Irish Protestants 1815–1922* (Dublin: Gill & Macmillan, 1988).

Bew, P. and G. Gillespie, *Northern Ireland: A chronology of the Troubles 1968–1999* (Dublin: Gill & Macmillan, 1999).

Bew, P. and H. Patterson, *The British State and the Ulster Crisis: From Wilson to Thatcher* (London: Verso, 1985).

Buckland, P., *The Factory of Grievances: Devolved government in Northern Ireland 1921–39* (Dublin: Gill & Macmillan, 1979).

Burgess, M., 'The British federal tradition', in A. Duff (ed.), *Subsidiarity Within the EC* (London: Federal Trust, 1993).

Callaghan, J., *A House Divided* (London: Collins, 1973).

Connolly, P. and M. Keenan, *The Hidden Truth: Racist harassment in Northern Ireland* (Belfast: Northern Ireland Statistics and Research Agency, 2001).

Dowds, L. *et al* (various dates), *Northern Ireland devolution monitoring reports* (London: Constitution Unit) available at:
www.ucl.ac.uk/constitution-unit/nations/monitoring.php

Eide, A., *New Approaches to Minority Protection* (London: Minority Rights Group, 2003).

English, R., *Armed Struggle: A history of the IRA* (London: Macmillan, 2003).

Fawcett, L. and R. Wilson, 'The media election: coverage of the November 2003 Northern Ireland Assembly poll' (Belfast: Democratic Dialogue, 2004), available at www.democraticdialogue.org/documents/Mediacover_000.pdf

Gibbon, P., *Origins of Ulster Unionism* (Manchester: Manchester University Press, 1975).

Hillyard, P., G. Kelly, E. McLaughlin, D. Patsios and M. Tomlinson, *Bare Necessities: Poverty and social exclusion in Northern Ireland — key findings* (Belfast: Democratic Dialogue, 2003).

Jarman, N. and A. Tennant, *An Acceptable Prejudice? Homophobic violence and harassment in Northern Ireland* (Belfast: Institute for Conflict Research, 2003).

Lijphart, A., *Democracy in Plural Societies* (New Haven, CT: Yale University Press, 1977).

Lijphart, A., 'Constructivism and consociational theory', *Newsletter of the American Political Science Association Organized Section in Comparative Politics*, 12(1): 11–13, (2001).

Ormsby, F. (ed.), *The Collected Poems of John Hewitt* (Belfast: Blackstaff Press, 1991).

Reynolds, A. (ed.), *The Architecture of Democracy: Constitutional design, conflict management and democracy* (Oxford: OUP, 2002).

Wilford, R., 'Northern Ireland: resolving an ancient quarrel?' in M. O'Neill (ed.), *Devolution and British Politics* (Harlow: Pearson Longman, 2004).

Wilson, R., 'Imperialism in crisis: the "Irish dimension"', in M. Langan and B. Schwarz (eds.), *Crises in the British State 1880–1930* (London: Hutchinson, 1985).

Wilson, R., *Northern Ireland: What's going wrong* (London: Constitution Unit, UCL and Belfast: Institute of Governance, Public Policy and Social Research, QUB, 2003).

5

The Regions at the Crossroads
The Future for Sub-National Government in England

Mark Sandford and Peter Hetherington

A strange sense of calm fell over the question of elected regional government on 5 November 2004. The referendum in the North-East, on the previous day, returned a vote against an elected assembly of such magnitude — on a respectable turnout — that both supporters and opponents were somewhat wrong-footed. Supporters were unable to point to any strong degree of public support for the proposals which happened to be outweighed by scepticism on the day, and opponents were emboldened to suggest a number of less-than-convincing alternative solutions to the region's problems which had appeared nowhere in the referendum campaign.

But the result also had wider ramifications. On a political level, the result killed off elected regional assemblies in England — formally speaking for seven years,[1] politically speaking for a generation. A large vote against in the North-East, generally agreed to be the hotbed of regional sentiment within the English regions, guarantees that no other region will be offered the opportunity in the lifetime of this Government. A vacuum was thereby opened up around the question of the sub-national government of England. However, the result, and much of the rhetoric and public attitudes visible during the campaign, suggest a wider distrust of and cynicism about politicians and politics. Voters appeared unconvinced that any new political structure would serve their interests.

This chapter outlines the events leading up to the referendum on 4 November 2004, including the campaign in the North-East, and also sets out the development of the Government's regional agenda during 2004. More importantly, however, it analyses the future direction of regionalism and other forms of sub-national government change within England, in the time-frame of the next ten years.

2004: STEADY PROGRESS HITS THE BUFFERS?

The period up till 4 November 2004 saw a continuation of 'creeping regionalisation', identified by Tomaney and Hetherington in their contribution to

---

[1] Regional Assemblies (Preparations) Act 2003, s6 (2).

Has Devolution Made A Difference?, the previous volume in the *State of the Nations* series.[2] This was caused by two main factors: a slow increase in the powers and standing of Regional Chambers and Regional Development Agencies (RDAs); and the continuation of the Treasury's interest in regions in the context of its macroeconomic policies.

The Planning and Compulsory Purchase Act 2004 marked a significant change, formalising the regional planning arrangements that have existed in England for some 15 years. Regional Planning Guidance is replaced by statutory Regional Spatial Strategies (RSSs), which will be written, monitored and enforced by formal Regional Planning Bodies. In all regions, the Regional Chamber has been designated the Regional Planning Body, although Chambers themselves are not mentioned in the Act. Local authorities will be obliged to take the new RSS into account in their local development plans.[3] The Regional Planning Bodies must monitor the implementation of the RSS, and regularly review it. The Act also abolishes county structure plans, and abolishes the *right* for county planning authorities to be heard at the examination in public which must be held as part of the RSS.[4] Regional Chambers have benefited from a one-off Planning Delivery Grant, in the region of £3–400,000 for each chamber for the current financial year, to allow them to develop their capacity to deliver the new statutory strategy. These extra funds, however, have in many cases been used for public engagement rather than for hiring new staff. The RSS has become the lead priority in almost all of the Chambers, and the entire process is expected to take about two and a half years (see Table 5.1 for the example of the South-East).

The slow march of regionalism goes wider than spatial planning, however, and again it has been most visible through the economic planning process and many reviews emanating from the Treasury. The 2004 Spending Review was also the first to benefit from Regional Emphasis Documents which had been prepared jointly by the RDA, Government Office and Regional Chamber in each region. These were prepared in the second half of 2003, and were expected to make recommendations for the reallocation of public money within the region (the institutions were strictly warned off asking for more money). Regional Emphasis Documents had been prepared for the 2002 Spending Review, but they had been limited documents lacking input from regional institutions. In 2003, many Chambers were still critical of the tight timescale of the Regional Emphasis Documents, and perceived domination of the process by Government Offices, but the fact that such a

    [2] J. Tomaney and P. Hetherington, 'English Regions: the quiet regional revolution?', in A. Trench (ed.), *Has Devolution Made a Difference? The state of the nations 2004* (Exeter: Imprint Academic, 2004), pp. 121–40.
    [3] Planning and Compulsory Purchase Act 2004, s19 (2) (b).
    [4] *Ibid.*, s8 (3).

process takes place at all demonstrates both the growing importance of the Chambers and of regional approaches in the eyes of the Treasury — the dominant department of central government.

Table 5.1:
Timetable for Production of South-East RSS ('South-East Plan')[5]

Autumn 2003 – May 2004	Development of vision and preliminary work to identify options Commission research projects Carry out sub-regional studies Stakeholder workshops
May – August 2004	Consideration of sub-regional strategies Development of spatial options Proposed sub-regional policies prepared
August – Nov. 2004	Preparation of draft South-East Plan
January – March 2005	Public consultation on draft South-East Plan by the South East England Regional Assembly
Summer/ Autumn 2005	The Assembly submits its draft South-East Plan to the Government
Spring 2006	Public consultation on the South-East Plan by the Government Office for the South East Public examination of South-East Plan proposals by the Government Office for the South East
Summer 2006	Expected Government approval of the South East Plan

The Treasury's response to the Regional Emphasis Documents indicated a considerable willingness to take recommendations on board — notably, where they concerned cross-departmental working. A joint Safer and Stronger Communities Fund, funded by ODPM and the Home Office, is promised.[6] Regional Skills Partnerships have been formally established in all regions, allowing pooling of budgets for adult skills between RDAs and local Learning and Skills Councils, as well as Jobcentre Plus and the Small Business Service. Extra investment from UK Trade and Investment, and from the Treasury as a result of the Lambert Review of business-university

[5] Source: www.southeast-ra.gov.uk. The Government Office carries out its own consultation in advance of submitting the final plan to the Secretary of State.

[6] HM Treasury, *2004 Spending Review; Meeting regional priorities* (London: The Stationery Office, 2004), p.10: available at www.hm-treasury.gov.uk

collaboration, will raise the RDAs' collective budget to £2.3 billion per year by 2007–8.[7]

The Treasury also supported the setting up of two pilot Regional Transport Boards, in the South-East and Yorkshire & Humber. These Boards have no formal power, but are expected to make non-binding recommendations for reorientation of public spending on transport within their regions. Each of the two pilots had a number of Regional Chamber representatives on them, but these representatives were not in a majority, neither did they chair the Boards. The Boards were also stymied by the claim of the Strategic Rail Authority (SRA) that it was unable to disaggregate any of its spending whatsoever on a regional basis, meaning that it could not be included in the Boards' deliberations. The South-East board pressed for a change to this response (the outcome of which is unclear following the abolition of the SRA). The Regional Transport Boards were themselves modelled on Regional Housing Boards, which have been set up in all regions to carry out a similar task with regard to housing capital spending (currently divided between the Housing Corporation and Government Office for the Region). Again, although these boards have hardly been revolutionary in their impact, permitting local and regional representatives any say at all in central spending decisions indicates a degree of influence for institutions of sub-national governance that is atypical of UK central government.

The Chancellor also announced in 2004 that the Business Link franchises, currently let by the Small Business Service, would come under the control of the RDAs from April 2005. The separation between these two agencies, handling economic development and business support, has long been criticised. Also, the Department of Environment, Food and Rural Affairs began the implementation of the Haskins Report of December 2003, leading to the transfer of many of the Countryside Agency's programmes to the RDAs and to the creation of the Integrated Agency[8] from three existing agencies (intended to be established in statute by 2007).[9] Though the new agency is intended to be a national non-departmental public body, Regional Rural Priority Boards are to be created to bring together rural stakeholders with the policy priorities of the new agency. RDAs also took on tourism responsibilities from the Department of Culture, Media and Sport in 2003, with the abolition of the English Tourist Board. Some regional tourist boards wound themselves up as a result, whilst others stayed in existence as shadow organisations alongside the RDAs. To sweeten the process of merger for Regional Tourist Boards, tourism funding was increased at the same time.

RDAs were therefore bulking up through 2004, reducing some of the overlaps between them and other organisations. The significance of this is

---

[7] HM Treasury, 2004.

[8] Draft Natural Environment and Rural Communities Bill, DEFRA, 2005.

[9] DEFRA, *Rural Strategy 2004*, annex C, p.10, available at www.defra.gov.uk/rural/strategy

not only better administrative joining-up in the regions, but also that once these functions are transferred to the RDA they become regional rather than outposts of national executive agencies. As organisations, RDAs are far less bound to national policy frameworks within departmental silos. Their responsibility to the centre is outcome- rather than process-based, and they have discretion, within their Regional Economic Strategies, to respond to regional priorities as they see fit.

Further evidence of incremental central government interest in regionalism and regional disparities comes in the form of various reviews. The McLean report into regionally disaggregated spending pointed up poor quality recording of public spending by region by many departments. It established, for instance, that some departments obtained regional or local spending figures by simply dividing their total spending in any given programme by the number of people living in the given area, with no reference at all to actual spending.[10] In other cases substantial discrepancies between claimed and actual spending were identified. The Treasury is pressing ahead with the recommendations of the Lyons report, for 20,000 civil servants to be moved out of London and the South-East.[11] The Barker Review of housing policy, commissioned by ODPM, made recommendations for the expansion of housing supply and for the merger of Regional Housing Boards with Regional Chambers, which is to go ahead.[12]

All of these developments, however, are the outgrowth of *regionalised centralism*: addressing England-wide macroeconomic issues in the context of regional disparities and differences. They are integral to the establishment, by the Treasury, of more centralised control within Whitehall over the priorities of spending departments. Directly-elected assemblies do not figure in this agenda. In 2004 the progress of Government policy on elected assemblies continued to move, as in previous years, at a snail's pace. Elected regional government remained a semi-detached policy, barely acknowledged by most Labour MPs and ministers nor referred to by policy on Government priorities such as health, education and crime.

THE NORTH-EAST REFERENDUM

The Campaign

Although almost everyone involved in the North-East referendum was taken aback by the size of the 'no' vote, the eventual rejection of a regional

---

[10] See I. McLean *et al.*, *Identifying the flow of public expenditure into the English regions* (London: ODPM, 2003), pp 151–69.

[11] See Sir Michael Lyons, *Independent Review of Public Sector Relocation* (London: HM Treasury, 2004).

[12] http://www.hm-treasury.gov.uk./media/0F2/D4/barker_review_report_494.pdf

assembly came as little surprise to campaigners and close observers alike. While, on the surface, support for the broad concept of devolution appeared high in the North-East, the more the details of John Prescott's package became clear — the potential cost to council taxpayers, the constraints likely to be exercised by Whitehall on the extremely limited powers on offer, and the perception of another tier of well-paid politicians — the more people moved initially into the undecided category and, finally, into the 'no' camp.

Few bargained for the success of devolution opponents operating under the umbrella of a North-East Says No campaign, which entered the fray relatively late in the day and was expected to provide only token opposition. Backed by elements of the North-East landed establishment, several leading businessmen who preferred to remain quiet, as well as by the Conservative and UK Independence Parties, NESNO, as it became known, struck a chord with a few catchy sound bites — notably 'vote no to more politicians.' The most enduring symbol was a huge, inflatable white elephant to give the impression that the proposed assembly would have few powers. It was engineered by a Euro-sceptical London-based group, the New Frontiers Foundation, which provided a campaign director and administrative support, and saw the campaign as a dry-run for a referendum on whether to endorse a European Union constitution.

The message from the opposing camp, Yes4theNorthEast, was more complex, and difficult to get across — namely that while powers were limited, more would assuredly follow as the new body bedded down.[13] Indeed, no doubt recognising the vulnerability of the 'yes' side, both John Prescott and his deputy Nick Raynsford appeared quite happy to volunteer that they were negotiating with ministerial colleagues, particularly the Transport Secretary Alastair Darling, for more powers.

It had all seemed so very different in the spring of 2004, with a 'Your Say' campaign, featuring Prescott and Raynsford, touring cities and towns throughout the three northern regions with the message that a 'great north vote' — the Deputy Prime Minister's label for the three planned northern referendums — would help shift the centre of gravity away from London and the greater South-East by creating strong regional institutions to challenge Whitehall.

On reflection, this was a top-down campaign, with little added weight either from activists on the ground or, crucially, from local MPs and councillors. Increasingly, it would be seen by many sceptical voters as an imposition

---

[13] Obtaining extra powers at a later date was not as straightforward as ministers (or campaigners) might have liked to imply. Many of the delivery agencies in the regions, such as the Learning and Skills Councils, the Environment Agency and the Highways Agency, are statutory bodies, and changes to their functions would require further legislation. That was unlikely to be forthcoming in the near future from a Government for which decentralisation was not a priority. The same is true of the GLA; it has gained no new functions since 2000, apart from the movement of some budgets into the London Development Agency, in line with all of the RDAs.

from central government, commanding little popular support. For the local press, it was viewed as a bureaucratic nightmare because of the UK Government's insistence that the introduction of single-tier, or unitary local government must go hand in glove with the creation of elected regional assemblies. Threatened county and district councils began fighting each other 'like ferrets in a sack', according to one bemused chief executive.[14] Local newspapers were consumed by county-versus-district bust-ups.

By the early summer, it became clear that Downing Street was increasingly concerned. Alerted to a letter from more than 20 Labour MPs to Prescott calling for the referendum in the North-West to be postponed, the Prime Minister apparently urged his deputy to think again. In Yorkshire, there were similar mutterings of disquiet among backbenchers. The chair of a 'Yes for Yorkshire' campaign, the Labour peer Lord Haskins, publicly raised doubts about whether a referendum could be won.

Consequently, late in July, referendums in the North-West and Yorkshire & Humber were 'postponed', officially because the Electoral Commission was uneasy about the prospect of all-postal voting in the regions. That left the North-East out on a limb and, by late August, it seemed Yes4theNorth-East had the momentum — but not for long.

Just as a disparate band of 'yes' campaigners in the 1979 devolution referendums in Scotland and in Wales suffered from the unpopularity of the then prime minister (James Callaghan), so their North-East successors were beset by the relatively unfavourable image of Tony Blair in particular and politicians generally. (The Prime Minister hardly helped by telling the Darlington-based *Northern Echo* that he had once been a devolution sceptic). There were other parallels, too. While the 1979 Scottish 'yes' campaign was undermined by arguments in the 'yes' camp — to the extent that there were two, polarised groups campaigning for devolution — Yes4theNorthEast was probably more divided than many realised. This is not so much a reflection on its leaders, who put together a credible organisation with an impressive range of supporters, as an indication that some in Labour's ranks appeared to want an exclusively party-based campaign and resented a more inclusive effort. In reality, apart from John Prescott, few prominent Labour or Liberal Democrat personalities, let alone MPs, were prepared to get involved. Privately, like counterparts in the North-West and Yorkshire & Humber, some were either lukewarm or opposed to the package on offer. Apart from an extremely brief intervention by the Prime Minister (a North-East MP, after all) with the Liberal Democrat leader Charles Kennedy at a photo-opportunity in Stockton, the Deputy Prime Minister appeared a lone voice.

Yes4theNorthEast gathered together an impressive list of regional personalities from the sports entrepreneur and commentator, former Olympic

---

[14] Interview with co-author, autumn 2004.

athlete Brendan Foster, to the president of Newcastle United FC and the independent mayor of Middlesbrough, Ray Mallon. Its campaign video, featuring a catchy song from the Manchester band M-People, emphasised pride and passion in the context of the strong regional identity of the North-East. On the publicity front, it appeared to be winning hands down.

But as *The Guardian* reported, many who assumed there would be an automatic 'yes' from the region's 1.9 million electors, slowly realised . . . 'that regional identity does not easily translate into political expression.'[15] Bill Lancaster, the North-East's most prominent social historian and director of the Centre for Northern Studies at Northumbria University, put it more succinctly:

> It's a region that has an identity based on a range of cultural factors and practices — dialect, the way you look at the past, shared history — but much of that is latent rather than manifest. It's there, people recognise it, but it does not necessarily prompt them into action.[16]

Recognising the need to take the debate beyond politicians, Yes4the-NorthEast generally eschewed the political class, to the chagrin of several North-East MPs. In reality, as the campaign gained momentum, there appeared to be two campaigns with only, it seemed, limited contact between them. True, the Labour 'yes' campaign borrowed Yes4theNorthEast's slogan, and the M-People anthem. But, essentially, the Deputy Prime Minister John Prescott pursued a lone campaign. Backed by the party machine and travelling on a campaign bus — even its slogan, 'This is your chance; don't waste it', betrayed a nervousness — he visited the area regularly over a four-week spell and took his message to street rallies, frequently engaging voters on walkabouts. Yes4theNorthEast appeared to be operating at a different level.

Predictably, friction came to the surface after the result. The Labour leader of Gateshead Council, Mick Henry, gave a hint of the Labour establishment view, claiming that Yes4theNorthEast 'for all its good intentions and celebrity support, did not communicate its vision so clearly . . . voters were not given a clear enough message of what the assembly was actually going to do.'[17]

Yes4theNorthEast could, perhaps, be forgiven for thinking that this criticism should be directed not at itself, but at the government for its failure to flesh out the powers of the proposed assembly beyond the white paper of

---

[15] 'Northern Exposure', *The Guardian*, 27 October 2004.
[16] *Ibid.* See R. Colls and B. Lancaster, *Geordies: Roots of regionalism* (Edinburgh: Edinburgh University Press, 1992) for a range of accounts of these factors.
[17] Mick Henry, 'Determined on devolution', *Public Finance*, 19 November 2004.

May 2002.[18] This white paper, which formed the basis of a draft bill (further outlining the extremely limited powers) published in July 2004, was always a messy compromise born out of the uneven gains made by Prescott in the Cabinet's Committee of the Nations and Regions (CCNR).[19] As it turned out, publication of the draft bill itself proved one of the major stumbling blocks for the 'yes' campaigners — the document came back to haunt them time and again. On every television debate, at every press conference, the main spokesman of the North East Says No campaign, Graham Robb — a former Conservative parliamentary candidate who runs a public relations business in Darlington and still acts as a PR adviser to the Tories — could be seen thumping the draft bill with the message that the powers on offer were not worth having.

The polling data available during the campaign indicated a considerable swing from approximately late July 2004 onwards. This was a surprise, as polls taken during the previous five years repeatedly indicated a solid majority in favour of an elected assembly in the North-East. The BBC's poll of March 2002 indicated that 72 per cent of respondents supported an assembly, whilst the County Councils Network poll of July that year suggested 51 per cent of respondents in favour and only 19 per cent against.[20] Even in February 2004, a MORI poll suggested that 39 per cent of respondents supported the establishment of an assembly and only 22 per cent opposed it. However, as the campaign gained momentum it became clear that these comfortable majorities were draining away. A further MORI poll, in July and August 2004, showed support and opposition evenly balanced, and also suggested that support for the concept in all three northern regions had fallen considerably in the previous year. Paradoxically, this poll also showed that the number of respondents claiming to understand the Government's proposals had fallen during 2003–4, suggesting widespread confusion in the electorate.

By mid-October, the 'no' camp had a seven-point lead in the *Northern Echo* and Prescott was spending half his weeks in the North-East. Local daily newspapers, the Newcastle-based *Journal* and the *Northern Echo*, devoted considerable space to the campaign, although the former became distinctly cooler towards the devolution package on offer while the latter

[18] DTLR/Cabinet Office, *Your Region, Your Choice: Revitalising the English regions*, Cm 5511, (London: The Stationery Office, 2002).

[19] Office of the Deputy Prime Minister, *Draft Regional Assemblies Bill*, Cm 6285 (London: The Stationery Office, July 2004).

[20] BBC poll data available to the author. The BBC poll was not formally published when it was conducted and is no longer available on the BBC website. It is discussed in J. Tomaney and P. Hetherington, *English Regions Devolution Monitoring Report*, May 2002, pp. 25–6, available at www.ucl.ac.uk/constitution-unit/nations/monitoring.php. On the County Councils Network poll, see C. Jeffery and A. Reilly, 'The English Regions Debate: What do the English Want?', *ESRC Devolution Briefing*, 3, (July 2003).

was by far the strongest supporter. Referendum campaign television broad-
casts, from both camps, were sharply contrasting, with 'yes' campaigners
producing an upbeat image of the North-East — 'be proud, be positive, vote
yes' — and the 'no' side presenting eerie images of politicians alongside the
none-too-subtle message of 'do you want more of them.' Combine this with
the cost of the exercise — £25 million annually in running costs for a
25-member assembly and, on government estimates, 5p per week for the
average council taxpayer — and it proved a potent, negative message.

But the message from some ministers visiting the North-East was hardly
positive either. Perhaps in recognition of the referendum, the BBC's *Question Time* was screened from Gateshead two weeks before polling day. It
seemed an ideal opportunity for the Government to field a high-profile
minister. Instead Harriet Harman QC, the solicitor general, was chosen. She
did not appear to understand the package on offer, and a rambling, hesitant
reply to one devolution question outraged Prescott supporters.

The Result

The referendum votes were counted by 2am on 5 November. The result and
question are shown in Table 5.2:

Table 5.2: The North-East Result
'Should there be an elected assembly for the North-East region?'

Yes	197,301	22.1 per cent
No	696,519	77.9 per cent
Spoiled	12,538	
Turnout	893,829	47.7 per cent

Every locality of the North-East voted against by a wide margin. However,
the overall figures concealed interesting regional distinctions.[21] The former
colliery areas of Durham and South-East Northumberland, and the conurba-
tion of Tyneside, were considerably more supportive of an assembly, with
support ranging from 25–30 per cent. The rural peripheries, Teesside, and
Sunderland were particularly strongly opposed, with support ranging from
12 per cent of voters in Darlington to 19 per cent in Sunderland.[22] Although
the strength of the 'no' vote renders these statistical distinctions virtually
irrelevant, it is interesting that they follow conventional wisdom about internal cleavages within the North-East. Teesside has been claimed to fear

---

[21] See www.electoralcommission.org.uk for the full figures.
[22] The area of Castle Morpeth borough council is the one authority area which does not fit this
analysis: it is really part of the rural periphery but 22 per cent of voters supported the assembly, more
than their peers in other parts of rural Northumberland.

domination by a Newcastle-based assembly, as has Sunderland, a traditional rival city to Newcastle. The rural peripheries of north and west Northumberland, and Teesdale (south-west Durham), are the only parts of the region where the Labour Party is weak — local and parliamentary elections return Conservative, Liberal Democrat or independent candidates — and this may explain in part the lack of support for a policy that became increasingly politicised throughout the campaign. There were also considerable local variations in the vote on unitary authorities. The two county seats, Morpeth and Durham, plus adjoining areas, voted quite strongly for a unitary county. Most other localities voted for the option of 2–3 unitary authorities, suggesting they felt more remote from the county council.[23]

It is historically interesting, though not necessarily instructive, to note the clear parallels between the North-East experience and the referendum for a Welsh Assembly in 1979. A confusing and relatively weak Assembly was proposed, meaning that the 'Yes' campaign's message was easily confused and less approachable than the simple opposition of the 'No' campaign. The sitting Prime Minister came from the region and was unpopular at the time of the referendum; the Labour Government was nearing a general election; Labour MPs were less than enthusiastic about the proposals (some, of course, were entirely opposed), and many of those supporting devolution wanted a party-based campaign. Local government reform was also a big issue in 1979 Wales, with many Labour supporters wanting to replace the then new counties which had been established by the Heath administration, but fearing the implications of the process to be gone through. There were also concerns, in 1979, about a Welsh Assembly leading to the 'break-up of Britain'. Nevertheless, there had been enough indications in opinion polls that voters were supportive enough to make the exercise worthwhile. There were indications in 1979 that part of the opposition was to the specific proposals rather than to devolution itself, though that appears *at this stage* to have been less of a factor in the North-East.[24]

THE FUTURE OF SUB-NATIONAL GOVERNMENT IN ENGLAND

The consequences of the 'no' vote in the North-East are not yet entirely clear, but there can be no doubt that they spell the death of elected regional assemblies at least for the time being. On 8 November John Prescott

[23] For full figures, see www.regionalvote.co.uk, and forthcoming work from C. Rallings and M. Thrasher at the Local Government Elections Centre, University of Plymouth, and from P. John and A. Tickell at the Universities of Manchester and Bristol respectively.

[24] All of these comparisons come from the extended analysis of the Wales 1978 campaign in D. Foulkes, B. Jones and R. Wilford (eds.), *The Welsh Veto: the Wales Act 1978 and the referendum* (Cardiff: University of Wales Press, 1983). Almost every chapter in this book contains marked similarities in events and developments to those of the North-East in 2004.

confirmed, after much press speculation, that the North-West and Yorkshire & Humber referendums would now be cancelled — a politically sensible decision given the size of the North-East 'no' vote. He did confirm, however (backed by the Prime Minister), that the regional agenda was still on track, including a continuing role for RDAs and Regional Chambers/Assemblies.[25] But in the small hours of 5 December, at a news conference near the counting centre in Sunderland, even Prescott appeared to be speaking the language of Downing Street. He volunteered that the government would continue its 'reform agenda' for local government, mentioning 'directly-elected mayors and community leadership' almost as an alternative. He acknowledged that the government had simply 'failed to get its case across'.

Asked how he felt to lose so badly, the Deputy Prime Minister replied:

> I have a strong view about regional assemblies, but the people have spoken. It's their choice. It was a manifesto commitment. I might be disappointed . . . the people have spoken and I recognise that. It's an emphatic defeat . . . the electorate felt comfortable with a Labour government . . . that came across often and I think that led them to feel 'why another tier of government?' They didn't feel threatened like they did under a Tory government.[26]

Ironically, one of the effects of the 'no' vote was a sudden increase in attention to the Regional Chambers, organisations hitherto little-known outside political circles. Conservative politicians attempted to argue that the 'no' vote should lead to the closure of the North-East Assembly (Chamber); this was argued by Linda Arkley, Conservative mayor of North Tyneside, and by Michael Howard, the party leader. One of the present authors noticed some public surprise at the fact that an assembly 'already' existed in the aftermath of the referendum. Although the Government reaffirmed its support for the Regional Chambers/Assemblies in November, their medium-to long-term future is not clear. But anecdotal evidence available to one of the authors suggests that the Conservatives believe that some form of regional-level forum would be useful, and it therefore appears unlikely that the party would abolish Regional Chambers outright if it is returned to power in 2005.[27]

It may be that the Regional Assemblies' decision to rename themselves 'Assembly' instead of 'Chamber' has caused much confusion. Despite calling themselves 'Assemblies', they have no real democratic credentials, being part-appointed and part-elected by limited electoral colleges of interest groups. Though many call themselves the 'voice of the region', they have

---

[25] HC Deb, 10 November 2004, col 838–9.

[26] Interview with co-author, 5 November 2004.

[27] Formally no government can abolish the Regional Chambers, as they are voluntary, membership-based bodies. A Conservative government could deprive them of funding, which would leave them where they were at their establishment in 1999 — reliant on small sums from their members, and ineffective.

very little connection with the general public. This confusion has been exploited by political parties who see regional institutions as a Labour Party or European Union 'plot', arguing that the existence of these little-known 'regional assemblies' demonstrates some form of conspiracy. In reality the Chambers are minor quangos. They spend some £20 million per annum collectively, a sum dwarfed by other quangos such as English Nature (£80 million), the Highways Agency (£5 billion) or the Housing Corporation (£2 billion). Their existence is called into question as much by their lack of democratic accountability as the work that they do, much of which is technical in any event.

In the immediate wake of the 'no' vote, few were prepared to defend the existing regional institutions openly. Instead, a number of alternative forms of change to sub-national government arrangements in England were briefly mooted. We explore these here in some detail, because they emanate from all sides of the political spectrum and indicate a degree of agreement that, whatever the merits of elected assemblies, there remains an 'English question'.[28] We argue that most of these, despite appearing superficially attractive, are actually less convincing ways forward than regional government (whether elected or unelected). They offer far less opportunity for improved and distinctive governance of the North-East (or any other region). We go on to use the comparison of London, the only elected 'regional' government in England, to point up what can be achieved by an elected regional tier.

The proposals set out here come from a variety of sources. Some were made by the North-East Says No campaign in the immediate aftermath of the referendum; some emanate from rumours in and around the 'Westminster village'; and some derive from previous reform attempts.[29]

1. A Minister for the North-East

The idea of 'regional ministers' has a long pedigree. Scotland, Wales, and Northern Ireland had cabinet ministers for much of the twentieth century, and this has become associated with their privileged financial settlements and the ability to vary UK policy to the benefit of the 'region'. Business, in particular, has supported the concept of a series of regional ministers alongside departmental ones, seeing them as one-stop shops to discuss policy or financial decisions.

If a minister for the North-East were in charge of a department of state, held Cabinet rank, and therefore had policy and financial discretion over a large part of the public spending in the North-East, their influence could be

---

[28] For a detailed examination of this, see R. Hazell (ed.), *The English Question* (Manchester: Manchester University Press, forthcoming).

[29] We have not mentioned the idea of an English Parliament here, which remains as far as ever from the political mainstream. See www.thecep.org.uk

considerable. The Scottish and Welsh Offices were able to influence substantially some of the Conservatives' policies of the 1980s and 1990s through this route, and Scotland in particular took a quite different approach to economic development. Both countries were able to put together strong inward investment packages for various international companies during this time.

The creation of a Department for the North-East, however, begs its own questions. If it were effective, other regions might well demand their own departments, implying a gradual reorganisation of Whitehall from a functional to a territorial division that would surely be fiercely resisted by civil servants and Ministers alike. At the same time, the existence of a powerful regional department would be sure, sooner or later, to lead to the renewal of calls for elected regional government — especially if the Conservative Party returns to power at Westminster. They would be torn between the likelihood of having to appoint a non-North-Easterner to the post (due to their low representation in the region) or abolishing such a department altogether.

Meanwhile, a minister beneath cabinet rank, or one with a political but no functional portfolio, would be extremely unlikely to have any effect whatsoever on behalf of the region. A leading spokesman for North-East Says No proposed 'a minister for the North-East based in either the Treasury or the DTI that can shake up the Government and get us the results we expect'.[30] But the political reality is that decision-making in Westminster rests with Ministers within their departmental policy areas, and is only rarely susceptible to change because of lobbying from a non-Cabinet minister in another department. Such a Minister might be able to 'stand up for' the region and 'call' for changes, but their actual impact would be negligible. Past experience, such as Lord Hailsham in the North-East in the early 1960s or Michael Heseltine in Merseyside in the early 1980s, demonstrates that only very limited benefits can flow from such an arrangement.

2. A Select Committee of North-East MPs

This proposal suffers from the same problems as those which would afflict a non-cabinet Minister for the North-East. It sounds initially attractive: a select committee containing all or some of the MPs of the North-East, like other select committees, would be able to summon witnesses and report on the problems and possible solutions for the region.

However, producing reports and calling for change is essentially all a territorial select committee could do. Select committees have no power to institute change, and the history of departmental select committees since their formation in 1979 demonstrates that they have never been able to

---

[30] '"No" group want North minister', *Newcastle Journal*, November 6 2004.

modify Government policy substantially.[31] Policy decisions rest with Government, and back-bench MPs alone or collectively cannot reverse them: they can only speak, lobby, and persuade. Furthermore, it is not certain that ministers would agree to appear before a Select Committee for the North-East, as they usually only agree to appear before their own departmental committee. It is not apparent that much of the electorate, or many of the opponents of regional assemblies, actually understand the degree to which MPs are powerless to reverse decisions made by a determined Government, even on matters which apply to their region or locality. MPs can lobby strongly and bring the public eye to bear on Government decisions, but they do not themselves take decisions. The advantage of an elected assembly in this respect is that it brings specific executive powers away from central government and into the region, freeing them from the indifference, misunderstanding or lack of time available to ministers.

The experience of Wales is again salutary here. The Welsh Affairs Committee was set up in the wake of the 1979 referendum (following the Conservative Party's election victory). This had been presented by some, in the referendum campaign, as an alternative to devolution: yet, as Jones and Wilford point out, its recommendations were almost entirely ignored by the government (1983: 232–3). A different potential 'model' is the Welsh Grand Committee, which sat regularly until devolution in 1999 and has continued to find a role for itself since then, holding seven sessions on four days in the 2003–04 session on such matters as the implications for Wales of the Government's Legislative Programme. The Grand Committee consists of all of the MPs representing Welsh constituencies. It is, however, a talking shop. The political make-up has long been heavily Labour, meaning that dissent is likely to be stifled under a Labour government and prioritised under a Conservative government. A similar lack of balance would very likely affect a North-East grand committee (though this would not be so true of other regions).

3. Unitary Local Authorities Across England

All elected regional assemblies, under the Regional Assemblies (Preparations) Act 2003, must be accompanied by a move to unitary local government in that region.[32] Since this provision was introduced, there have been rumours that the Government wanted to introduce unitary local authorities whether or not elected assemblies were introduced, as part of its third-term

---

[31] See G. Drewry (ed.), *The new select committees : a study of the 1979 reforms* (Oxford: Clarendon, 1989). See also the Hansard Society's report *The Challenge for Parliament: Making government accountable* (London: Vacher Dod, 2001).

[32] Regional Assemblies (Preparations) Act s 1(5) and s 13; see also DTLR/Cabinet Office, 2002, pp. 64–6.

programme.[33] Both Labour and the Conservatives have long been sympathetic towards unitary local government. The chaotic Banham review of 1992-95 started out as a means towards achieving unitary authorities. The 2002 White Paper gave several arguments in favour of unitary authorities, and claimed that cost savings would result.[34]

Paradoxically, a move to unitary local authorities is very likely to strengthen the case for a regional tier of government (whether elected or unelected) to take account of strategic issues which spill over boundaries. The move to unitary local government in Scotland and Wales in 1996 made devolution far easier to deliver. The unitary authorities proposed by the Boundary Committee review of 2004 were either counties (a politically expedient option) or merged districts ranging in size from 131,000 to 510,000, with an average population of 262,000. These merged districts would be smaller than county councils, strengthening the need for coordination between them on matters such as transport, land-use, waste and environmental issues.

4.   A Revival of Elected Mayors

Reviving the elected mayor idea would be politically brave, given the level of opposition from much of the Labour party and from many local electorates between 2000 and 2002. Elected mayors take on the executive functions of local authorities, and were promoted as increasing the visibility and hence the accountability of local council activities. However, elected mayors have not been given any additional powers to those available to all local authorities, and there is no sign of this happening. The elected mayor idea does not address the issues of coordination between authorities.

5.   City-Regions

There were some indications at the end of 2004 that city-regions were once again finding favour with government. The city-region idea is most clearly dealt with by Derek Senior (1969) and Michael Coombes (1996), both of whom proposed a wholesale reorganisation of local government into city-regions based on travel-to-work areas.[35] The concept has been somewhat conflated with the idea of elected mayors, though the two are not dependent on one another. The latest rise in the idea's popularity appears to

[33] See 'English councils braced for shake-up', *The Guardian*, 1 January 2005; 'Prescott's "super parish" revolution', *The Guardian*, 5 January 2005.

[34] DTLR/Cabinet Office, 2002, p. 65. This claim has been disputed: see A. Midwinter and N. McGarvey, 'Local Government Reform in Scotland: Managing the Transition', *Public Administration*, 75, (Spring 1997); M. Chisholm, *Structural Reform Of British Local Government: Rhetoric and reality* (Manchester: Manchester University Press, 2000).

[35] D. Senior, *Royal Commission on Local Government in England, 1966–1969 Vol. 2: Memorandum of Dissent* (London: HMSO, 1969); M. Coombes, *Building a New Britain* (London: City-Region Campaign, 1996).

have less to do with structural reorganisation and more to do with urban-based cooperation, particularly in the context of the 'Northern Way' growth strategy announced by the Deputy Prime Minister in 2003.[36] But this will not lead to any lasting changes in the central-local power balance unless it is partnered by some form of structural change.

THE TENACITY OF REGIONALISM

None of these possible alternatives, however, addresses a number of aspects of sub-national government which are addressed, if falteringly, by the existence of Regional Chambers and the option of elected regional assemblies.

First, although the dictum that 'some functions are best tackled at the regional level'[37] is in itself rather glib, there are issues of coordinating housing new build, transport plans and expenditure decisions on economic and business development which would be hard to handle at the level of the fragmented local government structure that exists in England. For instance, a large regional spending budget is simply more flexible than a multitude of local economic development budgets (for instance) and can allow a locality to progress with a significant development which it might not be able to afford if it had only its own, far smaller, budget. Regional allocation can also lessen considerably inter-local competition for economic investment, for instance. Transport plans relate frequently to neighbouring counties, whether road or rail, individuals or freight. Waste disposal within county boundaries is often hard to arrange. Policy areas continually spill over, leading to regional solutions of one kind or another.

Secondly, probably for one or more of the above reasons, government has for a long time found it convenient to establish a tier of offices between local and national levels.[38] The pattern of administration that has been used in the last forty years suggests that central government does not find dealing directly with around 45 county areas to be efficient without regional offices in between. Those regional offices then come under pressure to link their work up to their counterparts in other departments, to improve policy outcomes, and, where they disburse money, to make clear the criteria on which they do so. Precisely these pressures led to the formation of the Government Offices in 1994 and the beginnings of a number of partnerships which evolved into Regional Chambers in 1994-99. Wannop's 'regional imperative'[39] may be overstating the case, but the administrative reality of

---

[36] There is also no indication that a restoration of the metropolitan counties is being proposed.

[37] Labour Party, *Ambitions for Britain* (London, 2001), p. 32.

[38] B. Hogwood, 'Introduction', in B. Hogwood and M. Keating (eds.), *Regional Government in England* (Oxford: Clarendon, 1982), 16–19; F. Robinson and K. Shaw, 'Governing a Region: Structures and Processes of Governance in North East England', *Regional Studies* 35(5): 473–8, (2001)

[39] U. Wannop, *The Regional Imperative*, (London: Jessica Kingsley, 1995).

the last 60 years has been of a regional tier, of some kind, in England. The position of that tier — caught between centralised accountability and local-ised impact — guarantees that its activities will attract attention, and possi-bly opprobrium, where it makes mistakes.

A regional tier of administration has continued to appear and reappear in some form in England since at least 1960. It has been of little interest to the public and often to central government, but it has proved remarkably consis-tent and tenacious, especially considering the lack of regional identities or cultures within England and the absence of the regional tier from most government policy programmes. At present it looks likely that any future changes, including regionalism, will not include any form of democratic accountability. Does this matter for the sub-national government of England? Our answer is yes. To demonstrate this we examine briefly the one part of England not yet discussed, and examine its prospects in the medium term in the context of its own anaemic form of devolution.

GREATER LONDON COMES OF AGE

The sudden return of Ken Livingstone, Mayor of London, to the Labour fold on 6 January 2004 marked the beginning of a far more active partnership between his anaemic 'devolved' government and the UK. Livingstone was re-elected on 10 June 2004 with a reduced majority, and the Labour group lost 2 of its 9 seats in the London Assembly. This has consequences for the Mayor's budget, which can be overridden with a two-thirds majority in the Assembly. The Labour group is not now large enough to block that majority, which led to considerable horse-trading in the budget process of early 2005.

What is of interest in this context is what the Mayor has been able to achieve for London. The existence of the GLA, his personal mandate, visi-bility and the opportunity of making executive decisions have had consider-able impact — even if his powers are quite circumscribed. The Mayor's only real executive powers are transport and economic development, and his overwhelming focus has been on improving bus and underground services in London, plus the introduction of the congestion charge. The changes he has made to these services have in the main been low-cost, apart from the intro-duction of a large number of new buses, which has driven up his precept on the council tax. The 'strategic role' has had few publicly visible outcomes.[40]

However, the benefits of an elected assembly, in terms of lobbying central government from a coordinated perspective, were starkly demonstrated by the GLA in 2004. The Mayor was able to strike a series of deals with central

[40] M. Sandford, 'The governance of London: strategic government and policy divergence', in A. Trench (ed.), *Has Devolution made a Difference? The state of the nations 2004* (Exeter: Imprint Academic, 2004).

government which emphasise starkly what elected regional tiers of government can achieve through politics, negotiation and partnership. He was able to broker the establishment of the bid for the 2012 Olympics. He was able to obtain permission from the Treasury to borrow £2.9 billion in order to improve the light rail and underground network in East London, in preparation for London's Olympic bid. This is a particularly impressive sum given the Treasury's paranoia about public sector borrowing since 1997 — indeed, the devolved authorities in Scotland and Wales have not borrowed at all since their establishment. The Mayor's access to revenue through the precept and transport fares (giving him a source from which he can pay the loans back) is an important factor here — elected regional assemblies would not have had an ability to raise revenue in a similar way to this.

The Mayor's own Regional Emphasis Document, the 'Case for London', largely repeats the policy priorities of his first term, indicating his greater freedom in preparing a submission for 2004 Spending Review. Despite the Treasury stating in its letter to the regions about Regional Emphasis Documents that it would not listen to bids for extra cash, the GLA requested an extra £1 billion for Transport for London. Subsequently, Transport for London's grant was increased by £800m. The Mayor has also been able to increase fares to begin paying back the money borrowed: this is a controversial decision, but he has the power to make it. He has been able to institute a capital spending programme of £1.4 billion in total (£1 billion in transport); the total spend of the GLA 'family' in 2004–5 is £8.25 billion.

These are eye-wateringly huge figures compared to the £400–500 million that would have been available annually to a North-East regional assembly. The comparison is not entirely fair, as the size and expense of London Underground inflates the London figures. But consider even a twentieth of the London budget — £400 million that is not currently available — being borrowed and then spent in the North-East, by an accountable assembly in the public eye, for instance on transport infrastructure. The impact on the North-East would be huge. Without a representative body such as an elected assembly, it is hard to obtain such funds, because there is no other type of organisation that can combine public responsiveness (spending the money on matters of public concern), visibility (leading to accountability), technical expertise, and political impetus and leadership (including seeing the job through), not to mention the capacity to make the case for increased funding or negotiate loans in the first place. Under the current system of fragmented central government offices, local authorities focused on service delivery, and centralisation of executive power, it is almost impossible to ensure that projects like new road and rail services, new school and college buildings, or improved cultural facilities actually get done, on time, rather than remaining worthy aspirations. Local authorities and committees of MPs, not to mention national government ministers with vast numbers of competing priorities, would never be able to meet such a challenge.

Of course, some of the Mayor's achievements are explicable because London is London. The capital has long occupied a uniquely central place in public policy priorities in the UK.[41] This is demonstrated by the unproblematic way in which issues such as the Olympic bid, Crossrail, and the state of the Underground network move between being urban/local, regional and national news issues/public policy concerns. And not everything that the Mayor does relates to billion-pound projects: he also runs an assortment of far more minor policy programmes which have only a very attenuated effect on London life, due to his lacking the powers or money to back them up.[42] But the presence of an elected Mayor and Assembly, backed up by a considerable policy-making capacity, bolsters London's negotiating position with facts, analysis and political attention. The fact that England's only elected regional assembly exists in London, the capital city and dominant economic region, is a further reason why London's voice wins in comparison with the lagging regions of England and the UK. There will be no First Minister of Yorkshire or the North-East to act as a countervailing voice against the huge investment demands of the capital or against the central government tendency to be more receptive to demands from London than those from Durham or Wigan. The political voice of counties and cities is feeble by comparison.

CONCLUSION

In spring 2005, the upshot of the North-East referendum was not clear. The Government, and most of the media, had gone silent on the question of regional government. But the variety of problems to which elected regional assemblies were proposed as a solution remain. In particular, there is no sign that the numerous regional offices of executive agencies will be abolished. RDAs and Government Offices are not under threat; Conservative policy at the time of writing is to maintain RDAs in place. A raft of unelected regional government bodies, spending some £25–30 billion across England, is the outcome of the North-East 'no' vote. It is not certain, as some opponents of regional government claim, that all of the functions exercised by these offices could be transferred to local government and still be undertaken effectively.

---

[41] A. Amin, N. Thrift, D. Massey, *Decentering the Nation: A radical approach to regional inequality* (London: Catalyst, 2003).

[42] Sandford, 2004.

Regional government has been proposed not merely for administrative convenience but to enhance economic resilience, democratic accountability of some public services, and the flowering of disparate political voices in the hyper-centralised Westminster polity of England. The particular form of regional government proposed as a solution to these issues is open to much criticism. The ODPM Select Committee's report on the draft Regional Assemblies Bill, published in January 2005, suggested that 'general powers needed to be tied down with some more specific statements of assembly functions'.[43] In their absence, the likely prognosis for the regions of England is dependent upon political developments. Following Labour's victory in the 2005 general election, slow progress down the road of regionalisation is likely to continue, with little public awareness or accountability, and very little opportunity for any real degree of policy divergence. This suggests that the range of pressures towards regionalisation and hence regional account- ability will also remain in place, and hence a renewed interest in elected regional assemblies is not out of the question. Predicting future develop- ments, however, remains extremely difficult due to the very limited overt interest shown by the two main parties in the issue.

One scenario with unpredictable, but potentially significant, conse- quences is a serious breakthrough of the Liberal Democrats at Westminster, either in a coalition government or holding the balance of power under a minority government. Liberal Democrats have in the past been strongly supportive of moves towards a federal UK, including fairly autonomous English regions with tax-raising powers, though always with the caveat of public approval through a referendum. Following the referendum result it remains to be seen whether they will continue to promote this line with such enthusiasm (witness their 2005 manifesto, which omitted any reference to these policies). But it is not impossible that in the medium term, Liberal Democrat influence could lead to the resurrection of some form of elected regional agenda.

None of the pressures which gave rise to the current round of regional changes and proposals are likely to disappear in the medium term. Central- ised regionalisation is likely to continue on its course. But regionalism is likely to remain the answer that no-one wants to hear to the question that no-one wants to ask. Administrative pressures will continue to run up against public disinterest, and the Westminster state — and state of mind — has proved more resilient than expected. In that context, the lack of power (in terms of institutions and individuals) associated with the concept of elected regional assemblies may have been one of the most deep-laid problems of the whole policy. This is clear if we consider what would happen if a

---

[43] House of Commons ODPM Select Committee, First Report of 2004–5 Session, *The Draft Regional Assemblies Bill*, HC62–1, (London: House of Commons, 2005), para. 32.

North-East regional political party demanding devolution, and threatening Labour strongholds, had emerged or were to emerge: the impact of that on regional policy would be greater than everything in this chapter put together.

BIBLIOGRAPHY

Official Documents

DEFRA, *Rural Strategy 2004*, available at www.defra.gov.uk/rural/strategy

DTLR/Cabinet Office, *Your Region, Your Choice: Revitalising the English regions*, Cm 5511, (London: The Stationery Office, 2002).

HM Treasury, *2002 Spending Review* (London: The Stationery Office, 2001).

HM Treasury, *2004 Spending Review: Meeting regional priorities* (London: The Stationery Office, 2004): available at www.hm-treasury.gov.uk

ODPM, *Regional Assemblies (Preparations) Act 2003* (London: The Stationery Office).

ODPM, *Planning and Compulsory Purchase Act 2004* (London: The Stationery Office).

ODPM, *Draft Regional Assemblies Bill*, Cm 6285 (London: The Stationery Office, July 2004).

House of Commons ODPM Select Committee, First Report of 2004–5 Session, The Draft Regional Assemblies Bill, HC62–1 (London: House of Commons, 2005).

Secondary Sources

Amin, A., N. Thrift, D. Massey, *Decentering the Nation: A radical approach to regional inequality* (London: Catalyst, 2003).

Chisholm, M., *Structural Rreform of British Local Government: Rhetoric and reality* (Manchester: Manchester University Press, 2000).

Colls, R. and B. Lancaster, *Geordies: Roots of regionalism* (Edinburgh: Edinburgh University Press, 1992).

Coombes, M., *Building a New Britain* (London: City Region Campaign, 1996).

Drewry, G. (ed.), *The New Select Committees: a study of the 1979 reforms* (Oxford: Clarendon, 1989).

Foulkes, D., J. B. Jones, and R. Wilford, *The Welsh Veto: The Wales Act 1978 and the referendum* (Cardiff: University of Wales Press, 1983).

Hansard Society, *The Challenge for Parliament: Making Government accountable* (London: Vacher Dod, 2001).

Hazell, R. (ed.), *The English Question* (Manchester: Manchester University Press, forthcoming).

Hogwood, B., 'Introduction', in B. Hogwood and M. Keating (eds.), *Regional Government in England* (Oxford: Clarendon, 1982).

Hogwood, B., *Mapping the Regions: Boundaries, coordination and government* (York: Joseph Rowntree Foundation, 1995).

Jeffery, C. and A. Reilly, 'The English Regions Debate: What do the English Want?', *ESRC Devolution Briefing*, 3, (July 2003).

Labour Party, *Ambitions for Britain: General election manifesto*, (London: Labour Party, 2001).

Lyons, Sir Michael, *Independent Review of Public Sector Relocation* (London: HM Treasury, 2004).

McLean, I. *et al.*, *Identifying the Flow of Public Expenditure into the English Regions* (London: ODPM, 2003).

Midwinter, A. and N. McGarvey, 'Local Government Reform in Scotland: Managing the Transition', *Public Administration*, 75, (Spring 1997).

Robinson, F. and K. Shaw, 'Governing a Region: Structures and Processes of Governance in North East England', *Regional Studies*, 35(5): 473–8, (2001).

Sandford, M., 'The governance of London: strategic government and policy divergence', in Trench, A. (ed.) *Has Devolution Made a Difference? The state of the nations 2004* (Exeter: Imprint Academic, 2004).

Senior, D., *Royal Commission on Local Government in England, 1966–1969 Vol. 2: Memorandum of dissent* (London: HMSO, 1969).

Smith, B. C., *Regionalism in England 1: Regional institutions — a guide* (London: Acton Society Trust, 1964).

Tomaney, J. and P. Hetherington, 'English regions: the quiet regional revolution?', in Trench, A. (ed.), *Has Devolution Made a Difference? The state of the nations 2004* (Exeter: Imprint Academic, 2004).

Tomaney, J. and P. Hetherington, *May 2002 English Regions Devolution Monitoring Report* (London: Constitution Unit, 2002), available at www.ucl.ac.uk/constitution-unit/nations/monitoring.php

Wannop, U., *The Regional Imperative: regional planning and governance in Britain, Europe and the United States* (London: Jessica Kingsley, 1995).

Part II

UK-Wide Issues

6

Public Opinion and the Future of Devolution

John Curtice

One ingredient vital to the future success of devolution is that it should have legitimacy in the eyes of the public. By this we mean that the public accept that the institutional arrangements under which they are governed are an appropriate mechanism for making political decisions, such that they accept the right of a body to make a decision even when they disagree with the outcome.[1] If a set of institutional arrangements lacks such legitimacy then the decisions that emerge are likely to be more difficult to enforce, for those who disagree with the decisions will feel they have a moral right to challenge the right of the bodies in question to make the decisions they have. The result may at best be widespread flouting of the law or a campaign of civil disobedience, and at worse civil unrest and violence.

This chapter examines how far the new institutional arrangements involving the creation of elected devolved bodies in both Scotland and Wales in 1999 appear to have acquired, maintained or lost legitimacy during the first five years of their operation, the reasons why this happened, and the apparent implications of this analysis for the future prospects for devolution. In so doing it pays particular attention to ascertaining the role of two foundations upon which support for the devolved institutions could rest. One possibility is that people's support for devolution is contingent on its success in bringing about outcomes that they desire. The Scottish Parliament and National Assembly for Wales may be valued for what they have achieved. Alternatively, however, they might be valued for what they represent. They might be regarded, for example, as the expression of a distinctive national identity or more representative of distinctive national customs, mores or interests. If so, this might be thought to provide a more substantial and more permanent foundation of support for devolution, one that helps the devolution settlement to withstand any short term failure in delivering the outcomes that people value.[2]

---

[1] D. Easton, *A Systems Analysis of Political Life* (New York: Wiley, 1965); P. Norris (ed.), *Critical Citizens: Global support for democratic government* (Oxford: Oxford University Press, 1998).

[2] This distinction is of course similar to the distinction made by Easton, *ibid.*, between 'specific' and 'diffuse' support.

Our analysis comes in two parts. In the first part we examine the degree to which the Scottish Parliament and the National Assembly are accepted by the publics that they seek to serve. Do people in Scotland and Wales wish to keep the devolved institutions that they now have? And if so, do they value them for what they can achieve or what they represent? In the second half we turn to England. England itself does not enjoy any measure of devolution comparable to that implemented in Scotland or Wales. This obviously raises the possibility that even if the current devolution settlement is accepted in Scotland and Wales, it is still a bone of contention in England, which after all constitutes 85 per cent of the population of the United Kingdom. The chapter does not address the position in Northern Ireland where the devolved institutions have so far had no more than a fitful existence as a result of disputes about the security situation there (which is discussed by Rick Wilford and Robin Wilson in Chapter 4). While these disputes have affected the willingness of unionist politicians to participate in and thus lend legitimacy to the devolved institutions established by the Belfast Agreement, the disputes themselves were not about the operation of those institutions.

Our data come from a set of parallel surveys conducted by the National Centre for Social Research. In England the platform was the annual British Social Attitudes survey. This is a high quality annual social survey conducted throughout Great Britain whose sample typically includes at least 3,000 respondents in England each year.[3] In Scotland the data were collected as part of the companion Scottish Social Attitudes survey which since 1999 has annually interviewed around 1,500 respondents north of the border.[4] In Wales, separate surveys known as the Welsh Assembly Election Study in 1999 and the Wales Life and Times survey in 2001 and 2003 were conducted.[5] Many of the key questions asked on these surveys since 1999 were also included on surveys conducted before 1999, thereby enabling us to compare attitudes towards devolution once it was in operation with attitudes prior to its introduction.

PUBLIC OPINION IN SCOTLAND AND WALES

Our first question then is whether people in Scotland and Wales think that their devolved institutions should exist. Table 6.1 suggests that the simple answer to that question is an affirmative one. In Scotland devolution appears to have had a high level of support from before its inception and that support

[3] A. Park, J. Curtice, K. Thomson, C. Bromley and M. Phillips (eds.), *British Social Attitudes: the 21st report* (London: Sage, 2004).

[4] C. Bromley, J. Curtice, K. Hinds and A. Park (eds.), *Devolution — Scottish Answers to Scottish Questions* (Edinburgh: Edinburgh University Press, 2003).

[5] R. Wyn Jones and R. Scully, 'A Settling Will? Wales and Devolution, Five Years On', *British Parties and Elections Review*, 13: 86–106, (2003).

Table 6.1: Trends in Constitutional Preferences in Scotland and Wales[6]

SCOTLAND	May 1997	Sept 1997	1999	2000	2001	2002	2003
Scotland should ...	%	%	%	%	%	%	%
be independent, separate from UK and EU or separate from UK but part of EU	28	37	28	30	27	30	26
remain part of UK with its own elected Parliament which has some taxation powers	44	32	50	47	54	44	48
remain part of the UK with its own elected Parliament which has no taxation powers	10	9	8	8	6	8	7
remain part of the UK without an elected parliament	18	17	10	12	9	12	13
WALES							
Wales should ...							
be independent, separate from UK and EU or separate from UK but part of EU	na	13	9	na	12	na	13
remain part of UK with its own elected Parliament which has some law making and taxation powers	na	18	35	na	37	na	36
remain part of the UK with its own elected Assembly which has limited law making powers only	na	25	35	na	25	na	25
remain part of the UK without an elected assembly	na	37	18	na	23	na	20

na: not asked

has largely been maintained. Immediately after the 1997 UK general election, just over half of those surveyed (54 per cent), said that they favoured some form of devolution, with most of them in favour of the Parliament having some taxation powers. By 2003 the figure was much the same, at 55 per cent. In Wales, meanwhile, support for devolution is if anything now

[6] Source: Scottish Election Study 1997; Scottish Referendum Study 1997; Scottish Social Attitudes Surveys 1999–2003; Welsh Referendum Study 1997; Welsh Assembly Election Study 1999; Wales Life and Times Surveys 2001, 2003.

even higher than it is in Scotland. But this is a relatively new found legiti-macy. Whereas by 2003, 61 per cent favoured some form of devolved parlia-ment or assembly, just 43 per cent did so immediately after the 1997 referendum when Wales voted in favour of creating the National Assembly by the narrowest of margins.[7] However, the three-fifths of Welsh voters in favour of devolution are seriously divided between those who prefer the current assembly and those who would like a more powerful parliament.

So devolution has majority support in both countries, but equally it does not have much more than majority support. In both countries there are still significant bodies of apparent opposition. In Scotland just over a quarter persistently remain in favour of their country becoming independent, either inside or outside the European Union. In Wales, by contrast, the largest source of opposition, albeit one much diminished since 1997, comes from the one in five or so who would still prefer not to have any kind of elected assembly at all, while only around one in eight people in Wales support some form of independence. While those who support independence may not doubt the right of the devolved institutions to exist – unlike those who would prefer not to have any kind of parliament or assembly at all — they obviously still represent a challenge to their continued operation within the framework of the United Kingdom.

But what is the basis of the substantial support that does exist for the prin-ciple of devolution? The first possibility that we outlined was that people value the institutions for what they have achieved. If this were the case then, given the statistics in Table 6.1, we might anticipate that people in Wales have been particularly impressed by the performance of their institution while those in Scotland have at least been sufficiently impressed for them to have maintained the support for devolution they already exhibited even before the September 1997 referendum.

The evidence as presented in Table 6.2 does not however conform to these expectations. The Scottish Parliament was greeted at the time of the 1997 referendum with very high expectations. The perceived reality has been well short of those expectations. For example, at the time of the 1997 referendum, nearly four in five thought that the Parliament would give ordinary people more say in how they are governed. Within two years of its inauguration that figure had halved. On education standards the equivalent figures are seven in ten and around one in four. Only in respect of whether the Parliament is thought to give Scotland a stronger voice in the UK has the gap between expectations and perceived reality been less precipitate.

---

[7]   B. Taylor and K. Thomson (eds.), *Scotland and Wales — Nations Again?* (Cardiff: University of Wales Press, 1999).

**Table 6.2: Expectations and Evaluations of the Devolved Institutions
in Scotland and Wales[8]**

SCOTLAND	1997*	1999	2000	2001	2002	2003
	%	%	%	%	%	%
Perceived impact on Scotland's voice in the UK						
No difference	17	20	40	40	52	41
Weaker	9	7	6	6	7	7
Perceived impact on giving ordinary people a say in how Scotland is governed						
More	79	64	44	38	31	39
No difference	17	32	51	56	62	54
Less	2	2	3	4	4	4
Perceived impact on education						
Increase standards	71	56	43	27	25	23
No difference	19	36	49	59	58	59
Reduced standards	3	3	3	5	6	7
WALES	**1997***	**1999**	**2000**	**2001**	**2002**	**2003**
	%	%	%	%	%	%
Perceived impact on Wales' voice in the UK						
Stronger	50	62	na	49	na	52
No difference	33	32		45		42
Weaker	12	5		3		4
Perceived impact on giving ordinary people a say in how Wales is governed						
More	54	56	na	34	na	38
No difference	36	39		60		54
Less	4	3		3		6
Perceived impact on education in Wales						
Increase standards	50	42	na	22	na	27
No difference	37	48		64		53
Reduce	5	3		3		6

* Referendum. na: not asked. The questions were worded each year as follows:
    1997: Would a Scottish Parliament/Welsh Assembly increase ...
    1999: Will a Scottish Parliament/Welsh Assembly increase...
    2000: Is having a Scottish Parliament going to increase...
    2001, 2002, 2003: Do you think having a Scottish Parliament/Welsh
       Assembly is increasing...

[8] Sources: Scottish and Welsh Referendum Studies 1997; Scottish Social Attitudes Survey 1999–2003; Welsh Assembly Election Study 1999; Wales Life and Times Surveys 2001, 2003.

As one might have anticipated initial expectations of the National Assembly for Wales were not so high as they were in Scotland. Only around half expected it to have a positive impact on how much say ordinary people have, education standards or Wales' voice in the UK. But even so, on the first two of these three items at least, perceived reality has fallen short of expectations. Indeed on education the proportion who think the National Assembly has helped to increase standards is but half the proportion who in 1997 thought it would do so. Only on whether the Assembly has helped to strengthen Wales' voice in the UK do perceptions of the outcome match expectations.

True, few in Scotland or in Wales think that devolution is making things worse in respect of any of the items covered in Table 6.2. Even so, if support for the Scottish Parliament rested on what it could deliver (as some have argued it does)[9] one would have expected to have seen some decline in support for its continued existence. In practice support for devolution in Scotland has held steady while in Wales it has grown.

There is a relatively simple reason why support for the principle of devolution has not been undermined by people's disappointment with what it has achieved. This can be seen in Table 6.3, which shows how people's constitutional preferences vary according to their perception in 2003 of the impact of the Scottish Parliament/ National Assembly on the strength of their country's voice in the UK and on education standards. Those who think that the Parliament or Assembly has not made any difference do not in fact hold very different views about the merits of devolution from those that do. Across all four parts of the table the largest gap between those who say that devolution has improved matters and those who say it has not made any difference is just 17 points. (While those who think the Parliament or Assembly has actually made things worse are sometimes less supportive of devolution than those who think it has not made any difference, it should be remembered this group is always small and has not grown significantly.) In short, at any one point in time support for the principle of devolution has not been closely related to perceptions of the performance of the devolved institutions.

⁹ See for example, P. Surridge. and D. McCrone, 'The 1997 Scottish referendum vote', in B. Taylor and K. Thomson (eds.), *Scotland and Wales — Nations Again?* (Cardiff: University of Wales Press, 1999).

Table 6.3: Constitutional Preference and Perceptions of Effectiveness: Scotland and Wales 2003[10]

SCOTLAND	Perceived Impact on Stronger Voice in the UK		
Constitutional Preference	Stronger %	No Difference %	Weaker %
Independence	29	23	23
Devolution	64	47	49
No Parliament	3	22	28
	Perceived Impact on Education Standards		
Constitutional Preference	Increase %	No Difference %	Reduce %
Independence	33	24	19
Devolution	59	55	56
No Parliament	4	15	23
WALES	Perceived Impact on Stronger Voice in the UK		
Constitutional Preference	Stronger %	No Difference %	Weaker %
Independence	14	13	12
Parliament	43	28	22
Assembly	30	22	15
No Assembly	8	33	49
	Perceived Impact on Education Standards		
Constitutional Preference	Increase %	No Difference %	Reduce %
Independence	17	13	9
Parliament	51	35	17
Assembly	23	25	17
No Assembly	6	23	50

It is interesting however to note which is the issue on which the 17 point gap does arise. It is whether having a Scottish Parliament has helped strengthen Scotland's voice in the UK. Equally, we should note that in Wales too views on whether the National Assembly has given Wales a stronger voice are more strongly related to attitudes towards devolution than are perceptions of education standards. At the same time perceptions of the impact of devolution on their country's voice in the UK makes little difference to the chances of someone backing independence. Doubtless this reflects the fact that strengthening the position of Scotland and Wales within

[10] Sources: Scottish Social Attitudes Survey 2003; Wales Life and Times Survey 2003.

the UK is at least one objective of devolution that advocates of independence do not support. In any event we can now see that devolution has in fact come closest to matching expectations on the one issue, its impact on Scotland's and Wales' voices in the UK, where perceived failure had the greatest potential to undermine support for devolution.

So one feature of devolution that apparently shapes the nature of its support is that it attempts to combine improved advocacy of the interests of Scotland and Wales with continuing membership of the United Kingdom. That such a feature commands support would appear to require the existence of a dualism in the attitudes and identities of people in Scotland and Wales. On the one hand it suggests that people should feel in some sense distinctively Scottish or Welsh, and that they wish to see this distinctiveness represented in separate political institutions. On the other hand it also suggests that this distinctiveness is not necessarily regarded as being in opposition to a sense of Britishness that may be expressed through membership of the United Kingdom.

Having dual national identities, that is feeling both Scottish/Welsh and British, is certainly relatively commonplace. For example, when presented with a list of possible national identities and asked to indicate all those that they would use to describe themselves, 34 per cent of people in Wales said in 2003 that they were both Welsh and British, while no less than 47 per cent gave the equivalent response in Scotland. The degree to which people feel a dual identity is measured more systematically by a question about national identity commonly known as the 'Moreno' question.[11] This invites people to place themselves on a five point scale that at one end is (in, for example, Scotland) labelled 'Scottish, not British', and at the other end, 'British, not Scottish'. In between, are answers that indicate some form of dual identity; respondents can indicate that they feel equally British and Scottish or that while they feel both, they feel one more strongly than the other.

When asked about their national identity in this way, around three in five people in both Scotland and Wales claim to be some mixture of both Scottish/Welsh and British (see Table 6.4). However, in Scotland at least the proportion taking this view has been somewhat lower in the post-devolution era. The highest post-devolution reading of 60 per cent compares with 69 per cent in 1997 and no less than 76 per cent in 1992. There are also hints of a similar drop in Wales where the proportion with a dual identity was six points lower in 2003 than it had been in 1997. In both cases the decline has been accompanied by an increase in the proportion claiming an exclusively Welsh or Scottish identity. If dual national identity provides a foundation for support for devolution, it would appear that it is being undermined.

[11] L. Moreno, 'Scotland and Catalonia: The path to Home Rule', in D. McCrone and A. Brown (eds.), *The Scottish Government Yearbook 1988* (Edinburgh: Unit for the Study of Government in Scotland, 1988).

Table 6.4: Trends in Moreno National Identity: Scotland and Wales[12]

	1992	1997	1999	2000	2001	2003
SCOTLAND	%	%	%	%	%	%
Scottish not British	19	23	32	37	36	31
More Scottish than British	40	38	35	31	30	34
Equally Scottish and British	33	27	22	21	24	22
More British than Scottish	3	4	3	3	3	4
British not Scottish	3	4	4	4	3	4
WALES						
Welsh, not British	na	17	17	na	24	21
More Welsh than British	na	26	19	na	23	27
Equally Welsh and British	na	34	37	na	28	29
More British than Welsh	na	10	8	na	11	8
British, not Welsh	na	12	14	na	11	9

na: not asked.
1997 readings are for the general election of that year, except in Wales where it is for the devolution referendum.

But what difference does national identity make to people's preferences as to how they should be governed? As can be seen from Table 6.5, in answering this question we in fact uncover a paradox. Attitudes towards the full range of constitutional preferences are clearly related to national identity. Moreover, in Scotland at least they are clearly more related to national identity than they are to perceptions of the performance of the devolved institutions. However, this does not mean that attitudes towards devolution itself are strongly related to national identity.

[12] Source: Scottish Election Study 1992 and 1997; Scottish Social Attitudes Surveys 1999–2003. Welsh Referendum Study 1997; Welsh Assembly Election Study 1999; Wales Life and Times Surveys 2001, 2003.

Table 6.5:
National Identity and Constitutional Preference: Scotland and Wales[13]

SCOTLAND	National Identity				
Constitutional Preference	Scottish Only %	More Scottish %	Equal %	More British %	British Only %
Independence	47	22	8	5	10
Devolution	41	63	62	66	68
No Parliament	5	10	26	23	21
WALES	National Identity				
Constitutional Preference	Welsh Only %	More Welsh %	Equal %	More British %	British Only %
Independence	27	11	11	7	6
Parliament	40	44	31	38	22
Assembly	18	25	28	31	29
No Assembly	11	14	28	21	39

In both Scotland and Wales support for independence is far higher amongst those who feel exclusively Scottish/Welsh than it is amongst any other group. At the same time opposition to there being any kind of parliament at all is more marked among those who feel at least as British as they do Scottish or Welsh. Meanwhile the 40 point or so difference between the highest and lowest level of support for independence in Scotland is far higher than any difference in the first half of Table 6.3, though the same cannot be said of support for the existence of some kind of parliament in Wales.

But support for devolution itself crosses divisions of identity. Only among the exclusively Scottish is it not the single most popular option. Thereafter in Scotland its appeal is much the same irrespective of national identity. In Wales devolution has majority support in all groups, albeit that support for having a parliament with legislative power rather than just an assembly is relatively stronger amongst those who feel wholly or mostly Welsh. By contrast it cannot be said in either country that support for devolution in general is consistently higher amongst those who acknowledge a dual identity.

It would appear that the strength of the underpinning of support for devolution lies in not its ability to appeal to those with dual identities but rather to meet the aspirations of those with very different national identities. Those who feel predominantly Scottish or Welsh may feel inclined to want their

[13] Sources: Scottish Social Attitudes Survey 2003; Wales Life and Times Survey 2003.

own distinctive political institutions, but for many of them devolution appears to provide a sufficient means of expressing their country's distinctiveness. Meanwhile while those who feel mostly British may have an attachment to the UK, for many the fact that devolution means that Scotland and Wales retains its membership of the UK evidently means that they do not feel it compromises their sense of Britishness. Indeed it is interesting that further analysis reveals that in both Scotland and Wales, the perception that the Parliament/Assembly has strengthened their country's voice in the UK is more strongly correlated with constitutional preference amongst those who feel equally or predominantly British than it is amongst those who feel predominantly Scottish or Welsh. So long as it is thought to have this quality those who feel a relatively strong sense of Britishness are willing to give devolution their support. And of course if devolution has an ability to appeal to those with very different national identities, then it helps explain why levels of support for it have apparently been little affected by the recent decline in the proportion with a dual identity.

In Scotland and Wales then, people's constitutional preferences are linked both to national identity and perceived performance. But the performance that matters most is the degree to which the devolved institutions help strengthen the position of their country within the UK, and it matters most to those with a relatively strong sense of Britishness. This has had two important consequences. First it has enabled devolution, unlike independence or the *status quo ante*, to appeal to those with different national identities. For some devolution helps emphasise their nation's distinctiveness while for others it enhances their country's place in the UK. Second, it has meant that support for devolution has been relatively stable; it is largely immune to changes in national identity while strengthening their country's role within the UK is the one criterion on which perceived reality of devolution has not fallen so far short of expectations.

PUBLIC OPINION IN ENGLAND

If support for devolution appears to rest on relatively strong foundations in Scotland and Wales, what of England? Does England want devolution too? What parallels if any are there between the reasons why people in England do or do not support devolution and what we have learnt about the basis of support for devolution in Scotland and Wales? Meanwhile we have also to examine what England thinks of devolution in Scotland and Wales and whether the apparent strength of support for devolution in Scotland and Wales has to be set against antagonism towards it amongst those living in their near neighbour.

Table 6.6: Trends in Constitutional Preferences for England[14]

	1999	2000	2001	2002	2003
	%	%	%	%	%
England should be governed as it is now, with laws made by the UK Parliament	62	54	59	56	55
Each region of England should have its own assembly that runs services like health	15	18	21	20	24
England as whole should have its own new parliament with law-making powers	18	19	13	17	16

There are of course two very different forms that devolution could take in England.[15] One is for there to be some form of English Parliament that makes the law for key policy areas in England in much the same way that the Scottish Parliament now does for Scotland. The other is that regional assemblies be set up across England, most likely with fewer powers than a national parliament. In asking people in England how they would like to be governed, therefore, the British Social Attitudes survey has asked people to choose between these two possible forms of devolution as well as the status quo.

In any event, as Table 6.6 reveals, England has it seems been little persuaded by the example of Scotland or Wales of the merits of either form of devolution. Consistently more than half have said that they wish to retain the status quo with laws for England being made by the UK Parliament. There has been some growth in support for regional devolution, the option favoured by the UK Labour Government, but that growth proved too little to avert a heavy defeat when people in the North East of England, the region most in favour of regional devolution, were given the chance to say a referendum in November 2004 whether they wanted an elected regional assembly.[16]

[14] Source: British Social Attitudes Surveys 1999–2003

[15] R. Hazell (ed.), *The English Question* (Manchester: Manchester University Press, forthcoming).

[16] J. Curtice and M. Sandford, 'Does England want devolution too?', in A. Park, J. Curtice, K. Thomson, C. Bromley and M. Phillips (eds.), *British Social Attitudes: the 21st report* (London: Sage, 2004); J. Curtice, 'What the people say — if anything', in R. Hazell (ed.), *The English Question* (Manchester: Manchester University Press, forthcoming a).

Table 6.7: Perceptions of the Impact of Regional Chambers/Assemblies[17]

From what you have seen or heard so far do you think that having a regional chamber or assembly for [region] will give ordinary people (2003: is giving).... in how [region] is governed.

	All England			London			
	2001 %	2002 %	2003 %	2000 %	2001 %	2002 %	2003 %
More say	32	25	19	45	38	35	26
No Difference	55	59	62	45	51	51	53
Less say	2	3	4	6	2	3	8

...will the region's economy become better, worse or will it make no difference?

	All England			London		
	2001 %	2002 %	2003 %	2001 %	2002 %	2003 %
Better	29	21	23	34	24	27
No Difference	55	60	58	50	54	52
Worse	3	4	4	3	7	6

Not that the English regions do not have some form of devolution.[18] In particular, since 1998–99 each region has had an unelected chamber or assembly with responsibility for scrutinising the work of a Regional Development Agency. Meanwhile, following the restoration of London-wide local government institutions in 2000, London has its own elected regional assembly responsible for scrutinising the work of a directly-elected mayor. The perceived success or otherwise of these bodies could well be an influence of people's attitudes in England towards devolution.

Table 6.7 suggests however that the existing limited forms of devolution in England have done little to impress the public as to the merits of devolution. In England as a whole around three in five think that their regional assembly is not making any difference to how much say they have in how they are governed, while the same proportion think it will not have much impact on the strength of their region's economy. Moreover these figures are only a little lower in London where just over half share these sentiments so far as their elected assembly is concerned. In each case the proportion saying that their regional assembly is actually making things better is markedly lower than it is in Scotland and Wales where, as we have already seen in Table 6.2 , just under two in five think their devolved institution is giving

17 Sources: London Mayoral Election Study 2000; British Social Attitudes Surveys 2001–2003.
18 See Sandford and Hetherington, Chapter 5, this volume.

them more say and where in both cases around 35 per cent feel their devolved institution will help improve their nation's economy.

Table 6.8: Attitudes Towards Regional Government by Perceptions of Impact of Regional Chambers/Assemblies[19]

Now that Scotland has its own Parliament and Wales its own Assembly, every region of England should have its own assembly too

	Perceived impact of regional chamber on giving ordinary people a say		
	More Say %	No Difference %	Less Say %
Agree	45	27	27
Neither	24	25	18
Disagree	24	37	44
	Perceived impact of regional chamber on region's economic prospects		
	Better %	No Difference %	Worse %
Agree	42	28	18
Neither	25	25	12
Disagree	26	37	62

This lack of positive perceptions about the current regional institutions is certainly not doing anything to bolster support for devolution in England. This can be seen in Table 6.8 which shows how responses to a question that asked people directly about the merits of the English regions having their own institutions vary according to their perceptions of the effectiveness of their regional chamber or assembly. Those who think their regional assembly is giving them more say or feel that it will improve their economy are more likely to support regional devolution than those who do not. The differences are not however overwhelming – indeed they are not dissimilar to those we saw earlier in Scotland and Wales in Table 6.3 – and even among those who think that their regional assembly is having a positive impact, less than half express support for regional devolution. Evidently the lack of enthusiasm for devolution in England cannot simply be explained by the failure of the regional institutions that have been created so far to have much apparent impact.

[19] Source: British Social Attitudes 2003.

Table 6.9: Trends in Moreno National Identity: England[20]

	1997	1999	2000	2001	2003
	%	%	%	%	%
English not British	7	17	19	17	17
More English than British	17	15	14	13	19
Equally English and British	45	37	34	42	31
More British than English	14	11	14	9	13
British not English	9	14	12	11	10

What then of national or regional identity? How far might this provide a basis of support of some form of devolution? Table 6.9 shows that the pattern of national identity in England is very different from that in Scotland or Wales. Only just over one in three say they are mostly or exclusively English rather than British, much lower than the half in Wales who feel mostly or exclusively Welsh or the two thirds in Scotland who feel mostly or exclusively Scottish. A sense of being British is much more pervasive in England and that in itself might help explain why there appears to be relatively little interest in England in devolution. However, the proportion saying they are exclusively English has been at least somewhat higher since the advent of devolution in Scotland and Wales in 1999. So if having an English Parliament were regarded as a means of expressing such a distinct identity, this should have helped bolster support for such a body.

The difficulty is that in practice this is not the case, as Table 6.10 (overleaf) shows. Preferences as to how England should be governed vary little by national identity. While those who feel exclusively English are more likely to advocate an English Parliament, the difference is small. Even in this group almost as many are happy for England to be ruled by the UK Parliament as want either an English Parliament or regional devolution. National identity certainly seems to matter much less to how people in England would prefer to be governed than we have seen it does in Scotland or Wales.

[20] Source: British Election Study 1997; British Social Attitudes Surveys 1999–2003.

Table 6.10: Constitutional Preference by National Identity: England[21]

	National Identity				
	English only	More English	Equal	More British	British only
	%	%	%	%	%
Parliament	24	17	14	17	14
Regional Assemblies	23	24	24	25	26
No Change	46	55	57	52	55

Meanwhile relatively few people feel a close sense of attachment to their region. In 2003 just 22 per cent said they were 'very proud' of being someone who lives in their particular region of England, little different from the proportion who said the same three years earlier, whereas no less than 41 per cent said that they were very proud of being British, and 43 per cent, English. In any event, as Table 6.11 shows, how much pride someone has in their region makes little difference to their attitudes towards regional government. Even amongst the minority who say they are very proud of their region, only just over one in three back regional devolution.

Table 6.11: Attitudes Towards Regional Government by Regional Pride[22]

Now that Scotland has its own parliament and Wales its own assembly, every region of England should have its own assembly too

	Regional Pride			
	Very Proud	Somewhat	Not very/at all	Don't think that way
	%	%	%	%
Agree	36	32	32	27
Neither	18	29	22	27
Disagree	34	29	38	34

There is then a striking contrast between England and its two Celtic neighbours. Whereas in the latter national identity helps shape people's constitutional preferences, in England neither national nor regional identity seems to make much difference to people's views about how they should be governed. Of course we also discovered that attitudes towards devolution as opposed to independence or the *status quo ante* differed relatively little by national identity in Scotland or Wales. But this appears to be not because national identity does not make any difference to people's attitudes towards

---

21 Source: British Social Attitudes 2003.
22 Source: British Social Attitudes 2003,

devolution but rather because it appeals in somewhat different ways to those with different national identities. In England, by contrast, where relatively few give precedence to a sense of being English rather than feeling British and few have a strong sense of regional pride, it appears that few feel it necessary for their English or regional identity to be reflected in distinctive institutional structures.

Not least of the likely reasons for this is that people in England already feel their English identity is adequately represented and their interests sufficiently protected by existing structures in which they play a predominant role. For example, 30 per cent actually feel that the House of Commons is either 'English, not British' or 'More English than British'.[23] Moreover this perception is even more (nearly two in five) common amongst those who describe themselves in either of these two ways, that is amongst the group that might be thought to feel the greatest need for a distinctively English institution. At the same time, just over half of people in England say they trust the UK Government to work in the best long-term interests of England either 'just about always' or 'most of the time', whereas in both Scotland and Wales only just over one in five give the equivalent answer when asked how much they trust the UK Government to look after the interests of their country. If England feels that the current structure serves it reasonably well, why should it wish to imitate Scotland and Wales?

Indeed, people in England themselves appear to recognise that they may be in a different position from those in Scotland or Wales. For despite their apparent lack of interest in devolution for themselves, there is evidently little antagonism to the creation of the Scottish Parliament and National Assembly. As Table 6.12 (overleaf) shows, only between one in seven and one in eight of people in England appear to oppose the creation of any kind of distinctive political institutions in Scotland or Wales, a figure that seems to have fallen from around one in four prior to the establishment of the institutions in 1999. At the same time there is little appetite for having Scotland or Wales leave the Union with England.

Not that some features of the current asymmetric devolution settlement do not grate with people in England. In 2003 no less than three in five agreed that 'Scottish MPs should no longer be required to vote on English legislation', while nearly three quarter said that the Scottish Parliament 'should pay for its services out of taxes collected in Scotland'. But these sentiments receive considerable support in Scotland as well.[24] Making England feel

[23] J. Curtice and A. Heath, 'Is the English lion about to roar?', in R. Jowell, J. Curtice, A. Park, K. Thomson, L. Jarvis, C. Bromley and N. Stratford (eds.); *British Social Attitudes: the 17th report: Focusing on diversity* (London: Sage, 2000).

[24] J. Curtice, 'Brought together or driven apart?', in W. Miller (ed.), *Anglo-Scottish Relations from 1900 to Devolution and Beyond* (Oxford: Oxford University Press, forthcoming).

John Curtice

happier about some of the apparent inequities generated by the current asymmetric settlement would receive considerable support in Scotland too.

Table 6.12: Attitudes in England Towards How Scotland and Wales Should be Governed[25]

	1997	1999	2000	2001	2003
Scotland should ...	%	%	%	%	%
be independent, separate from UK and EU or separate from UK but part of EU	14	24	20	19	17
remain part of UK with its own elected Parliament which has some taxation powers	38	44	44	53	51
remain part of the UK with its own elected Parliament which has no taxation powers	17	10	8	7	9
remain part of the UK without an elected parliament	23	13	17	11	13
	1997	1999	2000	2001	2003
Wales should ...	%	%	%	%	%
be independent, separate from the UK and the EU or separate from UK but part of EU	13	20	17	17	16
remain part of the UK, with its own elected parliament which has law-making and taxation powers	37	34	35	39	37
remain part of the UK, with its own elected assembly which has limited law-making powers only	18	22	17	19	20
remain part of the UK without an elected assembly	25	15	20	14	15

CONCLUSION

In the early years of its existence devolution has retained the majority public support it has long had in Scotland while it has strengthened its support in Wales. It may not be wanted by the English for themselves but people in England have acquiesced in the creation of devolved institutions in the rest of Great Britain. The 1999 asymmetric devolution settlement can be regarded as having a satisfactory level of legitimacy across Great Britain.

It has acquired or retained that legitimacy despite some disappointments about what devolution has actually achieved so far. The key to attitudes towards devolution lies, however, in the pattern of identities and the nature

[25] Sources: British Election Study 1997; British Social Attitudes Surveys 1999–2003.

of the link between identity and constitutional preferences. Support for devolution in Scotland and Wales is founded on its ability to represent the aspirations of both those who feel predominantly Scottish or Welsh and the minority who feel predominantly British. The lack of interest in devolution in England reflects the fact that not only do relatively few have a distinctive English identity or a strong sense of regional pride, but also that those with such sentiments do not see how their identities would be better represented by some form of devolved structure.

So while some of the details of the current asymmetric system, such as the West Lothian question, how the Scottish Parliament is financed and the particular form that devolution should take in Wales, may yet be in the balance so far as public opinion is concerned, the broad structure of the current devolution settlement appears to rest on some solid foundations. In Scotland and Wales devolution would seem capable of bringing together those of disparate identities in a manner that independence as yet shows little sign of being able to do, though if this position is to be maintained devolution needs to make people feel their country is being better heard within the UK. In England there seems to be little chance of much demand for devolution until both more people feel a more distinctive sense of identity that they feel would be better represented by distinctive political structures. At present at least, there seems little immediate prospect of either development occurring.

BIBLIOGRAPHY

Bromley, C., J. Curtice, K. Hinds and A. Park (eds.), *Devolution — Scottish Answers to Scottish Questions* (Edinburgh: Edinburgh University Press, 2003).

Curtice, J., 'What the people say — if anything', in R. Hazell (ed.), *The English Question* (Manchester: Manchester University Press, forthcoming).

Curtice, J., 'Brought together or driven apart?', in W. Miller (ed.), *Anglo-Scottish Relations from 1900 to Devolution and Beyond* (Oxford: Oxford University Press, forthcoming).

Curtice, J. and A. Heath, 'Is the English lion about to roar?', in R. Jowell, J. Curtice, A. Park, K. Thomson, L. Jarvis, C. Bromley and N. Stratford (eds.), *British Social Attitudes: the 17th report: Focusing on diversity* (London: Sage, 2000).

Curtice, J. and M. Sandford, 'Does England want devolution too?', in A. Park, J. Curtice, K. Thomson, C. Bromley and M. Phillips (eds.), *British Social Attitudes: the 21st report* (London: Sage, 2004).

Easton, D., *A Systems Analysis of Political Life* (New York: Wiley, 1965).

Hazell, R. (ed.), *The English Question* (Manchester: Manchester University Press, forthcoming).

Moreno, L., 'Scotland and Catalonia: The path to Home Rule', in D. McCrone and A. Brown (eds.), *The Scottish Government Yearbook 1988* (Edinburgh: Unit for the Study of Government in Scotland, 1988).

Norris, P. (ed.), *Critical Citizens: Global Support for Democratic Government* (Oxford: Oxford University Press, 1998).

Park, A., J. Curtice, K. Thomson, C. Bromley and M. Phillips (eds.), *British Social Attitudes: the 21st report* (London: Sage, 2004).

Surridge, P. and D. McCrone, 'The 1997 Scottish referendum vote', in B. Taylor and K. Thomson (eds.), *Scotland and Wales — Nations Again?* (Cardiff: University of Wales Press, 1999).

Taylor, B., and K. Thomson (eds.), *Scotland and Wales — Nations Again?* (Cardiff: University of Wales Press, 1999).

Wyn Jones, R. and R. Scully, 'A Settling Will? Wales and Devolution, Five Years On', *British Parties and Elections Review*, 13: 86–106, (2003).

7

Intergovernmental Relations
Within the UK
The Pressures Yet To Come

Alan Trench

Intergovernmental relations in the UK have been remarkably relaxed since devolution. The framework for intergovernmental relations between the UK Government in London and the devolved administrations of Scotland, Wales and Northern Ireland created at the time of devolution involved a relatively informal set of arrangements, based largely on existing administrative and political practices, and making minimal use of any sort of formal institutional arrangements.[1] The first five years of devolution support two conclusions. First, that framework has by and large proved adequate for the demands placed on it so far. Those demands, it is true, have not been particularly difficult, helped by a benign climate of Labour-controlled or dominated governments in Scotland and Wales, and strong growth in public spending and (for much of the period) the economy more generally. Second, in fact things have gone so well that substantial elements of that modest framework have been allowed to fall into disuse. The plenary form of the Joint Ministerial Committee has not met, for example, for nearly two and a half years (at the time of writing). Instead, a combination of informal liaison at the political level and a high degree of integration between UK Government and devolved administrations where necessary at the working level have prevailed. Expectations that there would be endless disputes between government have proved to be wrong.

One set of questions for the future is whether this situation can last, what will cause change if the status quo cannot last, and what factors may influence the system that emerges afterward. What will trigger change depends on a variety of contingencies, but this chapter will survey three major areas: political parties and political change, financial and fiscal issues, and constitutional and institutional factors. While these are the main drivers of change as well as the main areas in which change is likely, other issues remain

[1] For more extensive discussions, see A. Trench, 'The More Things Change the More They Stay the Same: Intergovernmental Relations Four Years On' in A. Trench (ed.) *Has Devolution Made a Difference: The state of the nations 2004* (Exeter: Imprint Academic, 2004) and House of Lords Select Committee on the Constitution, *Devolution: Inter-institutional relations in the United Kingdom* (Session 2002-03, 2nd Report, HL 28) (London: The Stationery Office, 2003).

important. The involvement of the European Union is key – the extent to which it affects what the various governments in the UK can do, and to which it enables sub-national governments to be directly involved in its decision-making processes. These are discussed by Charlie Jeffery in Chapter 9, as well as by Scott Greer in Chapter 10. Similarly, economic issues and the persistence of regional inequalities as discussed by John Adams and Peter Robinson in Chapter 11 may drive policy, particularly from London, perhaps leading to attempts to persuade devolved administrations to adopt policies endorsed by the UK Government, perhaps leading the UK Government to devolve further functions to enable the devolved administrations and regional bodies in England to tackle such problems themselves. However such questions play out, they will both affect and probably be at least partly driven by the political, financial and institutional relations of the UK's constituent parts.

A second set of questions relates to the impact of intergovernmental relations on devolution as a whole. Intergovernmental relations (IGR) are a key part of the structure of the devolved UK state, because of the continuing role of the UK Government as the sole government for England (accounting for 85 per cent of the population of the UK as a whole), as well as its responsibility for reserved and non-devolved matters such as foreign affairs or the economy. The way functions are allocated between the two sorts of government means that few actions of the UK Government do not affect the devolved bodies, often profoundly. Conversely, many actions of the devolved institutions have some effect on the UK Government (if only by setting a potentially- embarrassing example). Governments therefore have to find ways to get along if they are to exercise their own functions, even if they are not inclined to do so. The various sorts of resources (financial, legislative, legal, constitutional, party-political) possessed by the UK Government gives it a number of ways to influence the devolved institutions. These range from referring the legal competence of various devolved actions or proposed actions to the courts, to introducing a financial system which includes conditional grants whose conditions shape recipient governments' policy. (The latter is a widely-used technique in many other systems, most notably Australia and the USA.) So far the UK Government has largely refrained from using the means that already exist and from seeking to develop new ones. Instead, it has allowed the devolved administrations largely to do what they wish – what one might call 'permissive autonomy'. Working out why the UK Government has taken this approach is harder. The lack of transparency with which IGR in the UK is conducted means that it is difficult to know whether this is due to a general consensus between governments or the use of covert back-channels to deliver agreement (although the author's interviewing suggests that in general the former is much more important).

The issue is important because it relates directly to the autonomy that the devolved institutions can actually exercise. If IGR enables the UK Government can grant limited autonomy to the devolved territories while in fact remaining able to secure its desired outcomes when it needs to, that implies that devolution is a very limited reform which has neither improved the ability to make policy locally nor to connect the people of Scotland, Wales or Northern Ireland with those who govern them. Alternatively, if devolution has reshaped the way in which the UK Government approaches politics within the UK, so that it accepts (and may even relish) the fact that many matters are beyond its control and are for the devolved institutions to determine, that suggests a far-reaching reshaping of the British state has happened.

The first three sections of this chapter look at three key areas that will shape intergovernmental relations in the next ten or fifteen years: party politics, and how that may change the context of intergovernmental relations; finance, a likely source of tension and control; and the institutions of intergovernmental relations and the role of constitutional debate. In the conclusion, it will return to the issue of how IGR affects devolution, rather than the forces at work within IGR itself.

PARTY POLITICS

As discussed in Chapter 1, one of the minor paradoxes of devolution is that it has created a set of new party systems without leading to major change in how the UK system as a whole works.[2] Both Scotland and Wales have distinct party systems following devolution, whereas before they could be said to be little more than distinct political settings. In both those systems, Labour is the largest single party but faces challenges from nationalist parties as well as revived Conservatives.[3] More importantly, in both it faces significant political challenges from the left as well as the right – in Scotland from the Greens or the Scottish Socialist Party as well as the Scottish National Party (SNP), in Wales from Plaid Cymru.[4] Those challenges are distinct from the supposedly more left-wing tendencies within the Labour Party in Scotland or Wales. Whether or not Labour is innately more left-wing in Scotland or Wales, it has to respond to the political environment

---

[2] This discussion focuses on the relations between the UK Government and Scotland and Wales, and leaves out Northern Ireland. This is partly because of the intermittent nature of devolution to Northern Ireland and partly because the different nature of political competition there means that party ties do not work in the same way, nor is party competition likely to drive policy divergence or affect intergovernmental relations in the same way.

[3] See M. Laffin, E. Shaw and G. Taylor, 'The Parties and Intergovernmental Relations', in A. Trench (ed.), *Devolution and Power in the United Kingdom: Intergovernmental relations after constitutional change* (Manchester: Manchester University Press, forthcoming 2006).

[4] Wales Forward, a party formed by John Marek AM (Deputy Presiding Officer of the Assembly) has failed to make appreciable headway since it was formed in 2003, however.

in each country. Consequently, that will fuel a tendency to move to the left for reasons of electoral competition whatever else happens.

At the same time, the party system of the UK appears to have changed to a minimal degree. The big national parties – Labour, Conservatives, Liberal Democrats – dominate the political landscape in Westminster and set the terms of general political debate. From a UK-wide perspective, the SNP or Plaid Cymru are interesting local diversions in a way similar to the UK Independence Party in some parts of southern England. Such parties can have only limited impact at Westminster, because of the geographic limits to where they can campaign aggravated by the first-past-the-post electoral system. Dominance of the UK Parliament by UK-wide parties is more than a tautology, as fragmentation along national or linguistic lines within a state is far from unknown in Europe; Belgium is the obvious example, but the CSU in Bavaria and CiU in Catalonia are others, and in all three countries such parties can hold office in the nation-state government in coalition with others. (A similar pattern can be seen in Canada, where the sovereigntist *Bloc Quebécois* formed the official opposition in the federal House of Commons between 1993 and 1997).

While change on such a scale in the UK appears exceedingly remote, the party systems of Scotland and Wales nonetheless work differently. There are strong pressures for that trend to increase, in a way that is likely to accentuate differentiation from the UK party within Labour and to benefit Plaid Cymru and the SNP. Elections to the National Assembly for Wales and the Scottish Parliament are best regarded as 'second-order' elections, in which electoral behaviour is likely to become uncoupled from that at Westminster elections or to act as a means of protesting what happens at Westminster (or to combine aspects of both).[5] That will fuel anti-UK Government votes in devolved elections, or anti-UK Government behaviour when (as with Labour at present) the same party is in office at both ends. This is illustrated well by the results of the 2003 elections, when Labour in Scotland stuck closely to the UK line and was punished electorally, with votes going to a rainbow of interests to its left including the Scottish Socialists and the Greens, while in Wales Labour sought to maintain 'clear red water' and was rewarded by a significantly better result than in 1999 (enabling it to govern alone rather than in coalition). The strong implication of this is that devolved elections are likely to produce substantially different results to Westminster ones, even when the same parties are running in both.[6] A second implication

---

[5] This section draws heavily on C. Jeffery and D. Hough, 'Elections in Multi-level Systems: Lessons for the UK from Abroad' in R. Hazell (ed.), *The State of the Nations 2003: The third year of devolution in the United Kingdom* (Exeter: Imprint Academic, 2003).

[6] Australia provides another example of similar behaviour, with State Premiers and governments (all presently Labor) concerned far more about ensuring their own survival, by acting in what they regard as the best interests of their State, than with helping the Australian Labor Party in federal elections even if a more sympathetic federal government might be helpful to the State in due course.

is that UK parties operating in Scotland or Wales will seek to distinguish themselves from their UK colleagues, because what works in UK elections will probably not work in Scotland or Wales. That in turn means that parties are likely to drive political divergence between Cardiff and Edinburgh on one hand and London on the other. The emergence of profound political difference between the UK Government and the devolved administrations is not simply an airy guess or an assumption that all things change over time, but is driven by the inherent political structure of devolution.

Such political change is likely to have a profound effect on intergovernmental relations. Much of IGR at present is based on assumptions of common interest and common ground, along with a desire to ensure that devolution is regarded as a success which is measured by the absence of public or legal devolution disputes. In the next ten years or so, whichever party is in office, the trend is likely to be quite different. Even Labour administrations in Scotland or Wales will become far more concerned with that territory, its government and its interests, not those of the Labour Party more generally. Pursuing Labour interests will only be an appropriate strategy if it can be shown to benefit Welsh or Scottish electors, rather than the party overall. All parties will seek to show that they are distinct from their dominant Westminster counterparts and that they will stand up strongly for the interests of their territory, to enhance their electoral position. Even if they are able to secure advantageous deals from the UK Government and do so behind the scenes, they need something to use in public to show how different they are. While the wheels of such a relationship may be oiled privately, more will have to take place in the public domain and in a more formal way.

That change will also expand what intergovernmental relations involves. At present, the main concerns are either political – and often party – matters, practical policy issues or constitutional and institutional matters. These categories are not hard and fast, and a particular matter tends to affect two or three of them. In terms of volume of interchange – formal interministerial correspondence, high-level official or ministerial meetings, as well as telephone calls or emails – policy matters account for the vast bulk of the business. Such issues are dealt with issue by issue, outside a broader context, although they may lead to institutional adjustments to ensure that the government actually dealing with a matter has the powers to do so. Issues with a party-political dimension tend to draw much of the attention and energy of the Secretaries of State for Scotland and Wales (rather than difficult policy matters requiring a ministerial decision for their resolution). Constitutional issues may have a high profile but are relatively rare, even in the case of the debate about Wales's constitutional future. However, once the issue becomes one of overall political relations rather than day-to-day management, structural issues will become prominent parts of the agenda and demand more involvement from politicians and senior officials. That will increase the importance of two issues in particular: finance and what welfare state entitlements mean in the modern context. The first of these is discussed in more detail below.

The question of welfare rights is potentially even more problematic, however. It arises for two reasons.[7] First, the devolved legislatures and administrations have competence for many of the *distributive* aspects of the welfare state, for health, education and housing if not for *redistributive* functions including social security or tax. Those distributive areas of policy are what is likely to change as a result of devolution. Second, the political dynamics of devolution and the desire of all parties to differentiate themselves from what the UK Government does means that policy divergence in these areas, which is already becoming plain, is likely to become very marked.[8] That will in turn create a very different set of packages of citizenship rights, in which there will remain talk of a common UK 'welfare state' but with very considerable variations in what that means between the various parts of the UK. Resolving such issues – which might mean establishing a common basic set of entitlements, which may be supplemented from jurisdiction to jurisdiction but which may not be reduced – will be a major issue as a result. Again, this issue will be fuelled by political divergence but will also drive divergence, with parties seeking to use their powers once they are established to differentiate themselves from the UK Government. It will also not be the only instance where lines of legal competence need to be clarified; many other issues will need that too.

A further dynamic political factor is what happens at Westminster. With clearer lines of competence for the devolved administrations, there may be a backlash at the centre. Part of this will arise from a concern about the powers of Westminster and Whitehall to govern 'the country', leading to attempts to clarify the demarcation of devolved and non-devolved competences. Partly it may derive from tensions, especially within the Labour Party and among Labour MPs from Scotland and Wales about their roles. This tendency is already emerging, and if governments in Scotland or Wales are using their powers to act in markedly different ways it is likely to become all the stronger. Unilateral attempts to roll back the powers of the devolved bodies are highly unlikely to succeed, as such steps will require the consent of the

---

[7] This issue has been raised most clearly by Charlie Jeffery. See in particular his paper 'Equity and Diversity: Devolution, Social Citizenship and Territorial Culture in the UK' presented at the British Academy's conference on Anglo-Scottish Relations, Edinburgh, November 2003, and his chapter 'Devolution and social citizenship: which society, whose citizenship', in S. Greer (ed.), *Territory, Democracy and Justice* (Houndmills: Palgrave, forthcoming 2005).

[8] For health, see S. Greer, 'Policy Divergence: Will it Change Something in Greenock? in R. Hazell (ed) *The State of the Nations 2003: The third year of devolution in the United Kingdom* (Thorverton: Imprint Academic, 2003); and generally M. Keating *et al.*, 'Does Devolution Make a Difference? Legislative Output and Policy Divergence in Scotland', *Journal of Legislative Studies* 9 (3), (2003).

devolved bodies themselves, but will ensure that there is a broader debate about what devolution means.

FINANCE AND FISCAL ISSUES

The Barnett formula may underpin devolution, but it constitutes a minimal change from the way funding was allocated to the Scottish and Welsh Offices before devolution. As David Bell and Alex Christie discuss in Chapter 8, it uses a historic baseline, and operates only in relation to changes to that baseline. These are calculated in relation to changes in similar functions for England, on a proportional basis driven by population; so Scotland, with about one-tenth of Britain's population, receives roughly a 10 per cent increase when spending on comparable functions for England (such as hospitals) increases. Thus, fiscal capacity or tax revenue raised in a territory plays no part in determining what funding a territory gets, nor do its needs.

The UK's financial arrangements for devolution are unique in having so far been remarkably uncontentious. Every other comparable system has regular and protracted disputes about funding issues. It is the essence of intergovernmental relations in most systems. Sometimes these are high-level political disputes (as often in Australia), but sometimes they involve the courts: litigation before the Federal Constitutional Court in Germany has led to renegotiation of the mechanism by which richer *Länder* subsidise poorer ones, reducing the contributions made by the wealthy.[9] Pressure from Canadian Provinces, especially Quebec, led the federal government in 2003 to acknowledge the existence of a 'fiscal imbalance' (the federal government collecting more than it needed, while Provincial governments have been under serious fiscal pressure), and to start to increase payments to the Provinces to support health-care.[10]

By contrast, the devolved administrations have remained remarkably quiescent about finance issues. Northern Ireland did express some criticisms about the Barnett formula especially in the run-up to the 2002 Spending Review, and ministers in the Welsh Assembly Government have voiced muted unhappiness about the formula, but no devolved administration has openly sought a full-scale review.[11] Criticism has come from academic quarters, with the emergence of a debate about the Barnett formula and its implications; from Westminster politicians, many of them concerned with what

---

[9] See BVerfG, 2BvF 2/98., 3/98, 1/99 and 2/99 of 11 November 1999, Absatz-Nr (1-347). For a discussion see M. Aziz, 'The Federal Constitutional Court Decision Concerning Financial Equalization Between the States of the Federal Republic of Germany: The Länderausgleich Judgement', *European Public Law*, 6 (2): 217-28, (2000).

[10] Details of the agreement are in the meeting's communiqué, available at: www.scics.gc.ca/confer04_e.html

[11] See Trench, 2004, pp. 172-5.

Lord Barnett (after whom the formula is named) called its 'terrible unfairness'; and from opposition parties in the devolved territories, particularly the SNP and Plaid Cymru, who think their country should do better than it does.[12] None of these criticisms has been particularly effective in bringing the debate to a wider public let alone in changing how finance is allocated.

The UK's second uniqueness lies in the nature of its arrangements. The use of a formula to calculate increases from a baseline of spending is not itself all that unusual; several countries allocate funds to constituent units using similar formulae, although such formulae (and the baselines to which they are applied) relate to a policy goal such as equalising public spending, service provision or the tax burden across the country as a whole. A formula based on population alone (rather than a range of indicators) is less usual, but not massively different to practices elsewhere. The UK's distinctiveness takes four forms. First, the mechanism used (both baseline and the formula) is not connected to need, or any form of equalisation of spending or service provision. Second, the formula provides increases for devolved spending on the basis of increases in spending for England. The devolved administrations have no control over whether they get increases in funding because of the Barnett formula, but receive them as an automatic consequence of decisions about spending needs taken for England. Third, all decisions about the allocation of funding are taken by central government, so the devolved administrations are dependent on another government to decide what funds are available to them. In principle at least, the Barnett formula can reduce their funding as well as increase it. Increases need not correspond to inflation or increases in costs of providing services. In extremis, the formula could be set aside entirely (it is only set out, after all, in a *Statement of Funding Policy*, and policy can change), and there would be little that the devolved administrations could do. This also means that the devolved administrations do not receive extra funding no matter how acute their need (unless they need to make a claim on the UK Reserve, which remains entirely in the Treasury's hands), and receive no benefit for themselves or their tax payers if they are able to reduce spending. They are not masters of their own financial destiny, and the master is another government which conceivably could be in an adversarial relationship with them.

The fourth part of the UK's distinctiveness is that the devolved administrations are not responsible for raising their own revenue. With a number of limited exceptions (the Scottish power to vary personal income tax by 3 per cent, and the possibility of increasing property-based local taxation, itself potentially subject to claw-back by the Treasury if used too much), the whole of the spending of the devolved administrations comes from Treasury grants.

---

[12] For debates on the formula in the Lords, see HL Deb, 7 November 2002, cols 225-64 and HL Deb, 6 January 2004, cols 81-3. In the latter at col 83, Lord Barnett himself described the formula as 'unfair and worthy of review'.

These grants are unconditional block grants, enabling the devolved adminis-trations freely to allocate money to policies as they wish, giving them very considerable room for manoeuvre and much policy discretion (certainly, much more than the Scottish or Welsh Offices had before devolution). However, the devolved administrations are not responsible for raising that funding. The decisions they, and their Parliament or Assembly, take about spending are not linked to what they raise. They are simply spending depart-ments, in that respect no different from a UK Government department like the Home Office except for the tighter territorial restrictions on what they can do and the fact that the Treasury acknowledges that it cannot impose Public Service Agreements on them.

In many respects, this is a very comfortable position for the devolved administrations, at least while funding appears to be adequate if not gener-ous. That has been the case so far, at least for Scotland, while funding for Wales is widely regarded as insufficient. Apart from Wales the main parts of the UK to lose out appear to be regions of England, most notably the North East, but also (it would appear) the West Midlands and the South West.[13] The losers have therefore been without a voice or reluctant to make a noise, while the winners have been happy to sit quietly enjoying their position.

This lack of disputes about allocating finance has depended to a very great degree on the very favourable circumstances of devolution's birth. However, it is unlikely to last. The likely dissolution of the present party-political consensus, as discussed above, means UK interests will cease to dominate Labour, and Labour may cease to dominate devolved governments. Whether under Labour or other control, the devolved administrations will have less interest in extolling the status quo and more interest in attacking the present arrangements in an attempt to secure more funds. Moreover, continued growth in public spending will fuel convergence in levels of spending across the UK on the English 'norm' and slow growth in spending for the devolved territories.[14] Little or no growth in spending will constrain the devolved administrations too; convergence will not happen, but the aggregate amount of spending available to them will be limited. Neither prospect is likely to win support for the UK Government from the devolved administrations; it is damned whatever it does. Calls for change will be fuelled further by the emergence of greater publicity about the effects of the present funding arrangements. This may be a consequence of the first factor, with govern-ments being inclined to criticise the formula. But the inherent qualities of the

---

[13] See D. Heald and A. McLeod 'Beyond Barnett? Financing devolution' in J. Adams and P. Robinson (eds.), *Devolution in Practice: Public policy differences within the UK* (London: Institute for Public Policy Research, 2002).

[14] Convergence on the English level of spending is an arithmetical function of the formula as nominal levels of public spending increase by a population factor. It appears to be an unintended consequence, but that does not alter its effect.

Barnett formula itself will also fuel it, as convergence becomes more apparent and therefore reduces the interest of Scotland in particular in defending the formula. It will therefore be all the harder for the pro-Barnett consensus to continue, and those seeking a review are likely to increase in number and volume.

The other reason for seeking change is the irresponsibility in spending decisions that block grant funding can encourage. This is not likely to convince the devolved administrations, but may have an effect on UK ministers, especially if they expect to face spendthrift devolved ministers. This system means that the devolved administrations are not answerable at the ballot box for the financial implications of their policy decisions. It is one thing to decide to fund a generous increase in teachers' pay or to provide free personal care for the elderly. It is something else to make expensive policy decisions which may not work and which, in not working, directly hit voters in the wallet or bank account. Take the example of the expensive disaster of the poll tax (community charge) of the early 1990s, which cost £1.5 billion to introduce, administer and dismantle, and a further £2 to £2.5 billion in unrecovered arrears.[15] A devolved administration venturing on a similarly disastrous policy would not face the same sort of response at the ballot box as the Conservatives then did, because the bill for the disaster would be paid out of its block grant, and so out of general UK tax revenue. The Treasury might not be happy at having to pay the bill, and the devolved administration would pay a price because it would have to make unappealing policy choices as a result – cutting into other programmes, most probably – but taxes would not immediately go up as a result. There would be little direct relationship between the disaster, the costs of the disaster and the electorate.

Such a lack of accountability for spending decisions may offend some democratic sensibilities, but does it have any broader significance? What, if anything, is likely to cause it to change? Here the pressure is likely to come not from the devolved institutions, but from London. While the devolved administrations are able to enjoy spending funds, they leave it to the UK Government to raise those funds. The devolved administrations have an ideal mechanism for avoiding blame, indeed transmitting it to the UK Government, when spending slows and hard financial decisions have to be taken. There have been many advantages in maintaining Barnett for the first years of devolution, as it enabled an easy transition to be made and was appropriate when there was an underlying consensus of approach between the UK Government and devolved administrations. As that changes, the Barnett-based block grant mechanism is less and less appropriate for the new

---

[15] D. Butler, A. Adonis and T. Travers, *Failure in British Government: The politics of the poll tax* (Oxford: Oxford University Press, 1994), p. 180.

political situation. There may well be strong objections from the Treasury to the loss of control that fiscal disaggregation would involve. It would also create a risk of dysfunctional tax competition between the devolved administrations and UK Government (a commonplace of fiscal federalism). Nonetheless, this approach would have a strong political attraction to UK politicians, especially ones less concerned to relieve Scotland of living with the consequences of its own decisions.

It is therefore possible to foresee a consensus emerging in favour of changing the funding mechanism, each seeking change for different reasons. Scotland will seek greater latitude to make policy free from Whitehall constraints; Wales, greater funding more commensurate with Welsh needs (and the same may apply in Northern Ireland); some English regions, an end to the over-funding of Scotland; and the UK Government, an end to having to pay the piper while not calling the tune.

The process of negotiating a change, when all involved have such radically different interests, will be a very difficult one. Suggestions for change involving some sort of impartial 'territorial grants commission' along the lines of the Australian Grants Commission may be misplaced. Such a commission would determine baseline allocations to the devolved administrations (and perhaps English regional governments), and the formula or formulae for their periodic uplift.[16] Such a body would be impartial with membership reflecting a variety of interests, be distinct from both the UK Government and devolved administrations and operate according to clear terms of reference and objective criteria. Proponents of such a commission consequently hope that it would be able to neutralise the political difficulties of arbitrating financial matters and improve transparency of such issues, and also the legitimacy of the solution reached. Such ambitions are laudable, but fail on two counts. They are likely to be politically unrealistic, when the negotiations involved will in any event be complex and fractious. A minimally acceptable solution is far more likely to come from an opaque and incomprehensible process. It is hard to reconcile a system where everyone can plausibly claim to have won with one which can easily be understood. One that is complex and confusing makes claims of success easier to sustain. These ambitions also fail because they fail to deliver the UK Government's likely objective of ensuring that the devolved administrations assume some direct fiscal responsibility for their decisions. A solution that tries to match finance with need will not necessarily deliver any sort of fiscal accountability as part of the package. A solution that does provide genuine fiscal

[16] See for example I. McLean and A. McMillan, 'The Distribution of Public Expenditure across the UK Regions', *Fiscal Studies*, 24 (1): 45-71, (2003) or R. Hazell and R. Cornes, 'Financing Devolution' in R. Hazell (ed.), *Constitutional Futures: A history of the next ten years* (Oxford: Oxford University Press, 1999).

accountability at the margin is likely to be a complex and messy solution, which will not make the devolution settlement more comprehensible but may make it more durable.

INSTITUTIONAL AND CONSTITUTIONAL ISSUES

So far, institutional relations between the UK Government and devolved administrations have been remarkable for their harmonious character. This author's interviewing supports what newspaper reports, the House of Lords Constitution Committee and other observers have found; by and large, informal behind-the-scenes contact works well and has dealt with some controversial issues, while many others have not developed as some expected.[17] Consequently, there has been no use of the Joint Ministerial Committee to resolve disputes, a declining use of the JMC for other matters, no intergovernmental litigation before the Judicial Committee of the Privy Council, and an overall climate of accord and agreement. There have been some disagreements between governments, but these have taken place and been settled out of the public sight, and these have not generally concerned issues of formal competence in any event.

The dominant role of the Labour Party has been crucial in underpinning this. Part of the reason for a lack of disagreement has been the shared outlook on the world and shared electoral interest that comes from being part of a single party operating at several levels of government.[18] That has fuelled a strong desire to make devolution appear a success, and to use the absence of disputes as an indicator of that success. It is therefore not an accident that there have been so few disagreements or disputes, but a consequence of a deliberate attempt by both UK Government and devolved politicians to find a compromise where there are differences between them. Such differences of approach as Rhodri Morgan's 'clear red water' with Westminster have to be viewed in this light. Morgan may have been signalling a difference of approach with the UK Government, but within an overall approach which Labour in London accepted. As the first part of this chapter has suggested, such a benign environment is unlikely to last. That will lead to the conduct of intergovernmental relations changing significantly as a result. This section will explore some of the key ways in which those changes are likely to manifest themselves. Many of those derive from the present framework of

17 See House of Lords Select Committee on the Constitution, 2003; G. Horgan, 'Inter-institutional relations in the devolved Great Britain: quiet diplomacy', *Regional and Federal Studies*, 14 (1): 113-35, (2004).

18 There is scant evidence of any use of Labour Party forums as an alternative to more formal governmental ones, although in October 2004 a meeting between the Scottish Health Minister and UK Health Secretary to discuss 'common issues' did take place.

devolution, and the extent to which its institutional working assumes (or has come to assume) 'goodwill' as an essential element of the relations between administrations which, in the nature of things, need to have a great many dealings with each other.

One key issue is determining the boundary between the competences retained by the UK Parliament and Government and those transferred to the devolved institutions. This boundary is perhaps more ragged in the UK than in comparable systems, as a result of the process that identified functions to be devolved in the first instance. That process drew heavily on what was already the responsibility of the Scottish and Welsh Offices or Northern Ireland departments, as revised following an internal bargaining process before the devolution legislation was finalised or came into effect. In other systems, the boundaries, once constitutionally established, become firm, and can only be altered either by the cumbersome mechanism of formal constitutional amendment or by decisions of the supreme or constitutional court. The UK is rather different, and the three devolution Acts contain provisions for adjusting the margins of competence of the devolved bodies without primary legislation. These take various forms under each of the sets of arrangements: a variety of order-making powers under the Scotland Act 1998 for Scotland, and arguably the Sewel Motion mechanism for Westminster legislation as well; the constantly-developing line using Westminster primary legislation for Wales, and transfer of functions orders under s. 22 of the Government of Wales Act 1998 for pre-1998 matters; and for Northern Ireland, a number of similar order-making powers to Scotland and the possibility of making 'reserved' matters under Schedule 3 of the Northern Ireland Act 1998 'devolved' (or vice versa).[19] In a climate of general agreement and desire to compromise to avoid public disagreement, this has assumed considerable importance in oiling the wheels of relations between the two governments. As all the order-making powers involved need the consent of the devolved administration as well as the UK Government, they do not create a way for the UK Government unilaterally to adjust the settlement. What they do create are convenient and well-used mechanisms for negotiating the boundaries of devolved competences when the parties involved can agree. However, if the present consensus breaks down, the use of such mechanisms is likely to provoke much greater controversy between administrations (and also the elected Parliament or Assemblies). The role of formal arrangements to decide how to use to such technical instruments would increase, and that is particularly likely to see an increase in the role played by the courts. Such a role could be undertaken by greater use of institutions such as the Joint Ministerial Committee, or of formal agreements between administrations

---

[19] For Scotland, the key provisions are sections 63, 30 and 107; and for Northern Ireland, ss. 84-86. Normally these require consent of both Westminster and the devolved parliament or assembly.

about how they will and will not use their powers, but in default of agreement between them the courts would have to fill the gap.

The prospect of an increased use of the courts to resolve thorny issues may itself create problems. It does not necessarily mean that all issues put before the courts are the subject of bitter antagonism, but that the courts will have to decide certain matters if they cannot be resolved otherwise. However, this would be a considerable shock for the UK's courts, as it involves tasks of interpretation and adjudication which the courts have not undertaken, and appear to have been reluctant to undertake. (Indeed, on the one occasion so far they have been asked to use their interpretative powers to clarify the devolution legislation and its relationship to other fundamental legislation, in that case the Human Rights Act 1998, they simply avoided the point.[20]) The novelty of such a role and the extent to which devolution has so far developed at a remove from the courts means that a major role for the courts would raise the possibility that judges would regard the legal structure of devolution as being quite different to the way politicians and administrators presently regard it.[21] The uncertainty of such an outcome would itself serve as a powerful incentive for politicians to retain charge of the process and keep it out of the hands of judges.

The implication would be, however, that intergovernmental issues would have to be handled in a different way. They would need to have a higher priority than they do at present and be handled in a more formalistic manner. Most importantly, clearer principles would have to be developed for dealing with thorny issues. One question would relate to Westminster legislation affecting a devolved matter where the devolved administration was not happy with what was proposed; how firmly would the UK Government comply with the principle of the Sewel convention, and ensure government bills did not affect such matters, if it disagreed profoundly with a devolved administration or there was a great deal – for example, an issue relating to the UK's security – at stake? How effectively would the UK Government seek to control private members' legislation, and how would it behave if it only had a thin Parliamentary majority? While the Sewel convention is clear as far as it goes, the question of how it will apply when there are real issues at stake

---

[20] In *Mills v. H. M. Advocate and Advocate General for Scotland* [2002] UKPC D2 the court was invited to fill a lacuna arising from the relationship of the Scotland Act 1998 and the Human Rights Act 1998, but declined to do so and dealt only with the narrower issue before it.

[21] One key question is whether legislation passed by the Scottish Parliament (or by implication the Northern Ireland Assembly) is primary legislation or merely a novel class of secondary legislation, legally more akin to a statutory instrument than an Act of Parliament. The political and legal implications of treating an Act of the Scottish Parliament or Northern Ireland Assembly as secondary legislation be most serious (and run contrary to a number of Commonwealth precedents). For a brief discussion, see B. Winetrobe, 'Scottish devolved legislation and the courts', *Public Law*, 31: 31-8, (2002).

and it is not simply a matter of deferring to devolved sensibilities, is so far unanswered, and unanswerable.

Similar considerations apply to a range of other matters. One is the general treatment of the devolved administrations in Whitehall and the extent to which, and ways in which, they are consulted about UK Government proposals that will affect them. The problem is not that good practice is not recommended to Whitehall departments, or that it is not often followed – there are many cases of departments consulting clearly and in good time, in a way that enables devolved views to be incorporated into the UK Government's proposals. The problem is that practice varies a good deal. Some departments are generally better than others; some individuals or sections are better than others, and even those who are regarded as 'good' may on occasion behave less well, because of the pressures they are under from ministers to provide quick solutions to ministerial problems.[22] This is fuelled by the general desire (coming from ministers in all governments) for their government to be helpful rather than unhelpful to the others. However, this state of affairs means that there is no significant sanction for any poor practice. The worst that can happen is some grumbling between officials. The issue is unlikely even to become a matter for concern between permanent secretaries, let alone ministers.[23] More politically-charged relations between administrations will mean that such issues will more often be raised formally. The costs of non-cooperation may increase too, with administrations perhaps trying to trip each other up, certainly not trying to stop each other from falling if they should trip of their own accord. The result will be a greater need for the principles set out in the Memorandum of Understanding of consultation, cooperation, coordination and confidentiality to be complied with by all involved, as a matter of routine and not just of courtesy.[24] That may in turn require more clearly defined and applied procedures for dealing with such matters, between governments but also within them, to ensure that the damage caused by a question (or administration) being accidentally overlooked does not arise.

There are other reasons for doing this too. One consequence of informal intergovernmental relations in general, and the non-meeting of the JMC in

---

[22] See A. Trench, 'Whitehall and the Process of Legislation after Devolution', in R. Hazell and R. Rawlings (eds.), *Devolution, Law Making and the Constitution* (Exeter: Imprint Academic, 2005).

[23] There are few meetings between the devolved permanent secretaries and their Whitehall counterparts; the main channel has been the weekly meeting every Wednesday of all permanent secretaries, but the present permanent secretaries in both Scotland and Wales are relatively infrequent attenders of those meetings. There appear to be no arrangements for regular routine meetings between officials running devolved departments, in the grades immediately below that of permanent secretary, and it is devolved (rather than UK) officials who initiate most of those meetings that do take place.

[24] *Memorandum of Understanding and Supplementary Agreements Between the United Kingdom Government, Scottish Ministers, the Cabinet of the National Assembly for Wales and the Northern Ireland Executive Committee*, Cm 5240 (London: The Stationery Office, 2001), paras 4-11.

particular, is that the channels by which the devolved administrations may express views (and be seen by their electorates to be expressing views) about non-devolved matters are limited. The JMC (Europe) is one arena where this happens, but there are many other areas of reserved or non-transferred functions where it does not. As John Curtice shows in Chapter 6 (see particularly table 6.2), the proportion of people in Scotland thinking that Scotland's voice in the UK has been made stronger by devolution has declined from 70 per cent in 1999 to 49 per cent in 2003. Those thinking that Wales's voice in the UK has been strengthened by devolution has declined from 62 per cent to 52 per cent over the same period. The numbers of those thinking that devolution has made no difference have increased, rather than those thinking that devolution has positively weakened Scotland's or Wales's voice. This indicates a sense that on the institutional level devolution has at least not lived up to the expectations it created. If influence exists but is exercised in private, the public are unlikely to believe that it exists at all. It would appear that a more formal approach to IGR, even if that were purely for reasons of public presentation, would address those concerns.

This assumes continued entanglement of the UK Government and devolved administrations regarding policy matters, the situation that exists at present and drives most interactions between governments. There are areas where disentanglement will have great attraction, however. The most notable of these relates to the constitutions of the devolved bodies themselves. These remain very largely controlled at Westminster rather than in Holyrood or Cardiff Bay. There is clearly a continuing UK interest in the nature of powers devolved, whether that relates to the functions devolved or transferred or to the nature of the powers that the devolved institutions can exercise over them. Thus deciding whether to alter the list of reserved matters in relation to Scotland, or to confer broader legislative powers on the National Assembly for Wales, is understandable.

The internal working of the devolved bodies is rather different. The implication of devolution is that these matters are for the devolved institutions themselves to deal with. It is hard to identify the UK interest in such issues as the internal arrangements or legislative procedures of the Scottish Parliament or the relations between legislative and executive parts of the National Assembly for Wales, let alone such domestic matters as their arrangements for legal advice or number of deputy presiding officers. At the same time, the continuing development of such institutions means that the need for change within the general framework created by the 1998 legislation will increase. The UK Government is likely to face continued calls to agree to change within the devolved institutions, and to find legislative time for such changes, when it claims also to have washed its hands of such matters. The example of the link between the number of Scottish MPs at Westminster and the number of MSPs indicates the nature of the problem. Although views in Scotland were clear that the number of MSPs should not be reduced as the Scotland Act 1998 provided, the consultation took nearly four months (between December 2001 and March 2002), the Secretary of State's deliberation on the consultation result a further seven months, and then a legislative slot had to be found. Between the issue coming onto the agenda and the passing of the Scottish Parliament Constituencies Act 2004, nearly four years passed. This was a case where the balance of opinion in Scotland was clear and there was no party-political opposition at Westminster, although many Scottish (Labour) MPs were concerned about the implications of a smaller number of seats. When there are real political differences with a devolved administration, the UK Government may be reluctant to make available time at Westminster or its Parliamentary majority. Even when it does, that may involve various difficulties and delay, and consequent irritation.

This does not necessarily mean that the UK's arrangements for intergovernmental relations would become more multilateral than they presently are. The asymmetries of the present devolution settlements, with different institutions responsible for varying functions in only certain parts of the UK, act as powerful incentives for relations remaining largely bilateral. For that to change would require a substantial reason for the UK Government to find it more convenient or effective to conduct them multilaterally, and to use forums such as the JMC more regularly. The devolved institutions themselves have much less interest in seeking a change given their own varying interests, and even if they wished to do so would need the active support of the UK Government. Predominantly bilateral arrangements suit both UK Government and devolved interests, and are likely to persist with the exception of financial arrangements.

A changed political climate will drive institutional relationships so that they become more carefully managed, and conducted according to more clearly demarcated rules. The existing informality will be unsustainable when it permits the sorts of variations and anomalies that it does at present. The UK Government will also need to decide with greater care what it needs to keep in its own hands, as otherwise relatively minor matters risk becoming sources of disproportionate tension, and get in the way of other matters that are of greater concern to it.

THE EFFECT OF INTERGOVERNMENTAL RELATIONS ON DEVOLUTION

Intergovernmental relations can affect the devolved administrations (and the broader process of devolution) in two ways – by affecting the autonomy of the devolved institutions, and by affecting their accountability.

Autonomy is not a straightforward concept, as its boundaries are hard to determine especially where the UK Government retains such a prominent role in relation to finance, legislation, reserved matters generally across the UK and its role as the sole government for England. The public expectation that underlies devolution (at least in Great Britain) is a simple one, however; that the devolved institutions should be responsible for dealing with devolved matters, and UK institutions should not be. What this means under each settlement varies, but the belief is that there should be a sphere of significant policy matters in which the devolved institutions are free to act autonomously.[25] What they achieve by their autonomy will vary. At one and the same time, there appear to be expectations that autonomy is good in itself and to be valued highly as a result; that devolution will permit policy divergence and diversity (while not allowing 'postcode lotteries' and the like to run unchecked); that devolution will protect the welfare state (even though it affects few redistributive functions); and that it will promote economic development and promote regional competitiveness. Achieving any of these goals may be difficult, and collectively they are contradictory. But the legitimacy of the UK state after devolution rests in part on the ability of the devolved institutions to pursue them.

What IGR creates are multiple means by which a UK Government that was so inclined could block some devolved ambitions, subvert and frustrate others and influence policy choices more generally so as to limit that autonomy very considerably. Perhaps the best way of putting the question is by asking whether the devolved institutions are capable of acting as 'institutional veto players' in relation to the UK Government.[26] Their formal powers and practical capabilities suggest that they are not, although in certain respects the UK Government has such powers both formally and (more important) practically and could therefore be such a player in relation to the devolved administrations.

The problem is not so much that one party to IGR can obstruct the other, but what the consequences of such action are. There can be no real argument that the UK Government can in the practical sense undermine the autonomy

---

[25] This is evident from data gathered by the British and Scottish Social Attitudes surveys, showing a strong public belief that devolved governments should be the most influential government in their lives, but presently is not. See J. Curtice, 'Restoring Confidence and Legitimacy? Devolution and Public Opinion' in A. Trench (ed), *Has Devolution Made A Difference? The state of the nations 2004*, (Exeter: Imprint Academic, 2004) especially Figure 9.1.

[26] The term is used in the sense developed by George Tsebelis, meaning an individual or collective actor whose agreement is required for a change in policy; G. Tsebelis 'Decision Making in Political Systems: Veto Players in Presidentialism, Parliamentarism, Multicameralism and Multipartyism' *British Journal of Political Science* 25 (3): 289-325 (1995), p. 301. Alfred Stepan, in a wide-ranging survey of veto players in federal and unitary systems, considers that devolution has not added to the number of veto players in the UK; see A. Stepan 'Electoral Generated Veto Players in Unitary and Federal Systems' in E. L. Gibson (ed.) *Federalism and Democracy in Latin America* (Baltimore, Md: Johns Hopkins University Press, 2004).

of the devolved institutions, at least as matters stand in 2004. The question is what prevents it from doing so. Here the fact that the UK's constitution remains largely unwritten becomes key. At present the constraints are vague in nature and unenforceable in form; a set of principles and aspirations, of which there is no the effective guardian and which no-one polices, coupled with a highly technical body of law and administration which is arcane and inaccessible. The only real enforcement is likely to be from the public belief that autonomy for the devolved bodies was established or re-established in 1999. That can only become manifest if that autonomy is denied (of which, as John Curtice shows in Chapter 6, there are already signs), and will be subject to confusion and delay before it takes tangible form.

All this places a heavy burden on the UK Government. Faced with the practical pressures of dealing with multiple and complex challenges, it asks a great deal to expect it to restrain how it responds to those challenges by accepting that some things cannot be done at all and others can only be done with the support of the devolved institutions. The question is of the extent to which devolution has moved from being a policy of the 1997 Labour government to a new way of working for the UK as a whole. If the UK finds devolved autonomy unappetising or simply unduly cumbersome, it may seek to unpick its worse effects; but doing so raises the issue of why devolution was introduced in the first place, and that may prompt a resurgence in support for the nationalist parties whom devolution was intended to undermine.

Accountability manifests itself more immediately than do issues of autonomy. Intergovernmental relations in a variety of systems have been criticised for the way they can hamper the ability of governments to deal with policy issues. Accountability can be a particular problem. In Canada, where intergovernmental relations are of great concern for all governments, this problem can be especially acute. Here, the problem of decisions being taken in intergovernmental forums, by agreement between governments, has become a source of concern and controversy.[27] The problem with such decisions is that there is no clear way of holding anyone accountable for these decisions. Governments are largely autonomous in how they conduct IGR. There may even be problems within governments: ministers for health, say, reach an agreement with each other, but this may cause difficulties for their ministerial colleagues. The agreement, however, will be fixed and incapable of being unpicked. In some cases, the nature of agreements reached may itself

---

[27] Perhaps the clearest statement of this view can be found in R. Simeon and D. A. Cameron, 'Intergovernmental Relations and Democracy: An Oxymoron if Ever There Was One?' in H. Bakvis and G. Skogstad (eds.) *Canadian Federalism: Performance, effectiveness and legitimacy* (Toronto: Oxford University Press, 2002).

be unknown, as the agreements may be confidential or at least unpublished, and even the fact of the meeting hard to establish.

In such circumstances it can be hard for parliaments to hold their ministers to account. The information and resources necessary may be lacking and possibly even outside the public domain. Legislators may lack the knowledge, skills or time necessary to pursue such issues. Governments may be reluctant to talk about intergovernmental matters (which commonly fall under an exemption in freedom of information legislation). Intergovernmental agreements not only fall between the two stools of accountability at devolved and central levels, but by their nature put themselves beyond accountability at either.

These criticisms are only partly appropriate in the case of the UK. Information about intergovernmental activities is hard to obtain, even by Parliament. The informality of many contacts means that those contacts are simply not recorded, but publicity about even high-level meetings is scarce and hard to find. However, even at this early stage of devolution several major inquiries into aspects of the working of devolution have been carried out. At Westminster, these have been by the Constitution Committee in the Lords (both on *Inter-Institutional Relations in the United Kingdom* and on *Devolution: Its Effect on the Practice of Legislation at Westminster*), the Welsh Affairs Committee in the Commons (on *Primary Legislation affecting Wales* and *The Powers of the Children's Commissioner for Wales* in the light of the legislation creating a commissioner for England. [28]The Procedures Committee in the Scottish Parliament has been carrying out an inquiry into the Sewel convention during the spring of 2005.[29] Curiously, however, the Commons Scottish Affairs Committee has carried out no major inquiries into devolution. The UK's other saving grace is that relatively few decisions or agreements are reached by intergovernmental discussions. So far they are of the information-sharing or consensus-reaching variety, and result in few formulations of policy. That may change, and is indeed likely to if the suggestions made above about the conduct of intergovernmental relations come to pass. At that point legislators may become aware that important decisions are being reached on behalf of their government in which they have no say and over which they have no control.

Such a development could lead to three sorts of outcome. One would be the degradation of parliamentary control over the executive, with

[28] House of Lords Select Committee on the Constitution, 2003; House of Lords Select Committee on the Constitution, *Devolution: Its Effect on the Practice of Legislation at Westminster* (Session 2003-04, 15th Report, HL 192) (London: The Stationery Office, 2004); House of Commons Welsh Affairs Committee, *The Primary Legislative Process as it Affects Wales* (Session 2002-03, 4th Report, HC 79) (London: The Stationery Office, 2003); House of Commons Welsh Affairs Committee, *The Powers of the Children's Commissioner for Wales* (Session 2003-04, 5th Report, HC 538) (London: The Stationery Office, 2004).

[29] See: www.scottish.parliament.uk/business/committees/procedures/currentInquiries.htm

governments free to act as they wished subject only to the sorts of rather distant and blunt controls that generally apply to governments: the possibility of votes of no confidence in the legislature or being thrown out of office at a general election. That has happened in a number of systems, notably Canada. A second would be the development of proper scrutiny and control mechanisms within legislatures: attempts to summon ministers, limit their mandates to negotiate before meetings, obtain statements after meetings, and so forth. That has occasionally happened in some Australian States. The third would be the absence of change within the legislature coupled with the development of public attention and concern. That would lead to a broader challenge to legitimacy at decisions made with no-one able to scrutinise them or hold those responsible to account, with consequences for the devolved institutions and the objective of connecting the public to those governing them more closely, and for democracy much more broadly.

CONCLUSION: DEVOLUTION AND THE DYNAMICS OF INTERGOVERNMENTAL RELATIONS

The soft ride the UK's intergovernmental relation have had so far will end in the foreseeable future. While many of the difficult issues have not yet materialised, and relations overall have been smoothed over by the underlying political consensus, intergovernmental relations will become more formal and contentious as parties in office become more conscious of, and responsive to, their particular electorates. That does not necessarily presage a full-scale restructuring of intergovernmental relations so they become more like those found in an asymmetric devolved state like Spain or a federal system like Australia, but it does mean a substantial change from the present state of affairs.

The big issue for the future is partly for governments to manage the transition to a newer mode of IGR where greater formality is the norm and disputes are something to be resolved not avoided, and partly to ensure that IGR does not become a means of undermining the autonomy of the devolved administrations or the broader goal of bringing government and electors closer together. It is regrettable that the response to easy times has been to relax rather than to prepare for more troublesome times ahead. If IGR becomes a back-door mechanism for the UK Government to reassert control over matters that are believed to be devolved, the problems created for the future will be all the worse.

BIBLIOGRAPHY

Official Documents

HM Treasury, *Funding the Scottish Parliament, National Assembly for Wales and Northern Ireland Assembly: A statement of funding policy*, available at www.hm-treasury.gov.uk/documents/public_spending_and_services /devolve/pss_devolve_devolveUK.cfm

House of Commons Welsh Affairs Committee, *The Powers of the Children's Commissioner for Wales* (Session 2003-04, 5th Report, HC 538) (London: The Stationery Office, 2004).

House of Commons Welsh Affairs Committee, *The Primary Legislative Process as it Affects Wales* (Session 2002-03, 4th Report, HC 79) (London: The Stationery Office, 2003).

House of Lords Select Committee on the Constitution, *Devolution: Inter-institutional relations in the United Kingdom* (Session 2002-03, 2nd Report, HL 28) (London: The Stationery Office, 2003).

House of Lords Select Committee on the Constitution, *Devolution: Its effect on the practice of legislation at Westminster* (Session 2003-04, 15th Report, HL 192) (London: The Stationery Office, 2004).

Memorandum of Understanding and Supplementary Agreements Between the United Kingdom Government, Scottish Ministers, the Cabinet of the National Assembly for Wales and the Northern Ireland Executive Committee, Cm 5240 (London: The Stationery Office, 2001).

Secondary Sources

Aziz, M., 'The Federal Constitutional Court Decision Concerning Financial Equalization Between the States of the Federal Republic of Germany: The Länderausgleich Judgement', *European Public Law*, 6 (2): 217-28, (2000).

Bell, D. and A. Christie, 'Finance – The Barnett Formula: Nobody's Child' in A. Trench (ed.), *The State of the Nations 2001: The second year of devolution in the United Kingdom* (Exeter: Imprint Academic, 2001).

Butler, D., A. Adonis and T. Travers, *Failure in British Government: The politics of the poll tax* (Oxford: Oxford University Press, 1994).

Greer, S., 'Policy Divergence: Will it Change Something in Greenock? in R. Hazell (ed) *The State of the Nations 2003: The third year of devolution in the United Kingdom* (Thorverton: Imprint Academic, 2003).

Hazell, R. and R. Cornes, 'Financing Devolution' in R. Hazell (ed.), *Constitutional Futures: A history of the next ten years* (Oxford: Oxford University Press, 1999).

Heald, D. and A. McLeod 'Beyond Barnett? Financing devolution' in J. Adams and P. Robinson (eds.), *Devolution in Practice: Public policy differences within the UK* (London: Institute for Public Policy Research, 2002).

Horgan, G., 'Inter-institutional relations in the devolved Great Britain: quiet diplomacy', *Regional and Federal Studies*, 14 (1): 113-35, (2004).

Jeffery, C. and D. Hough, 'Elections in Multi-level Systems: Lessons for the UK from Abroad' in R. Hazell (ed.), *The State of the Nations 2003: The third year of devolution in the United Kingdom* (Exeter: Imprint Academic, 2003).

Jeffery, C., 'Equity and Diversity: Devolution, Social Citizenship and Territorial Culture in the UK' presented at the British Academy's conference on Anglo-Scottish Relations, Edinburgh (November 2003).

Jeffery, C., 'Devolution and Social Citizenship: Which Society, Whose Citizenship?', in S. Greer (ed.), *Territory, Democracy and Justice* (Houndmills: Palgrave, forthcoming 2005).

Keating, M. *et al.*, 'Does Devolution Make a Difference? Legislative Output and Policy Divergence in Scotland', *Journal of Legislative Studies*, 9 (3), (2003).

Laffin, M., E. Shaw and G. Taylor, 'The Parties and Intergovernmental Relations' in A. Trench (ed.) *Devolution and Power in the United Kingdom: Intergovernmental relations after constitutional change* (Manchester: Manchester University Press, forthcoming).

McLean, I. and A. McMillan, 'The Distribution of Public Expenditure across the UK Regions', *Fiscal Studies*, 24 (1), (2003).

Simeon, R., and D. A. Cameron, 'Intergovernmental Relations and Democracy: An Oxymoron if Ever There Was One?', in H. Bakvis and G. Skogstad (eds.) *Canadian Federalism: Performance, effectiveness and legitimacy*, (Toronto: Oxford University Press, 2002).

Stepan, A., 'Electorally Generated Veto Players in Unitary and Federal Systems' in E. L. Gibson (ed.) *Federalism and Democracy in Latin America* (Baltimore, Md: Johns Hopkins University Press, 2004).

Trench, A. (ed), *Has Devolution Made A Difference? The state of the nations 2004,* (Exeter: Imprint Academic, 2004).

Trench, A., 'The More Things Change the More They Stay the Same: Intergovernmental Relations Four Years On' in A. Trench (ed.), *Has Devolution Made a Difference? The State of the Nations 2004* (Exeter: Imprint Academic, 2004).

Trench, A., 'Whitehall and the Process of Legislation after Devolution', in R. Hazell and R. Rawlings (eds), *Devolution, Law Making and the Constitution* (Exeter: Imprint Academic, 2005).

Tsebelis, G., 'Decision Making in Political Systems: Veto Players in Presidentialism, Parliamentarism, Multicameralism and Multipartyism', *British Journal of Political Science*, 25 (3): 289-325, (1995).

Winetrobe, B., 'Scottish devolved legislation and the courts', *Public Law*, 31: 31-8, (2002).

8

Finance

Paying the Piper, Calling the Tune?

David Bell and Alex Christie[1]

INTRODUCTION

Most of the devolved institutions have some physical form. Yet one of devolution's most influential institutions exists only as a mathematical formula. Its impact on the devolution process, however, has been pervasive. It determines the major part of the resources that are available to the Scottish Parliament, the National Assembly for Wales and to Northern Ireland and therefore constrains the ability of the devolved authorities to meet commitments and to follow new policy initiatives. This is the Barnett formula — the device by which funding is allocated to the 'territories' of Scotland, Northern Ireland and Wales.

First introduced in 1978, it has continued largely unchanged through the establishment and initial operation of the devolved institutions.[2] Its fundamental importance is that it is used, in conjunction with the biennial Spending Reviews, to determine the annual grant that comprises the majority of the funding of the devolved institutions. These then allocate this grant, using the powers available to them, to programmes such as health, education, transport and local government. There are other actual and potential sources of finance: European funding, local and business taxation, user charges and in Scotland the Parliament's power to vary the standard rate of income tax by 3p in the pound. Yet these instruments are of second-order importance compared with the Barnett-determined annual block grants that are sent to Edinburgh, Cardiff and Belfast. Thus, although devolution substantially extended legislative powers in Scotland and administrative powers in Wales and Northern Ireland, the funding mechanism to support these new powers did not change. What can the devolved governments do now that they couldn't do before? 'Remarkably little' is the honest answer. The financial constraint remains the same, so the economics of devolution are little

---

[1] Scottish Economic Policy Network.

[2] D. Heald and A. McLeod, 'Public Expenditure' in *The Laws of Scotland — Stair Memorial Encyclopaedia*, para. 480–552, (Edinburgh: Butterworths, 2002).

different to the economics of pre-devolution Britain. Policy differences are the result of output choice, rather than input change.

This chapter examines how the Barnett formula rests within a devolved government system and how it has affected the ways in which the devolved territories of the UK have managed public spending and economic policy since devolution. It seeks to answer two questions: does the fact that the devolved countries still receive the great majority of their funds from Westminster limit the extent of devolution, and is it still Westminster that calls the shots?

The chapter looks briefly at the Barnett formula and then asks what difference devolution made to what the devolved territories can do in terms of resource allocation. It also asks whether devolution has changed the scope of economic policy pursued across the UK. It then explores the alternatives to Barnett formula funding — needs assessment and fiscal autonomy — and how they would alter the balance of power and influence between the devolved governments and Westminster. The chapter concludes with a discussion of the possibility of the effect of different parties being in control in Cardiff or Edinburgh and London.

THE BARNETT FORMULA

Joel Barnett, then Chief Secretary to the Treasury, introduced the Barnett formula in 1978. It continued in existence throughout the Conservative administrations of the 1980s and 1990s and has been supported by the present Labour administration both before and after devolution. The resources to support public spending in Scotland, Northern Ireland and Wales are determined as a by-product of agreements between the Treasury and the major spending departments in Whitehall. Agreements with the Treasury to increase spending on 'comparable' programmes result in 'consequential' increases in the budgets for Scotland, Northern Ireland and Wales. The increase for the devolved territories is proportionate to their population shares. Thus for the 2002–5 period, Scotland received an additional £10.32m for every additional £100m that the Treasury agreed to spend on comparable programmes in England; the figures for Wales and Northern Ireland were £5.89m and £3.40m respectively.[3]

The effects of the Barnett formula are now well understood.[4] Its outcome is to deliver widely differing levels of per capita public spending in the

[3] HM Treasury, *Spending Review 2002: Opportunity and security for all*, Cm 5570 (London: The Stationery Office, 2002).

[4] D. Bell, 'The Barnett Formula' unpublished mimeo, Department of Economics, University of Stirling (2001); D. Bell and A. Christie, 'The Barnett Formula — Nobody's Child?', in A. Trench (ed.) *The State of the Nations 2001: The second year of devolution in the United Kingdom* (Exeter: Imprint

territories. Its relative generosity depends mainly on the success of each of the territories in striking a favourable deal with the Treasury when it was set up in the late 1970s, on bending of its rules, such as how to calculate population shares and on how successful the territories have been in 'formula bypass' — attracting central government funding outside the Barnett formula which then is built into subsequent baseline allocations. However, these rules have been progressively tightened, and the mathematical logic of the formula is that it will eventually lead to convergence towards equal levels of per capita public spending in each of the territories. The key issue is how long that will take.

Many people in Wales, and some sections of opinion in England believe that Scotland and Northern Ireland benefit unfairly from Barnett. Simultaneously, the supposed gainers believe both that their relative spending advantages are justifiable and that these advantages are being eroded. As a result, Bell and Christie described the Barnett formula as 'Nobody's Child'.[5] However, it still has allies in the Treasury and is defended whenever questioned; thus in December 2003, in a written answer to Win Griffiths MP, the Leader of the House replied that 'Government has no current plans to review the Barnett formula, which has produced fair and transparent settlements over the years.'[6]

Why should the Treasury defend the Barnett formula? Even though it has faults, it also has features that make it attractive. These include:

1. It is simple and relatively transparent. As we shall see, any alternative is likely to be more complex and understood by only a small group of experts.

2. It costs little to calculate. The internal resources devoted to the determination of the Barnett formula are modest. Not only would any alternative be substantially more costly, it might also be delegated to a new body if no political consensus supporting a dominant role for the Treasury in determining territorial allocation could be achieved.

It disposes rough justice to the territories — and in 1978 that doubtless seemed a suitable justification for its introduction — and it continues to do so, though perhaps not as well as it once did. That is not the formula's fault as it operates now as it did then. What has changed is relative economic conditions in the now-devolved territories. It was designed, ultimately and through its correct application, to lead to identical spending allocations per head across all four territories of the UK. If that is no longer what public policy wishes to achieve then blame lies not with the formula, but with those

Academic, 2001); I. McLean and A. McMillan 'The Distribution of Public Expenditure across the UK Regions' *Fiscal Studies*, 24: 45–71, (2003).

  [5] Bell and Christie in Trench (ed.), 2001.
  [6] HC Deb, 10 December 2003, Col. 459W.

who continue to defend its use. It is clear that due to differences in costs, equal provision of public services throughout the UK would require differences in public spending per head across the territories.[7] One would expect that policy differentiation under devolution strengthens the argument for differential per capita spending between territories. But the Barnett formula is a mechanism for equalising per capita spend and hence is largely inappropriate in meeting the objective of providing scope for variation in the size of the public sector across the territories. But of course it was introduced as a politically expedient solution to a pressing problem. The potential costs of its removal may well make its retention expedient for some time to come.

HOW HAS IT OPERATED SINCE DEVOLUTION?

The first two years of the Labour administration were marked by extreme restraint in public spending. The period since then has seen an almost unprecedented growth in spending fuelled by a desire on the part of the Labour Government to enhance and extend public services, funded by a relatively buoyant UK economy. The Barnett constraint has therefore been relatively weak in the first few years of the devolved institutions. Public support for devolution would have been jeopardised in an environment of tight constraints on public spending. In Scotland, the reputation of devolution has suffered from disenchantment with the profligacy of spending on the new parliament building: it would have suffered much more had the Scottish Executive been forced to spend its first few years closing schools and hospitals.

Although overall the British economy has performed well, the Scottish and Welsh economies have lagged behind that of England. Neither Scotland nor Wales could have sustained such a rapid increase in public spending based on their own economic performance; as a result Scotland and Wales have benefited from the existence of the Barnett formula and their relative lack of fiscal autonomy at least insofar that it has sustained public spending at higher levels than would have otherwise been possible. On the other hand, there is an argument that is being increasingly aired in Scotland that high levels of public spending are crowding out private sector activity. In Wales, such arguments are more muted, and the political imperative is on the need for improved services, particularly in areas with Objective 1 status.

The 2003 Public Expenditure Statistical Analysis show that Scotland and Wales both received a broadly constant share of identifiable UK public

---

[7] HM Treasury, *Needs Assessment Study: The report of an interdepartmental study coordinated by HM Treasury on the relative public expenditure needs in England, Scotland, Wales and Northern Ireland* (London: HM Treasury, 1979).

Figure 8.1: Territorial Gross Value Added Relative to England = 100

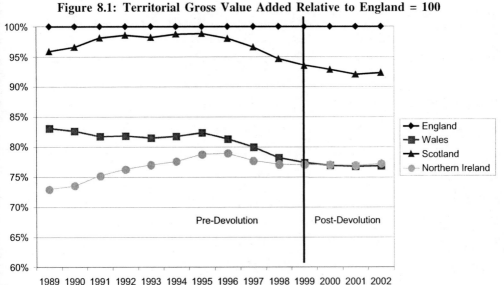

Source: Office of National Statistics

expenditure between 1997/98 and 2002/3.[8] During this period Scotland's population share drifted down from 8.74 per cent to 8.61 per cent of the UK total, while its share of identifiable public expenditure remained almost constant at 10.3 per cent of the UK total. The implication of a relatively constant share of aggregate identifiable public expenditure and a continuing decline in Scotland's relative population, is that spending per head in Scotland rose relative to other parts of the UK between 1997/98 and 2002/3. Indeed the data suggest a rise from 17 per cent above the UK average to 20 per cent above over this period.

The Barnett formula works by allocating to the devolved territories their population share of increases agreed with Whitehall departments on comparable programmes (such as health and education). A logical consequence of the formula is that the share of aggregate public expenditure to each should decrease — the so-called 'Barnett squeeze'. Therefore, taken at face value, these data suggest that the Barnett squeeze has not occurred, or has somehow been offset. For example, the Barnett formula applies to only a proportion of total identifiable expenditure and hence a potential explanation is that other spending programmes have risen to compensate for the Barnett Squeeze.

The social security programme is by far the largest component of public spending in Scotland that is not covered by the Barnett formula. Over the

---

[8] HM Treasury, *Public Expenditure: Statistical analyses 2003–2004*, Cm 6201 (London: The Stationery Office, 2004).

Figure 8.2:
Social Protection Spending per Head (1998–2003); England = 100

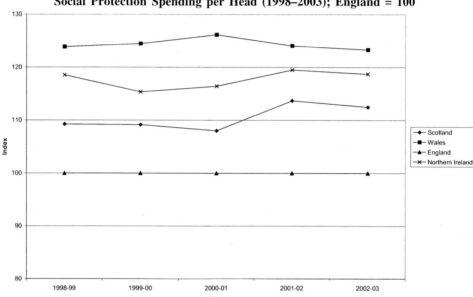

Source: Public Expenditure Statistical Analysis (HM Treasury, 2004)

period, expenditure per head on social security in Scotland rose from 9.2 per cent above the level of expenditure per head in England to 12.4 per cent. In Wales the figure has fluctuated around 24 per cent above the English level , while in Northern Ireland the figure is around 20 per cent above the English figure, barring a slight dip in 2000. This is consistent with the relative worsening of Scotland's economic performance, as measured by growth in GDP since devolution and the relative stability of the Northern Irish and Welsh economies. Thus, part of the explanation of the paradox of increased per capita spending in Scotland since devolution is due to the automatic stabiliser effects of social security. Many commentators outside Scotland argue that the outcome of the Barnett formula is too generous a provision to Scotland — but when Scotland's relative prosperity is declining, it is the social security system, rather than the Barnett formula, which provides an automatic countercyclical response.

We have argued that the Barnett formula largely determines the resources available to the devolved bodies, and that its operation since devolution has resulted in little relative change in spending levels. It follows that the latitude for policy divergence between them has also been extremely limited — at least where policy divergence will result in the devolved territories bearing significant public expenditure costs. Constraints on policy divergence include:

1. Limitations on borrowing powers reduce the devolved administrations' flexibility to fund spending programmes from sources other than the Westminster grant, though this problem is lessened, marginally, in Northern Ireland through the borrowing powers granted under the Reinvestment and Reform Initiative.

2. The fact that in both Scotland and Wales governing coalitions thus far have been dominated by the Labour Party has implicitly reduced the willingness of these bodies to diverge from a Labour-controlled Westminster Parliament, although there have been noticeable exceptions such as free prescriptions in Wales and free personal care in Scotland.

3. The original devolution settlement reserved powers to the Treasury to intervene if, for example, the devolved bodies raised local taxation to punitive levels.[9]

4. Proposed policies have themselves been subject to intense media scrutiny based on an extension of the 'postcode lottery' argument and its economic implications, particularly for household and factor mobility. As an example, the introduction of free personal care for the elderly was accompanied by a number of media stories suggesting that large numbers of the frail elderly would migrate to Scotland, a possibility that has not developed yet into a reality.

5. The nature of incremental budgeting, inherited from Westminster, has restricted the ability of all the devolved governments to alter greatly the allocation of public spending. Even in a period of high public spending growth and low inflation, the scope for radically altering the distribution of spending between various public services is limited.

CAN ANYTHING BE DONE NOW AS A RESULT OF DEVOLUTION THAT COULDN'T BE DONE BEFORE?

Public spending resources have grown much more since 1999 than they did in the five years prior to devolution. It has been shown that it is during periods of large public spending growth that the Barnett squeeze is most keenly felt. [10]Even though the absolute sums available to the devolved governments have increased, the ratio of spending per head in each devolved territory to

[9] See HM Treasury, *Funding the Scottish Parliament, National Assembly for Wales and Northern Ireland Assembly: A statement of funding policy* (London: HM Treasury, 1999).
[10] Bell, 2001.

that in England should have decreased. On the assumption that different levels of spending are needed in different parts of the UK to achieve the same level of service — as detailed in the Treasury's Needs Assessment — then the devolved administrations should have started to feel financial strain (relative to England), irrespective of the policies they chose to pursue.[11]

Nowhere was this more apparent than in Wales. The crisis over European Objective 1 support, and the stark fact that Wales could not afford the required match funding to secure European funds without cutting its existing service provision, highlights well the constraints on devolution without revenue raising powers. The UK Government made a 'formula bypass' — money that goes from Westminster to a devolved territory without going through the Barnett formula — in order to ensure sufficient funds to allow the European funding to be claimed. The power of the Westminster government over the Welsh administration was clear. Only Westminster had access to tax revenues, and by diverting those to Cardiff they became, in effect, a specific grant.

The Barnett formula is passed as a block, to be distributed as the devolved administrations see fit, as in theory could be done by the previous secretaries of state. The Welsh crisis allowed the UK Government, and the Welsh electorate, to place two implicit constraints on the additional monies given to the National Assembly: they had to spend the additional funds on matching European funding, and they had to maintain the existing spending obligations to secure sufficient match funding. Of course there were no statutory conditions attached to the additional funds; as with other funds they could have been spent at the discretion of the Welsh Assembly Government. What differed was that the additional funds were provided as a response to a particular — and embarrassing — financial shortfall. Having pleaded hard for the funds, it would have been near impossible for them to be used for any other purpose than match funding the EU support. When and if the squeeze bites it is likely that special pleading will become more common and that is likely to weaken the devolved institutions relative to Whitehall.

A further constraint on devolution is the nature of the UK's budgeting process. Devolution has not altered this process, but the process has conditioned devolution. Incremental budgeting does not allow for rapid policy divergence between the different administrations within the UK. By its nature, incremental budgeting demands that in periods of economic prosperity budgets rise by inflation, wage demands and a little more in addition as a result of increases in government revenue based on economic growth. There is seldom scope for revolutionary new policies unless they merely replace another policy, both in terms of desired outcome and cost. This is reinforced by the powers the devolution acts have given to Northern Ireland, Scotland

[11] HM Treasury, 1979.

and Wales. All three are limited to intervening on the supply side of the economy, in areas such as education, training, supporting enterprise and developing infrastructure. Apart from free personal care in Scotland and free prescriptions and eye examinations in Wales, the devolved governments have preferred to assert their degrees of independence through forms of social policy which are cheaper to implement and more visible to the electorate. The plan to ban smoking in public places in Scotland, subsequently forced onto the agenda in England, is an example.

THE FUTURE

Those who feel that the Barnett formula does not provide sufficient resources have argued in favour of alternative funding strategies. Two that are commonly proposed are a needs assessment and greater fiscal autonomy. This section looks at each in turn, and at how altering the status quo may lead to a change in the relationships between the devolved administrations and Westminster.

A needs assessment would entail determining how much it would cost to provide a standardised level of service across a wide range of public services in different parts of the UK. Such procedures are followed outside the UK in countries such as Canada and Australia. The mechanisms used in these countries tend to be based on the principle that public provision should reflect local need. Greater fiscal autonomy would involve the devolved administrations collecting more revenue and consequently receiving less support from central government. At present there is a significant disparity between the allocation of revenue raising powers and spending responsibilities within the UK. Darby, Muscatelli and Roy find that sub-central government in the UK receives over 70 per cent of its revenue in the form of grants, with taxation and other charges such as user charges making up the difference.[12] Historically, social services have been provided at local level in the UK, but the vast bulk of taxation is controlled by central government. Other than the variable taxation rate permitted in Scotland and extended borrowing powers in Northern Ireland, devolution has done little to alter this.

Needs Assessment

A needs assessment was conducted in the UK prior to the failed devolution proposals of 1979.[13] It sought to establish the cost of providing the same level of provision of government services across the four constituent parts of the UK. It established that to do so Northern Ireland, Scotland and Wales

---

[12] J. Darby, V. Muscatelli and G. Roy, 'Fiscal Federalism and Fiscal Autonomy: Lessons for the UK from the other industrialised countries', *Scottish Affairs*, 41, (Autumn 2002).

[13] HM Treasury, 1979.

would require £131, £116 and £109, respectively, for every £100 spent on comparable services in England. This is not a system like the Comprehensive Spending Review that seeks to determine the cost of introducing and maintaining policies; it seeks solely to determine the costs of implementing the same programmes to provide the same standard of service across the UK. There are a number of reasons why public service provision in Scotland, Northern Ireland and Wales is more expensive than England, with rurality, poorer health and lower overall income levels being key drivers.

Needs assessments are used beyond the UK; the two most common examples are those set by the Commonwealth Grants Commission in Australia and the Equalization Fund in Canada. Both differ in their application, but they seek to achieve a broadly similar level of funding for the public services between the states or provinces each country. It is a generally-held principle in such federal states that there will be differences in public services between their constituent units, but that these differences should be mediated by some form of transfer between richer and poorer units. The transfers can be made from central government revenue, or they can be made directly from the richer to the poorer units (as in Germany). Either way, there is generally argument about the method or amount of transfers, but an acceptance (albeit sometimes grudging) that it is for the benefit of the nation as a whole. However, one thing marks out Canada, Australia and other federal states that make transfers from the UK — they tend to have a greater number of constituent units and no single unit dominates the others in terms of size. This is an important difference. In economic terms Scotland, Wales and Northern Ireland are minnows compared with England. Funding mechanisms must accommodate the size issue; the Barnett formula does this quite successfully by determining outcomes in the Celtic fringe as a by-product of decisions made about spending in England. Giving Scotland, Wales and Northern Ireland more of a political stake in the determination of funding could lead to serious conflict between the centre and periphery.

Needs assessments do exist within the UK and are found in local government financial settlements, and most commonly within the allocation of health resources. These systems are far from simple and lead to protracted conflicts. Invariably the total amount to be allocated is already determined and the system only deals with the allocation of this between authorities. Those involved with such processes realise the outcomes are zero-sum games. It is difficult to reconcile such systems with the Barnett formula, which takes no account of the policy choices made by the administrations in Edinburgh, Cardiff and Belfast. Within health allocations, for instance, there is little policy leeway, and the combination of targeting and allocation system means that different health boards are expected to provide similar health outcomes in dissimilar circumstances.

Given that a key principle of devolution is to allow policy divergence, it is very difficult to determine matters of fact and matters of policy — are free personal care for the elderly in Scotland and free prescriptions in Wales needs or choices? Both Wales and Scotland would doubtless argue that they are policies that 'need' funding; the UK Government may well disagree.

The issue returns to one of size. The Barnett formula is, very indirectly, a needs assessment. The UK Government has to finance its existing policies, provide an increment to cover inflation and fund new policies. These funding requirements are determined by the policies that it introduces, many of which are applicable to England alone. The Treasury and UK Government departments are involved in decisions that determines both the size of the government expenditure 'cake' and the size of the slices into which it is to be cut. The Barnett formula ensures that the devolved administrations receive a reasonably predictable share of that cake, but it is not clear how that would change under a needs assessment.

Presuming needs assessments were to be conducted for the four governments of the UK, it is hard to imagine a circumstance where they could agree on suitably objective measurement criteria. Divergence in policies will increase with time, and it is difficult to envisage the Barnett formula being replaced before the next set of devolved elections. In those circumstances it becomes more difficult to find a consensus making it more likely that a Barnett formula replacement would be more complicated and more expensive. It would also probably lead to the establishment of some new body to determine funding allocations, a body that the devolved territories would demand was at least one degree removed from Westminster. However, when Scotland and Northern Ireland begin to feel the Barnett squeeze take hold, as Wales arguably already has, they may prefer to take their chances with a new allocation system than maintain the Barnett formula. Since each of the three devolved territories started off with different per capita spending levels, so should converge at different rates on English spending per head, and their own minimum sustainable spending per head levels at different rates (the latter being more important), this will not happen to all devolved territories at the same time. Wales has already received a formula bypass in the 2002 and 2004 Spending Reviews to accommodate the need for match funding for EU projects that follow from its partial designation as an Objective 1 area. Northern Ireland continues to receive the highest per capita spending level in the UK. It will most likely be the funding situation in Scotland that determines the timing of a switch to a new mechanism. This may give the Scottish Executive a lever over the UK Government — were Westminster to try and impose a funding change that Scotland did not want, it may prove difficult to set aside previous claims by the UK Government that the Barnett formula offered a fair method of resource allocation.

Fiscal Autonomy

Given the issues associated with needs assessments, what alternative is there? The starkest alternative is to adopt full fiscal autonomy; that is, to allow the devolved governments to raise sufficient taxes to fund the policies they wish to maintain and implement. At its extreme this would involve distinct fiscal systems for Scotland, Wales and Northern Ireland, and by implication England. A different degree of fiscal separation could involve the devolution of certain tax bases or rates to the devolved administrations: essentially an extension of the Scottish variable rate of income tax, backed up by a revenue transfer from the UK Exchequer.

The UK is rare, although not unique, in the low level of own source revenue collected by devolved territories.[14] Other than the council tax, the business rates and user charges the devolved territories have little fiscal power, barring the as-yet-unused Scottish variable rate of income tax. Canada's provinces collect just over 50 per cent of their own revenue, Australia's states over 30 per cent. In both that remains below the share of total government expenditure made by the states, requiring transfers to continue, but it does make the devolved states more responsible for the funding decisions they make. One of the charges against the current funding system within the UK is that the devolved administrations are not forced to link their spending decisions with the decisions to tax. This is true, and there are good reasons why responsibility for spending should be linked to the requirement to justify taxation, but it is a mistake to suppose that the Barnett formula leads to reckless spending. The devolved administrations remain responsible for the opportunity cost of their spending decisions — they have a fixed sum to allocate and more demands on those funds than they can meet, so they do have to justify their priorities to their assemblies/parliament and more especially their electors.

More likely than fiscal autonomy is a form of fiscal separation, with control over some tax bases or rates being given to the devolved territories.[15] However, the arguments against fiscal autonomy remain. Different tax rates and bases, with mobile factors of production, could lead to those factors moving to the lowest tax/greatest benefit jurisdiction. This argument, first put forward by Tiebout, argues that such a policy can lead to a race to the

---

[14] See Darby, Muscatelli and Roy, 2002, for a discussion of the relationship between revenue collection and spending responsibility.

[15] A full discussion of the economic case for the devolution of tax rates and bases is beyond the scope of this chapter. For an extensive discussion of the issues surrounding the most appropriate devolved taxes see T. Ter-Minassian (ed.), *Fiscal Federalism in Theory and Practice* (Washington DC: International Monetary Fund, 1997).

bottom in the provision of public services.[16] The rich will migrate to those areas with the lowest tax rates, and equally the lowest rates of government good provision. The higher tax and spend areas will attract those seeking government goods, but the tax base will not be able to provide for such a level of demand given its relative shrinking. Although this is an argument more applicable to a large state such as the USA than to the UK, there remains a fear that divergence in taxation could affect location decisions.

The UK Government has retained the right to intervene in territorial funding allocations where it believes the UK's macroeconomic interests are at stake. Given the Treasury's faith in Public Service Agreements as a method of ensuring public service delivery and value for money, they would doubtless find it difficult to allow Northern Ireland, Scotland and Wales a free, or at least partly free, hand in tax policy. Given the Scottish Parliament is reluctant to use its tax-varying power, to the extent that the Labour Party felt obliged to state it would not use it during the first and second Scottish Parliament election campaigns, it may yet be the case that where the Treasury leads, the devolved territories follow.

Much depends on the ability of the devolved territories to borrow. The regional economies of the UK do not move perfectly in cycle, largely due to their differences in composition, so they may not be able to satisfy all their spending requirements throughout the cycle without borrowing. Where this is the case, the relationships between the devolved administrations may hinge on borrowing powers rather than taxation powers. Since the Treasury has explicit borrowing targets, fiscal separation may not enhance the independence of the devolved territories, but rather inhibit it. It would also require a change in the devolution legislation. Borrowing remains a reserved power, apart from the borrowing concession given to Northern Ireland under the Reinvestment and Reform Initiative, and to allow the other devolved territories to borrow would probably require some form of independent adjudicator, be that a physical institution or a set of borrowing rules. Much like a needs assessment, the devolved territories would doubtless put great pressure on the UK Government to ensure such an institution was at arm's length from Westminster.

The arguments surrounding fiscal divergence are essentially extensions of the debate surrounding policy divergence and the Barnett formula. A fear that free personal care for the elderly would lead to an influx of potential claimants to Scotland failed to materialise, but divergences in business rates or corporation tax could have an effect on where businesses choose to locate at the margin. Business rate changes could be introduced, but given the poor business start-up and success rates in Scotland, Wales and Northern Ireland,

---

[16] C. M. Tiebout, 'A pure theory of local expenditures', *Journal of Political Economy*, 64: 416–24, (1956).

the pressure would be to reduce business rates, and therefore revenue, in the short term at least. Fiscal policy divergence is also increasingly constrained by the European Union. It has long been keen to see greater harmonisation in sales taxes. Standard economic theory suggests that in the face of restrictions on sales and consumption taxes, and with mobile factors of production, the best fiscal option is to tax non-mobile factors — primarily land and housing. Although at present largely the domain of local councils through council tax, this may represent the best way forward, in the short term at least, to extending devolved fiscal independence and power. The ability to alter council tax rates and bases is devolved under the devolution Acts, and suggests that allowing councils more scope to raise their own revenue may ease the pressures of a tightening Barnett formula. However, this is clearly constrained by the increasing unpopularity of council tax and the vociferous lobby against business rate increases.

Fiscal autonomy or separation does not solve the problem of fiscal deficits. Of the devolved administrations, only the Scottish Executive attempts to quantify whether there is a gap between Scotland's contribution to the Exchequer and its receipts in block grant. The latest figures, for 2001-02, estimate the fiscal deficit to be between £8.1 billion and £2.9 billion, depending on the treatment of North Sea Oil revenue (Scottish Executive, 2003). Under full fiscal autonomy this deficit would have to be financed, either by continued borrowing, by increased taxation or by reduced spending. Recurrent borrowing — not to fund cyclical deficits but structural ones — would rapidly become unsustainable, and is anyway not permitted under the present devolution settlement; increased taxation would be unpopular; and reduced spending impractical. In short there is no easy solution. Any alternative funding arrangement to the Barnett formula would have to overcome this perennial problem, not just for Scotland, but also for the fiscal deficits that may exist in Northern Ireland and Wales.

ELECTIONS IN 2007 — TIME FOR CHANGE?

The devolved territories are due to hold their third set of elections (Northern Ireland excepted) in 2007. It is possible that either Scotland or Wales could have a non-Labour administration, should the opposition parties find sufficient common ground to form a broad coalition and Labour's share of the vote decrease. Alternatively, the UK Government may change from a Labour administration in 2009. Should either scenario happen, the relationships between Cardiff or Edinburgh and London may change quite dramatically. The majority Labour devolved administrations have introduced policies that differ from those of Westminster, even though party ideology is broadly similar across the UK. Those policy differences would become much more radical were contrasting parties to be in control. Administrations of different hues in Cardiff or Edinburgh have a strong incentive to mark themselves out as different and cause as many problems as possible for a Labour government in Westminster, presuming it will not have a detrimental effect on their funding allocation — as would be the case if the Barnett formula remains. A different Westminster government, especially a Conservative government, would have little to lose from antagonising Wales and Scotland if it increased votes in England and did not pose an immediate threat to the Union.

A further issue is perhaps hypothetical, but it is unclear how much of post-devolution intergovernmental relations is based on a strong UK party system and inter-party connections as opposed to formal institutional structures.[17] The Barnett formula, due to its simplicity and transparency, prevents party politics from influencing the allocations. Where the Barnett squeeze has started to bite, as in Wales, party politics may be the deciding factor as to whether Westminster helps out the devolved administration in trouble. While a still broadly generous Barnett formula, at least to Scotland and Northern Ireland, allows the devolved territories an almost-free hand, any alternative would probably constrain them. Change would allow the dominant government to have its way, or at least its way most of the time, in determining the outcome of an alternative system, and the dominant government is most likely to be Westminster.

THE BARNETT FORMULA, POWER AND THE FUTURE

The Barnett formula is not under threat, at least at present. The UK Government and the devolved administrations all support its continued use, in public if less strongly in private. It will come unstuck, and lose supporters, where there is a repeat of an event such as the European funding issue in Wales. No direct repetition is possible, however, given that EU funding will increasingly focus on new EU members when the next set of allocations is agreed in 2006. While politicians regularly support the formula with statements about how it offers a fair settlement, these will stop when the same politicians have to justify spending cuts on the basis of reduced block grants. A possible solution in the face of such a prospect would be formula bypasses to ensure sufficient funds for agreed public service delivery, but at this point economic theory would be dismissed in favour of political influence and this would greatly reduce the independence of the devolved territories from Whitehall. That is not imminent, but it may be coming uncomfortably close

[17] See for discussions A. Trench's chapter in this volume and the chapter by M. Laffin, E. Shaw and G. Taylor in A. Trench (ed.), *Devolution and Power in the United Kingdom* (Manchester: Manchester University Press, forthcoming).

for Wales. At this point the Barnett formula will be as much a millstone around the necks of Westminster politicians as it will be for the devolved administrations.

While there are divergences in economic polices and institutions between the four governments within the UK, seldom does a debate concerning the economy, especially in Scotland, not return to a debate around the Barnett formula and fiscal freedom. There remains the assumption that the Barnett formula is a constraint imposed by Westminster that retards economic growth and limits policy freedom. In Wales, where there is much less interest in fiscal autonomy, the debate instead concerns the problem it has already faced — what to do when funding through the Barnett formula no longer allows the National Assembly to meet its spending pledges. Irrespective of the economic development polices followed by any of the devolved governments, or by their agencies such as Scottish Enterprise, the Welsh Development Agency or InvestNI, the Barnett formula is involved in some form.

The Barnett formula is done a disservice. It should, when allowed to operate unhindered, tend towards allocating equal expenditure per head across the territories. It has not changed since devolution. Because it is effectively a lump-sum transfer it does not directly distort markets — in contrast to many proposed forms of fiscal autonomy. What have constrained policy divergence in the territories and maintained the focus on the policies that the UK Government is pursuing are incremental budgeting, a strong national media and governments of the same political party. Determining who holds power in such a relationship is not easy, but the Barnett formula certainly does not diminish the power of the devolved territories, unless like Wales they have reached a point where the allocation is no longer sufficient to support their existing public funding obligations. Since they had to go cap in hand to Westminster they were limited in their options, but Westminster also felt obliged to pay.

The alternatives, fiscal autonomy, or at least fiscal separation of some kind, and needs assessment are untried in a situation similar to that in the UK. They are found in many other countries, and within parts of the UK itself, but not in a situation where one party to the agreement is so much larger than any other. It is not clear that a move to either alternative will be any better than the present situation, for Scotland and Northern Ireland at least. Change would allow the Treasury to impose conditions that it cannot while the Barnett formula remains in operation, and it is not clear the constraints they would seek to impose would be of benefit to the devolved territories, and may allow the Treasury a control over devolved policies it would otherwise not have had.

When the Barnett formula does come to be replaced, the UK Government and the devolved administrations will have to make hard choices. Economic theory will, as always, have to be tempered with political reality. Should elected regional government for England return to the political agenda, the number of administrations involved in any future funding settlement will increase as will the complexity of devolution, if their powers and remit are to be different again from those of the existing devolved nations and from each other. However one thing is clear: no replacement will be as simple, yet as misquoted, as the existing institution.

BIBLIOGRAPHY

Official Documents

HM Treasury, *Needs Assessment Study: The report of an interdepartmental study coordinated by HM Treasury on the relative public expenditure needs in England, Scotland, Wales and Northern Ireland* (London: HM Treasury, 1979).
HM Treasury, *Funding the Scottish Parliament, National Assembly for Wales and Northern Ireland Assembly: A statement of funding policy* (London: HM Treasury, 1999).
HM Treasury, *Spending Review 2002: Opportunity and security for all*, Cm 5570 (London: The Stationery Office, 2002).
HM Treasury, *Public Expenditure: Statistical analyses 2003–2004*, Cm. 6201 (London: The Stationery Office, 2004).
Scottish Executive, *General Expenditure and Revenue in Scotland 2001–2002*, (2003).

Secondary Sources

Bell, D., 'The Barnett Formula' unpublished mimeo, Department of Economics, University of Stirling (2001).
Bell, D and A. Christie, 'The Barnett Formula — Nobody's Child?', in A. Trench (ed.) *The State of the Nation 2001* (Exeter: Imprint Academic, 2001).
Darby, J., V. Muscatelli and G. Roy 'Fiscal Federalism and Fiscal Autonomy: Lessons for the UK from the other industrialised countries.' *Scottish Affairs*, 41, (Autumn 2002).
Heald, D. and A. McLeod, 'Public Expenditure' in *The Laws of Scotland — Stair Memorial Encyclopaedia*, para. 480–552, (Edinburgh: Butterworths, 2002).
McLean, I. and A. McMillan, 'The Distribution of Public Expenditure across the UK Regions', *Fiscal Studies*, 24: 45–71, (2003).
Ter-Minassian, T. (ed.), *Fiscal Federalism in Theory and Practice* (Washington DC: International Monetary Fund, 1997).
Tiebout, C. M., 'A pure theory of local expenditures', *Journal of Political Economy*, 64: 416–24, (1956).
Trench, A., (ed.), *Devolution and Power in the United Kingdom* (Manchester: Manchester University Press, forthcoming).

9

Devolution and the European Union
Trajectories and Futures

Charlie Jeffery

INTRODUCTION

The combination of devolution and European integration creates some odd multi-level dynamics in the EU's member states. Many of the competences devolved in 1999 to Scotland, Wales and Northern Ireland concern issues previously transferred to and already regulated by the European Union. If the devolved institutions wanted purchase on those issues — and to give meaning in practice to the powers formally devolved to them — they had to find ways of accessing EU-level decision-making. In the few years they have had so far, they have made considerable strides in doing so, establishing an effective practice of cooperation on EU matters with UK central government, seeking to influence debates at the EU level, and even leaving a mark on the Treaty Establishing a Constitution for Europe.[1] Seen comparatively, those strides are quite remarkable in that there have been few overt tensions between the UK central government and the devolved governments as the latter have 'mobilised' for Europe.[2] Elsewhere in the EU there have been rather more conflictual relationships between central and regional governments, with central government seeking to preserve an exclusive role in external affairs, and only grudgingly, if at all, allowing space for regions to shape member state EU policy.[3]

---

[1] The fullest account so far of the devolved institutions' involvement in EU decision-making is in S. Bulmer *et al.* (eds), *British Devolution and European Policy-Making* (London: Palgrave, 2002), though this has a focus on pre-devolution thinking between 1997 and 1999, and only the first eighteen months or so of devolution in practice. The same team has since developed its work further, including an impressive range of papers on their website at les1.man.ac.uk/devolution/. See also C. Jeffery and R. Palmer, 'The European Union, Devolution and Power', in A. Trench (ed.), *Devolution and Power in the United Kingdom* (Manchester: Manchester University Press, forthcoming 2005). On the impact of the devolved regions on the EU Constitution negotiations, see C. Jeffery, 'Regions and the Constitution for Europe: German and British Impacts', *German Politics* 13 (4): 605–24, (2004a).

[2] L. Hooghe, 'Subnational Mobilisation in the European Union', *West European Politics* 18 (3): 175–98, (1995).

[3] See C. Jeffery, 'Sub-national Mobilisation and European Integration: Does it Make any Difference?', *Journal of Common Market Studies*, 38 (1): 1–23, (2000). Note also that although the terminology of 'regions' is contested when applied to sub-state nations like Scotland and Wales, it is a

There have been two main reasons for the untroubled way in which devolved administrations have managed to work with the UK Government domestically and to raise a profile in EU matters externally. The first is a recurring theme in this volume: excepting Northern Ireland there has been party political congruence at central and devolved levels with the Labour Party leading government in Westminster, Scotland and Wales.[4] Labour's pre-eminence has smoothed out most of the territorial frictions which usually pervade intergovernmental relations in decentralised states. The second, reflecting the absence of the Conservatives from the intergovernmental equation, is that all governments, at UK and devolved levels have been broadly pro-European. 'Europe' has not been a complicating factor in intergovernmental relations. These benign circumstances for intergovernmental cooperation on Europe are discussed more fully below. The point for now is that they are not enduring circumstances. They will change. Labour will lose an election somewhere, sometime, and — connected with governmental change or independent of it — differences of territorial interest will emerge to complicate intergovernmental relations, and attitudes to the benefits and priorities of European integration may come to diverge at central and devolved levels away from the current, general Europhilia.

Given the extraordinary circumstances in which the first few years of devolved engagement with the EU have unfolded, this chapter begins with a brief comparative exploration of how regions elsewhere have, over a longer time period, developed their engagement with EU decision-making. The purpose is to get a sense of the longer term trajectories that the devolved administrations in the UK might end up following, including situations where partisan conflict, conflict over territorial interests, or conflict over the purposes of European integration complicate relations between regional and central governments. The chapter then sets out the evolving practice of devolved-central government-EU relationships in the UK hitherto, before exploring some of the parameters which may shape that practice in future.

REGIONS AND THE EU:
FAREWELL TO THE 'THIRD LEVEL', BACK TO THE MEMBER STATE

Scotland, Wales and Northern Ireland are 'legislative regions'. This terminology is relatively new, and largely associated with the lobby group 'Regions with Legislative Power', or RegLeg, established in 2000 (in which Wales and Scotland have been active members; the Scottish First Minister

standard shorthand for comparative analysis and, indeed, for the self-presentation of the Scottish and Welsh governments – both members of the group of 'Regions with Legislative Power' – in EU matters.

[4] The party system in Northern Ireland is distinct from that in the rest of the UK. Only modest reference to Northern Ireland can be made in this chapter as for most of the period since devolution the Northern Ireland Assembly has been suspended.

Jack McConnell was RegLeg President in 2003–4). 'Legislative regions' do what it says on the tin: they have elected parliaments which make laws with direct effect on the public goods and services provided to citizens in the region. Most of the bigger EU member states have legislative regions — Germany, Spain, Italy and the UK — as do Belgium and Austria (plus special status island regions in Finland and Portugal). Most of these make laws on health, education, environmental policy, local government and regional economic policy, and some do on internal security matters and taxation.

The qualifier 'legislative' was introduced to mark out such regions as a special group with interests in European integration distinct from other kinds of regional and local authority across the EU. The essence of that distinctive interest is to preserve the meaning of regional law-making powers in the context of European integration. There have been two 'preservation' strategies. The first, and now largely abandoned strategy was one of participation, focused on the formal recognition of the regional level — the 'third' level, after member states and the union itself — as a participant in EU decision-making.[5] Regions would become fully-fledged partners in EU-level decision-making, sharing responsibility for those competences allocated to them under domestic law in a European frame. The second, and now predominant strategy for legislative regions has been defensive: preventing the further 'Europeanisation' of issues falling under their domestic legislative powers, even rolling back the reach of EU regulation. The concern is to retain autonomy, and increasingly legislative regions have viewed a strong member state structure as the best guarantee of that autonomy. The old 'third level' strategy was in part about escaping the member state and finding new policy-shaping opportunities at the EU level; the newer, defensive strategy is about working with member-state central governments to hold Europe in check.

Table 9.1 summarises with a broad brush why legislative regions shifted away from the third level to the member state strategy. The story is one in which a divergence of interest compared to non-legislative regions and local authorities has become embedded in distinctive strategies for Europe. That interest has to do with power. European integration, by absorbing regional level competences at the EU level has tended to disempower legislative regions, to *reduce* their scope to influence public policy on their territory. The domestic functions of non-legislative regional and local authorities are not typically law-making, but rather the coordination and implementation of central government policies in regional and local contexts, often within tightly-defined frameworks allowing only limited decision-making

---

[5] U. Bullmann (ed.), *Die Politik der dritten Ebene. Regionen im Europa der Union* (Baden-Baden: Nomos, 1994).

autonomy. Engagement with EU decision-making has typically opened up new policy-shaping and learning opportunities whose effect is to *increase* the scope to influence public policy on the regional or local territory.

These are quite significant differences in the impact of European integration. But they did not initially become manifest as political differences in the wave of regional and local activism on EU matters which started around the mid-1980s; in fact a broadly common front held until around 1995. That this was so was in part because the different dynamics of (dis)empowerment only slowly became politically salient as the acceleration of integration unfolded following the 1986 Single European Act. But it was also more generally because of a wider optimism that the European integration process was opening up into something less focused on member states and therefore more accessible to non-central government actors. That optimism, and the lobbying effort it helped to mobilise, produced a concrete outcome in the 1991 Maastricht Treaty: the Committee of the Regions (CoR).

The establishment of the CoR in 1994 was a turning point. It threw legislative regions and non-legislative regional and local authorities together in an institution that few listened to with extremely modest powers.[6] Legislative regions were in a minority and were unable to mobilise even the modest powers of the CoR to help shape decision-making on issues at the EU level which impacted on their competences at the domestic level. From the perspective of non-legislative regions and local authorities, though, the CoR opened up new possibilities for exchange of experience, coalition-building and — at the margin — policy-shaping. The legislative region evaluation of the CoR led to the abandonment by the legislative regions of any serious attempt to establish a formal structure for engaging an EU-wide 'third level' with EU decision-making. They increasingly broke away from the wider mass of regional and local authorities which remained committed to — and benefited from — EU-level action outside the framework of the member state. The legislative regions instead 'returned' to the member state, placing a new emphasis on member-state channels as the most effective way of shaping or — increasingly — deflecting EU policies with an impact on domestic regional competences.

---

[6] C. Jeffery, 'Social and Regional Interests', in J. Peterson and M. Shackleton (eds.), *Institutions of the European Union* (Oxford: Oxford University Press, 2002).

Table 9.1: The Emergence of the Legislative Regions' 'Member State' Strategy

Legislative Regions	Other Regional and Local Authorities
Disempowerment: the competences problem	Empowerment: new policy-shaping opportunities
Differences bridged in initially shared 'third level' strategy, but then:	
Committee of the Regions ineffective	Committee of the Regions valuable
Working through the member state	Working beyond the member state

REGIONS AND THE EU: WORKING THROUGH THE MEMBER STATE

The 'member state strategy' had always been a parallel track for the Belgian and German regions, and by the time the CoR was in operation, formal rights had been established in both countries for the regional level to shape and in some cases determine the member state's policy on EU matters falling under the domestic competence of the regions. Similar rights were established in Austria on its accession to the EU in 1995. Less formalised and generally less far-reaching practices of central-regional coordination in EU policy have also been established in Spain (though with a more formalised system of access emerging), and in the UK. The main mechanisms of central–regional government coordination within these member states are set out in Table 9.2.

Regions in Belgium, Austria, Germany and Spain all have rights of access to relevant information on EU matters, and in all cases a routinised system has been established for forwarding information on from the EU, via central government, and onward to the regions. And in all these cases arrangements have been established to formulate regional opinions, and to feed these into the EU decision-making of central government authorities. These arrangements vary widely. In Belgium, following a radical decentralisation process, there is no hierarchy of status between regions and central government.[7] The lead role in EU policy-making varies by issue; the level of government which holds the corresponding domestic competence for the issue concerned takes the lead. But in order to maintain a coordinated Belgium-wide position

[7] Belgium has two largely overlapping forms of regional government, Regions, and Communities. For simplicity's sake we use 'region' to include both.

across issue areas, in practice each level of government is involved in all issue areas. All governments, central and regional, are therefore involved as equal partners in a systematic, collective EU policy formulation process, and each represents Belgium in the EU Council whenever it holds the domestic competence for the issue area concerned.[8]

Table 9.2: Working with the Centre

Mechanism	Belgium	Germany	Austria	Spain	UK
Full information on EU developments	✓	✓	✓	✓	✓
Decisions have binding effect on centre in fields of regional competence	✓	X	✓	X	X
Participate in meetings to instruct Permanent Representative	✓	✓	✓	X	✓
Represent member state in Council of Ministers in fields of regional competence	✓	✓	✓	X	✓
Contribute to member state decision-making in Convention/IGC	✓	✓	✓	X	?
Run Presidency of EU Council jointly with the centre	✓	X	X	X	X

In Austria and Germany, policy formulation has two stages: a first in which the regions come to a collective viewpoint; and a second where the collective regional position is connected with central government's decision-making process. That process is constitutionally codified in both countries, and allows the regions a 'decisive' voice where EU matters directly affect regional competences. In those cases (subject to caveats at the margins), a collective regional opinion is binding on central government, and the centre must represent that opinion in EU bodies. Equally the regions have the right to lead delegations in the EU Council on issues which touch on the 'heartland' of their exclusive legislative competences in the domestic arena. It should be noted that neither the Austrian nor the German federal

---

[8] For a detailed account of the complex procedures and rotas which makes this system work see B. Kerremans and J. Beyers, 'The Belgian Sub-national Entities in the European Union: Second or Third Level Players?', *Regional and Federal Studies*, 6 (2): 41–55, (1996).

system allocates a wide range of exclusive legislative competences to the regions; so Austrian regional participation in the Council is rare and German participation limited to four main areas, education, culture, media, and justice and home affairs (with a periodic presence also on research matters).[9] In both cases the real 'meat' of participation in EU matters is in domestic coordination processes between centre and regions, not in the Council.

In Spain central governments have traditionally resisted the award of *rights* of participation in EU affairs to regions. So while a range of intergovernmental conferences exist for regional-central exchanges of views, these lack constitutional underpinning and have as a result at best an advisory role. There is no obligation for the centre to represent any collectively-held regional view nor to allow a regional presence in the EU Council. In any case the Spanish regions have been slow to develop a practice of collective opinion-formation on EU (and, indeed, other) matters, not least because asymmetrical regionalisation has encouraged inter-regional competition and bilateral deal-making with the centre.[10] A new deal struck early in 2005 appears to have established new formal procedures for the representation of regional views in core areas of competence, and to allow the regions access to the EU Council. It remains unclear as to whether the traditional patterns of central-regional suspicions and inter-regional competition will be overcome sufficiently to give the new procedures the clout their equivalents have in Austria and Germany.

One issue the Spanish case points to is that of trust. The central government has not shown sufficient trust in the regions to allow them (until 2005) genuine access to EU decision-making, in part no doubt because of the separatist undertones of Basque Country and, sporadically, Catalan government policy. Territorial interests at the regional level stood in conflict with those of the state-wide government. The problem of trust was most marked under the period of Popular Party central government under Jose Maria Aznar, which was generally suspicious of regionalism. Its replacement by the Socialist-led Zapatero government in 2004 appears to have ushered in more trustful relations, in part because a Socialist-led government had also taken over in Spain's most dynamic region, Catalonia. These developments show how differing perspectives on the purposes and legitimacy of regional government together with partisan (in)congruence can affect intergovernmental relations in EU policy.

Neither of those problems have played a role in Belgium or Austria where practices of intergovernmental negotiation and consensus decision-making characteristic of the domestic political arena have been smoothly transposed to EU decision-making. In Germany the situation is somewhat different. The

[9] T. Börzel, *States and Regions in the European Union* (Cambridge: Cambridge University Press, 2002), p. 81.
[10] *Ibid.*, pp. 98–100.

central government has traditionally been suspicious of regional attempts to access EU decision-making; at each stage the regions have had to fight hard to extend their rights, at times amid open threats to veto the ratification of EU Treaties.[11] So what appears at first sight a routine extension of standard practices of intergovernmental coordination to Europe has in fact a persistent undercurrent of tension. At times this has been reinforced by party-political difference: for almost all of the last fifteen years, the central government coalition has been faced by a set of governments in the regions dominated by the opposition.

That persistent tension explains one significant contrast with Belgium and Austria (and why in this case Germany lines up with Spain in Table 9.2): the German regions do not have access to the regular meetings which bring together central government departments to coordinate policy and issue instructions to the Permanent Representative. In Belgium and Austria the regions do have access; in Germany they are held at arm's length.

There are, in other words, quite significant variations in the structures and spirit with which regions contribute to EU decision-making. In Belgium all regions are involved individually in all significant EU policy decisions (to the extent that the last Belgian EU Presidency was run as a joint operation of central and regional governments). In Austria the regions are collectively involved in a consensual decision-making process. In Germany the regions are involved collectively in a fuller range of policy fields than in Austria, but in a less consensual manner. And in Spain regional-central relations in EU policy have traditionally been fractious and only weakly institutionalised.

These variations provide some context for evaluating how devolved–central relations in EU decision-making work now, and for thinking through the ways they might develop in future. Some of the variables underlying these variations — levels of institutionalisation, territorial interests and questions of central-regional trust, party politics, and inter-regional competition — can also be applied fruitfully to questions on the future dynamics and trajectories of devolved engagement in EU decision-making in the UK. The next section reviews briefly the practice of devolved-UK intergovernmental relations on Europe against the comparative background set out above, before moving on to explore some future scenarios.

THE UK: THE PRACTICE SO FAR

Compared to experience elsewhere, the practice so far in the UK has been remarkable trouble-free. Generally, central governments have been reluctant to grant regional governments access to EU decision-making, because they

---

[11] See the outstanding collection of regional policy documents assembled in U. Leonardy (ed.), *Europäische Kompetenzabgrenzung als deutsches Verfassungspostulat* (Baden-Baden: Nomos, 2002).

viewed the EU as an integral part of their competence for foreign policy.[12] The UK Government by contrast planned on devolved input to its EU policy formulation practices from the outset. Though unusual, that openness to devolved input is easily explicable. There had been a territorial dimension to UK EU policy formulation before devolution, in which territorial departments of state for Scotland, Wales and Northern Ireland contributed, as did other UK-level departments within their remits, to EU policy formulation (the Scottish Office rather more than the other two).[13] Devolution essentially democratised the functions of the territorial departments, transferring responsibility for them (with relatively minor exceptions) to the devolved institutions.[14] In those circumstances it was logical to adapt prior practices of accommodating territorial concerns in UK EU policy positions to the new situation. The old *intra*-governmental process for accommodating territorial concerns therefore became a new *inter*-governmental process run on the basis of the same procedures.

This adaptation explains the characteristic feature of central-devolved relations in EU policy (and indeed in most other matters): its informality. There are formal statements of how UK and devolved governments work together in EU matters, as expressed in Concordats, but these do not really guide intergovernmental relations; rather they simply describe the conventional pre-devolution practice in post-devolution terms.[15] The Concordats have no legal weight, unlike equivalent statements of modus operandi in Austria, Belgium and Germany. They have been supplemented by 'guidance notes', largely on the bilateral relations of Whitehall and devolved departments, which set out 'good practice' rather than rules. The emphasis has been on creating 'an environment conducive to the sharing of intelligence', as captured in the mantra that there should be 'no surprises' in intergovernmental relations on EU matters.[16]

This informal and incremental adaptation of pre-devolution practice has supported a rather fuller practice of multilateral intergovernmental coordination on EU matters than in any area of domestic policy. The only Joint Ministerial Committee which has taken on a regular meeting rhythm is the JMC (Europe), which has emerged as a forum for strategic policy formulation in the run-up to quarterly EU summits. Likewise, outside of the JMC framework, UK and devolved agriculture ministers — whose business is

---

[12] C. Jeffery, 'Conclusions: Sub-national Authorities and "European Domestic Policy"', *Regional and Federal Studies*, 6 (2): 204–19, (1996a), here p. 215.

[13] Bulmer *et al.* (2002), pp. 15–32.

[14] The most notable exception being the 'reserved' functions in Northern Ireland government, which were to be retained by the Northern Ireland Office until the stabilisation of the security situation.

[15] C. Carter, 'The Formulation of UK EU Policy Post-Devolution: A Transformative Model of Governance?', *Manchester Papers in Politics, Devolution and European Union Policy Making Series*, 3, (2002)..

[16] *Ibid.*

almost exclusively EU-driven — meet multilaterally even more regularly, roughly on a monthly basis; similarly intense working relationships have developed in fisheries policy too between UK and Scottish departments (given that much of the UK fishing industry is located in Scotland, and within the competence of the Scottish Parliament). Significantly, though these relationships appear increasingly institutionalised they have no legal weight. There are no rights to sit on a JMC, there is only a practice of doing things in this way.

Nonetheless that practice has created surprisingly effective channels for the devolved administrations to influence EU decision-making which bears up well in comparison with the situations elsewhere depicted in Table 9.2. The devolved administrations do get access to all relevant EU documentation (not necessarily straightforward for a UK political mentality when another political party — the Liberal Democrats in Scotland and, for a time, in Wales — is involved). Fisheries (on a bilateral UK-Scottish basis) and agriculture (on a multilateral UK-devolved basis) are in effect joint policies where, if not with binding effect, devolved administrations do genuinely shape UK positions. In other areas too — in particular special pleading for the protection of local economic interests — devolved administrations have been able to swing the UK member state behind their concerns.[17]

The 'Friday' meetings convened by the UK Cabinet Office European Secretariat to establish the tactics for the UK Permanent Representative in Brussels are open to the devolved administrations, echoing Austrian and Belgian practice and moving one step ahead of the German Länder (in addition, and again unlike the German case the devolved representative offices in Brussels form part of the 'UKRep family' and senior staff have full diplomatic accreditation). Scottish and (to a lesser extent) Welsh ministers have appeared for the UK in the EU Council, notably on Justice and Home Affairs (reflecting the distinctive legal system in Scotland), Rural Affairs and Fisheries. They do so on an ad hoc basis, not by right, and at times reflecting diary contingencies when a UK minister was unable to attend. And they do so bound by an agreed UK position. As in the other cases summarised in Table 9.2 there is no possibility of developing a 'Scottish line' in negotiations. Council attendance is in all cases largely symbolic.

Finally, via the JMC (Europe), perhaps unexpectedly, the devolved administrations displayed a capacity to shape UK contributions to the European constitutional debate.[18] This is the one field in which some notes of tension did fleetingly appear in the UK-Scottish relationship on Europe, notably in 2001 when the then Scottish First Minister Henry McLeish signed up to a legislative regions declaration which in some respects went beyond

---

[17] Jeffery and Palmer, forthcoming 2005.
[18] *Ibid.*

the reach of even an accommodating UK Government policy.[19] The problem point was the idea of a regional right of appeal to the European Court of Justice on supposed subsidiarity infringements which, if awarded, could conceivably pit the Scottish government against European legislation approved by the UK Government in the Council. Subsequently, McLeish's successor as First Minister, Jack McConnell — who presided over the RegLeg grouping in 2003–4 — has played down such issues as priorities of other regions and inappropriate to the UK constitutional tradition.[20] Equally the UK Government moved to address other RegLeg concerns, seeking ways, stumblingly at first, to provide a UK platform for others of the RegLeg concerns.[21] The eventual outcome was its January 2003 paper to the European Convention on 'Europe and the Regions', which committed the UK Government to extend the subsidiarity 'early warning system' proposed for the EU's national parliaments to the devolved legislatures in the UK.[22] There appeared to be an instinct on each side to bracket out a contentious issue and find a way of moving ahead jointly. This may have the effect of setting a precedent for the devolved administrations, within accepted parameters, to claim a role in shaping UK policy on future EU institutional reforms which have a bearing on regional issues.

Once again, though, the central point is that there are no *rights* to any of these practices of devolved access to UK EU decision-making. The UK looks quite good in comparison in Table 9.2, but the situation could easily change. Before turning to circumstances in which such change might happen, there is one further notable dimension to devolved engagement with EU decision-making in the UK: it is executive-dominated. The devolved legislatures self-evidently enough stand outside a system which works through informal and/or behind-closed-doors processes of intergovernmental coordination. That in itself is not unusual; regional engagement in EU decision-making is everywhere executive-led. Where the UK stands apart is in the attempts by the Scottish Parliament to hold the Scottish government to account. This has in part to do with the role of the Scottish National Party as the leading opposition party in the Scottish Parliament. Fired by its imagery of 'independence in Europe' it has sought to press the Scottish government

[19] As discussed in C. Jeffery and R. Palmer, 'Stepping (Softly) onto the International Stage: The External Relations of Scotland and Wales', in R. Hrbek (ed.), *Aussenbeziehungen von Regionen in Europa und der Welt* (Baden-Baden: Nomos, 2003), pp. 168–9. See also 'Holyrood wins right to greater say on Europe', *Scotsman*, 22 June 2001.

[20] J. McConnell, 'Speaking Note, Florence Conference of Minister-Presidents of Regions with Legislative Power, 14 November 2002'. The note stressed that while McConnell was 'particularly supportive' of certain points on the RegLeg agenda, 'there are others – such as calls for regional access to the ECJ, or for guarantees of representation in the Council of Ministers – which apply less to Scotland's particular circumstances'.

[21] Jeffery, 2004a.

[22] P. Hain, 'Europe and the Regions', paper submitted to the European Convention on behalf of the UK Government and the devolved administrations in Scotland and Wales (2003).

into explicit statements of how distinctive Scottish interests were reflected (or not) in UK positions, notably on fisheries. The last two Convenors of the Parliament's European and International Affairs Committee have been senior SNP figures who have attempted to work beyond party discipline in pressing the government to account for its actions.

More generally the Parliament has sought to claim a distinctive role alongside the government in EU matters, reflecting some of the founding spirit of not succumbing to Westminster-style majoritarianism. It has given itself some of the wherewithal for that distinctive role, setting up an inter-regional pressure group, NORPEC (Network of Regional Parliamentary European Committees), as a 'forum for sharing ideas and experience on parliamentary procedures and practice',[23] and establishing its own Brussels office, distinct from that of the Scottish government, designed to improve parliamentary intelligence on EU matters.[24] The Parliament is also manoeuvring itself into a position to contribute purposefully to the 'early warning system' on subsidiarity proposed in the European Constitution. In Germany, Belgium and Austria access to the early warning system for regional 'parliaments' seems to be understood (assuming the Constitution is ratified) as an additional route for *governments* (legitimated by a parliamentary majority) to influence EU decision-making. This is no doubt how the UK Government views the role of Westminster; to support government policy by mobilising a government parliamentary majority. But in Scotland the *Parliament* is staking its own claim, looking at possibilities of cooperation with the European committees of the two UK Houses of Parliament, and developing an outline system for flagging issues it considers important to the Scottish government.[25]

No other regional government in the EU faces this kind of consistent pressure for parliamentary scrutiny and accountability as that in Scotland. This too could be an important factor in setting parameters for future UK-Scottish (and in stimulating equivalent UK-Welsh or UK-Northern Irish) interactions in EU decision-making.

SCENARIOS

The earlier comparative analysis gave some useful indications of the variables that might affect future intergovernmental relations in EU matters: institutionalisation, territorial interests and trust, party politics, and inter-regional competition. Of these it appears unlikely that the UK will see the kind of inter-regional competition, based in conceptions of differential

---

[23] www.scottish.parliament.uk/business/committees/europe/norpec/Norpec.pdf
[24] www.scottish.parliament.uk/corporate/elu/brussels.htm
[25] www.scottish.parliament.uk/business/committees/europe/papers-04/eup04-14.pdf (Convenor's Report, Annex C).

status, as in Spain. That might have been the case if the North-East had voted 'yes' to elected regional government, opening up the prospect of a lower status regional tier in England, but the voters in the North-East have taken that variable out of the equation. Of the other variables, as is made clear elsewhere in this volume, perhaps the most significant for the development of any variant of intergovernmental relations will be the partisan composition of future governments. Partisan change away from the current pan-GB dominance of Labour will have direct implications for inter-governmental trust. And the timing of any partisan change will be important in terms of institutionalisation: continuing incremental institutionalisation — and perhaps, in due course, fuller formalisation — of intergovernmental coordination practices may provide a framework for better managing partisan difference in the UK's EU policy-making. Two broad scenarios seem conceivable:

1. Incremental Development of the Status Quo

Incremental change is the most likely scenario. Its main precondition is absence of partisan change in government composition for some years ahead. The 2005 UK general election secured for Labour its unprecedented third term. The electoral systems in Scotland and Wales are not designed to make change away from Labour-led government easy. If there is Labour-led government everywhere (excepting Northern Ireland of course) for another Westminster term, it seems likely that current arrangements will be further embedded and systematised, much on the lines that Alan Trench suggests for the wider system of intergovernmental relations in Chapter 7 of this volume. There would likely be a further embedding of established practices of coordination through JMC (Europe), agricultural and fisheries ministerial meetings, and through the 'Friday meetings' which deal with immediate priorities. If the Constitution for Europe is adopted, the 'early warning system' will bring new procedures. Though perhaps unlikely to be embedded in law, those procedures will need to be clearly articulated, not least because the short, six-week timetable for responding to EU legislative proposals will demand clarity on who has to do what by when. Experience elsewhere — in all the countries in Table 9.2 — suggests a tendency over time for such practices and procedures of coordination to become institutionally formalised.

One might object at this point that the tendency to formalisation elsewhere might reflect different constitutional traditions where formal codification of political behaviour — and its concomitant, the justiciability of those codes — comes rather more naturally than in the UK. There are two considerations though which point beyond that objection and in the direction of formalisation. The first is that it may well be in the devolved administrations' interest.

There is perhaps a seductive attraction to the argument that Scotland and Wales have very quickly come to a very favourable position in comparative terms (see Table 9.2), and that the sheer flexibility of the British constitutional tradition has made this possible. There is a counterargument, though. Unformalised arrangements have been the rule in Spain hitherto and have allowed a Spanish central government suspicious of regional priorities (and abetted by inter-regional rivalries) to hold the regions at arm's length. It would be entirely straightforward for a UK central government to do the same. The flexibility of unformalised arrangements is double-edged. The devolved administrations may feel a need to entrench what they have — especially if they look ahead to the possibilities of a non-Labour government at UK level (see below).

But the devolved administrations may still favour entrenchment to ensure adequate channels of territorial interest representation even if Labour pre-eminence is maintained. As others show elsewhere in this volume, inter-governmental conflict is quite conceivable even among Labour-led governments. A tighter fiscal situation — which most commentators expect — could produce central-devolved conflict over the allocation of resources within the UK. Though this would have little direct impact on EU matters it could encourage a more explicit articulation of territorial interests capable of challenging intra-party loyalties and spilling over into unrelated matters such as the EU. The EU's own 'spillovers' can also cause territorially differentiated impacts in the member states which might lead devolved governments to prioritise territory over party. We have arguably been close to this on the EU Working Time Directive, which has had unanticipated implications for staffing patterns in hospitals by limiting the on-call hours of junior doctors. The implications are easier to deal with in a mostly urbanised England, where pooling of cover between hospitals is feasible. It is not, for example, in the Scottish highlands, where the Directive poses severe implications for staffing costs and for the delivery of on-the-job clinical training. These territorially differentiated implications were not anticipated, and have been difficult to manage. Arguably a difficult UK-devolved territorial conflict on the matter has been avoided only through systematic discussion of the issue in the JMC (Europe), out of which has emerged a territorially more nuanced UK position in debates about the implementation of the Directive.[26] The instinct appears to have been to move in the direction of systematisation in order to manage an issue with the potential to drive a wedge between UK and devolved governments, in other words to set aside some of the inherited flexibility of unformalised intergovernmental arrangements.

---

[26] I am grateful for insights on this issue from Scott Greer and from officials in the Scottish Executive. The latter confirmed that all JMC (Europe) meetings in 2004 discussed the Working Time Directive.

The issues raised by the Working Time Directive point to a devolved interest in more formalisation. A second impetus to formalisation may well come from the centre. It is striking that it is *only* in EU matters that there has been both a quite systematic and a multilateral coordination of UK and devolved governments. This has something to do with the external demands of representing the UK state's interests in the EU. Those demands have encouraged a logic of internal coordination. There may be peculiarly British concerns about national sovereignty and national interests at play here, which place a premium on a single, clear policy line; other member states are rather more ambiguous — or 'polyphonous'[27] — in the definition and pursuit of the 'national' interest. The willingness of the FCO, through UKRep, and the Cabinet Office to induct the devolved administrations into the single national line suggest an explicit concern with 'monophony'. The way that the fleeting tensions over Scotland signing up to an ambitious RegLeg agenda — by Scotland bracketing out problem issues and the UK Government embracing the rest of the regional agenda — confirms a UK instinct to establish a single line (as indeed did the co-option of UK regional and local government Brussels offices into a 'Team UK' common line in Brussels even under a Conservative government in the early 1990s).[28] This emphasis on establishing and holding a common line may itself prompt, or support, moves over time to a more formalised process of EU policy coordination — though it is likely, looking at the pattern elsewhere, and notwithstanding the early warning system, that fuller formalisation will be about bringing governments, not legislatures, into more systematic interaction. This would remain an executive-driven process, with legislative authorities (still) stuck on the outside.

2. Partisan Conflict

Academics routinely argue that the absence of formalisation of intergovernmental relations leaves the UK's devolved system of government vulnerable to changes of government, which would inject party competition into a process smoothed hitherto by the absence of party competition.[29] The House of Lords, in an influential Select Committee report, agreed in its very first recommendation:

[27] S. Bulmer, C. Jeffery and W. Paterson, *Germany's European Diplomacy: Shaping the Regional Milieu* (Manchester: Manchester University Press, 2000), pp. 22–51.

[28] Cf. C. Jeffery, 'Regional Information Offices in Brussels and Multi-Level Governance in the EU: A UK-German Comparison', *Regional and Federal Studies*, 6 (2): 183–203, (1996b), here pp. 200–1.

[29] See on this point: R. Hazell, 'Conclusion: The Devolution Scorecard as the Devolved Assemblies Head to the Polls', in R. Hazell (ed.), *The State of the Nations 2003* (Exeter: Imprint Academic, 2003), p. 296; A. Trench, 'The More Things Change the More They Stay the Same. Intergovernmental Relations Four Years on', in A. Trench (ed.), *Has Devolution Made a Difference? The state of the nations 2004*, (Exeter: Imprint Academic, 2004), pp. 189–90.

> We recommend that further use should be made of the formal mechanisms for intergovernmental relations, even if they seem to many of those presently involved as excessive ... Such mechanisms are likely to become increasingly important when governments of different political persuasions have to deal with each other.[30]

Governments just as routinely dismiss and ignore such arguments, arguing that practices of coordination are robust enough to cope with partisan difference.[31] That is an ambitious assumption generally, but perhaps in EU matters in particular. When we envisage partisan change, the most likely scenario is one of a Conservative UK Government, with Labour-led administrations remaining in Scotland and Wales (in partisan terms Northern Ireland, with its own party system(s) is a special case). Governmental incongruence may bring different kinds of challenge to the operation of the devolved political system:

- It may make more difficult the operation of some of the convenient devices used so far for making devolution work, such as Sewel Motions under which the Scottish Parliament allows Westminster to legislate, normally to ensure uniformity of provisions, in fields of Scottish competence, or the practice of 'piggy-backing' Welsh clauses onto Westminster bills to empower the National Assembly to take action in a particular field. This would not necessarily be a matter of a UK Government obstructing devolved wishes; it is simply easier to make such conveniences work within the same ideological tradition.[32]
- A future Conservative UK Government may in addition inject a different perspective on the value of devolution into inter-governmental relations. The Conservative Party has generally been 'devosceptic', and though largely resigned to the current set of devolved arrangements, may seek a more robust articulation of the UK union — much indeed as did the Aznar governments in Spain. Such concerns, which may challenge the autonomy of the devolved administrations — for example by failing to consider and consult about the linkages and spillovers of UK Government policy for England to the devolved nations — may import tensions into intergovernmental relations.
- Finally, a future Conservative Government might well be avowedly Eurosceptic and at the very least would be unlikely to share what is now a

[30] House of Lords Select Committee on the Constitution, *Devolution: Inter-institutional Relations in the United Kingdom* (Session 2002–3, 2nd Report, HL 28) (London: The Stationery Office, 2002), p. 5.

[31] See, for example, the Government's response to the House of Lords Select Committee on the Constitution report, published as Cm 5780 (London: The Stationery Office, 2003) and available at www.dca.gov.uk/constitution/devolution/pubs/odpm_dev_609018.pdf.

[32] C. Jeffery, 'Richard's Radical Recipe', in J. Osmond (ed.), *Welsh Politics Comes of Age* (Cardiff: Institute of Welsh Affairs, 2004b), p. 27.

fairly well-embedded elite-level consensus in Scotland and Wales about the desirability of European integration.

These challenges could of course be mutually reinforcing, with ideological difference, a different perspective on the meaning of devolution, and a Eurosceptic-Europhile divide each laying on top of one another. That would be an especially difficult scenario for operating the kind of informal practice of coordination we have now. The Spanish experience showed that the absence of formal rights can be used to exclude regions from meaningful input into the member state's policy formulation. A devosceptic *and* Eurosceptic UK Government would be less inclined to share information with the devolved administrations, would be less likely to admit them into central government thinking in JMCs, Friday meetings or other formats, and would be deeply wary about the symbolism of devolved ministers speaking for the UK in the EU Council. Mutual trust, so central to current practice, would be extremely difficult to achieve.

Moreover, a restrictive approach such as this would match with a devosceptic agenda; by excluding devolved administrations from input to decision-making on their domestic fields of competence — such as agriculture, fisheries, or regional policy — a UK Government would effectively re-centralise aspects of those policies through its ability in the EU Council to shape them. The outcome, especially if matched by a devosceptic approach in domestic policy would be to promote territorial conflict in UK politics (which might of course have an electoral logic: the Conservatives do not win many seats in Scotland and Wales, so might well feel disinclined to accommodate devolved territorial interests from parts of the UK where the electoral returns are slight). One implication of such an outcome would be a convergence of perspectives of executive and legislative branches at the devolved level. Both would be 'outsiders', opening up possibilities for a shared sense of territorial interest and disadvantage to bridge government-opposition divides and for avowedly secessionist parties to establish a common platform with others traditionally committed to UK statehood. In those circumstances the appeal of the old Scottish nationalist slogan of 'independence in Europe' might gain wider currency. Significantly Paolo Dardanelli sees the nexus of independence and European integration as important in explaining the 'Yes'-majority in the 1997 devolution referendum in Scotland. Dardanelli's premise is that voting for devolution where there is a strong secessionist party like the SNP entails an element of risk that independence will be a (long-term) outcome. Unlike in 1979 — when the then EEC was regularly decried as a 'capitalist club' — pro-devolutionists in 1997 had less to fear about the risk of devolution inadvertently opening up a path to independence because the contemporary, more 'social' EU was held to provide a more congenial environment for the eventuality of Scottish independence.[33]

DEVOLUTION'S VULNERABILITY

Governmental incongruence need not of course have such an outcome. Levels of acceptance of devolution may deepen. Notions of 'Team UK' in EU matters may leave open some of the procedures for accommodating devolved concerns in UK EU policy that have been developing. Those procedures even if remaining largely informal may, as the UK Government hopes, be malleable enough to accommodate partisan difference:

> The Government continues to believe that devolution is far more likely to be a success if ministers and officials in all administrations see such informal contacts [as have developed] as second nature irrespective of the political persuasion of the administration involved.[34]

But again the Spanish experience of central-regional distrust warns against this reliance on informal practices. And the German experience argues for formalisation. For most of the last fifteen years there has been partisan conflict between central and regional levels in Germany. This may have prevented the emergence of a consensual system on EU matters such as those in Austria and Belgium, and may have led to the regions in some respects being held at arm's length (not least by being excluded from the German equivalent of the UK 'Friday' meetings). But there have been codified channels for accommodating the interests of Social Democratic regions under Christian Democratic central government and, since 1998, vice-versa, in forums which bear some resemblance to the JMC (Europe). Those channels are justiciable, should any of the participants feel the need. But there is little recourse to law, because there is a general acceptance — trust, in other words — that a German member state position should reflect the democratically articulated territorial interests of the German regions. It is not clear that any such general acceptance of combining state-wide and territorial interests exists in the UK outside of a situation of governmental congruence of Westminster with Holyrood and Cardiff Bay. It might develop with a fuller formal articulation of the purposes of intergovernmental coordination under Scenario 1 above. But the absence of clarity on the ground rules of managing state-wide vs. territorial interests remains devolution's great vulnerability. We will only know how just vulnerable when we encounter Scenario 2. Michael Keating's analysis of that scenario at the very least shows how high

---

[33] P. Dardanelli, *Between Two Unions: Europeanisation and Scottish devolution* (Manchester: Manchester University Press, 2005).

[34] www.dca.gov.uk/constitution/devolution/pubs/odpm_dev_609018.pdf, p. 3

the stakes could be: 'A sharp turn to Euroscepticism on the part of a British government could polarise the issue [European integration] on national lines and force Scottish political, economic and social elites to choose between the UK and Europe.'[35]

BIBLIOGRAPHY

Official Documents

House of Lords Select Committee on the Constitution, *Devolution: Inter-institutional Relations in the United Kingdom*, (Session 2002–3, 2nd Report, HL 28) (London: The Stationery Office, 2002).

The Government's Response to the 2nd Report of the Select Committee on the Constitution, Session 2002–3 (HL 28), *Devolution: Inter-Institutional Relations in the United Kingdom*, Cm 5780 (London: The Stationery Office, 2003).

Secondary Sources

Börzel, T., *States and Regions in the European Union* (Cambridge: Cambridge University Press, 2002).

Bullmann, U. (ed.), *Die Politik der dritten Ebene. Regionen im Europa der Union* (Baden-Baden: Nomos, 1994).

Bulmer, S. *et al.* (eds.), *British Devolution and European Policy-Making* (London: Palgrave, 2002).

Bulmer, S., C. Jeffery and W. Paterson, *Germany's European Diplomacy. Shaping the Regional Milieu* (Manchester: Manchester University Press, 2000).

Carter, C., 'The Formulation of UK EU Policy Post-Devolution: A Transformative Model of Governance?', *Manchester Papers in Politics, Devolution and European Union Policy Making Series*, 3, (2002).

Dardanelli, P., *Between Two Unions: Europeanisation and Scottish Devolution* (Manchester: Manchester University Press, 2005).

Hain, P., 'Europe and the Regions', paper submitted to the European Convention on behalf of the UK government and the devolved administrations in Scotland and Wales, (2003).

Hazell, R., 'Conclusion: The Devolution Scorecard as the Devolved Assemblies Head to the Polls', in Hazell, R. (ed.), *The State of the Nations 2003* (Exeter: Imprint Academic, 2003).

Hooghe, L., 'Subnational Mobilisation in the European Union', *West European Politics*, 18 (3): 175–98, (1995).

Jeffery, C., 'Conclusions: Sub-national Authorities and "European Domestic Policy"', *Regional and Federal Studies*, 6 (2): 204–219, (1996a).

[35] M. Keating, 'Independence in an Interdependent World', in J. Murkens (with P. Jones and M. Keating), *Scottish Independence: A practical guide* (Edinburgh: Edinburgh University Press, 2002), p.295.

Jeffery, C., 'Regional Information Offices in Brussels and Multi-Level Governance in the EU: A UK-German Comparison', *Regional and Federal Studies*, 6 (2): 183–203 (1996b).

Jeffery, C., 'Sub-national Mobilisation and European Integration: Does it Make any Difference?', *Journal of Common Market Studies*, 38 (1): 1–23, (2000).

Jeffery, C., 'Social and Regional Interests', in J. Peterson, M. Shackleton, *Institutions of the European Union* (Oxford: Oxford University Press, 2002).

Jeffery, C., 'Regions and the Constitution for Europe: German and British Impacts', *German Politics*, 13 (4): 605–24, (2004a).

Jeffery, C., 'Richard's Radical Recipe', in J. Osmond (ed.), *Welsh Politics Comes of Age* (Cardiff: Institute of Welsh Affairs, 2004b).

Jeffery, C. and R. Palmer, 'Stepping (Softly) onto the International Stage: The External Relations of Scotland and Wales', in R. Hrbek (ed.), *Aussenbeziehungen von Regionen in Europa und der Welt* (Baden-Baden: Nomos, 2003).

Jeffery, C. and R. Palmer, 'The European Union, Devolution and Power', in A. Trench (ed.), *Devolution and Power in the United Kingdom* (Manchester: Manchester University Press, forthcoming 2005).

Keating, M., 'Independence in an Interdependent World', in J. Murkens (with P. Jones and M. Keating), *Scottish Independence: A practical guide* (Edinburgh: Edinburgh University Press, 2002).

Kerremans, B. and J. Beyers, 'The Belgian Sub-national Entities in the European Union: Second or Third Level Players?', *Regional and Federal Studies*, 6 (2): 41–55, (1996).

Leonardy, U. (ed.), *Europäische Kompetenzabgrenzung als deutsches Verfassungspostulat* (Baden-Baden: Nomos, 2002).

Trench, A., 'The More Things Change the More They Stay the Same. Intergovernmental Relations Four Years on', in A. Trench (ed.), *Has Devolution Made a Difference: The state of the nations 2004* (Exeter: Imprint Academic, 2004).

Part III
Public Policy

10

Becoming European
Devolution, Europe and Health Policy-Making[1]

Scott L. Greer

Once there seemed to be a lot to the idea of a 'Europe of the Regions'. An intrinsically exciting concept attractive to a wide range of activists, scholars, and politicians, the idea arose in the early 1990s in response to developments in territorial and constitutional politics across and outwith the EU and still lives on in unexamined assumptions and of regional leaders and journalists. The Europe of the Regions was to be a Europe in which regional governments, closer to their populations, and the EU, more able to project power and reap economies of scale, would take greater political roles. States, too small for the big things and too big for the small things, would cede at least some of their powers to this combination.

The problem is that the Europe of the Regions has turned out to be something much milder and more qualified — multi-level governance, at best.[2] In this model, the EU level is one of several interpenetrated, interdependent levels of government that cannot act alone and that shape each other's environment and autonomy. In other words, students of multi-level governance in the EU arrived at the insight of students of comparative federalism that no system allows governments to do something on their own. It is almost impossible to find a real policy problem that can be solved by one tier of government alone. In other words, like federations, the EU cannot hope to be a 'layer cake' with cleanly divided levels of government. Practical policy-making requires that it be a 'marble cake' with heavily interdependent levels of government.[3]

[1] University of Michigan, Department of Health Management and Policy, School of Public Health, and the Constitution Unit, University College London. I would like to thank the Nuffield Trust for its support of the research underlying this chapter and Alan Trench for very useful and interesting comments that do not absolve me from any surviving mistakes.

[2] G. Marks, L. Hooghe, and K. Blank, 'European Integration from the 1980s: State-Centric v. Multi-level Governance', *Journal of Common Market Studies*, 34 (3): 341–78, (1996).

[3] S. L. Greer, 'The politics of policy divergence', in S. L. Greer (ed.) *Territory, Democracy, and Justice* (Basingstoke: Palgrave Macmillan, 2005 forthcoming); M. Grodzins, *The American System: A new view of government in the United States*, 2nd ed., (New Brunswick, New Jersey: Transaction, 1984[1966]); R. L. Watts, 'Origins of Cooperative and Competitive Federalism', in Greer (ed.), 2005 forthcoming.

This means that policy is now more complex. It does not mean, however, that the drivers of policy-making in a complex multi-level continent are ones that defend or promote regional autonomy. Instead, the development of multi-level governance has created some serious challenges to the stability of devolution and to the policy autonomy of the different UK health systems.

The challenges come from the interaction of two different political arenas. One is the internal arena — the manner in which the UK (or any other state) structures its territorial politics and intergovernmental relations. This is the classic locus of devolution debates — how much power should regional governments have, how should relations between different governments be structured, and what institutions will defend the balance of power and autonomy politicians desire?[4] The other arena is that of the EU, in which a shifting cast of characters including 25 member states, the Commission, the Parliament, and other EU institutions, all with their own internal divisions, jockey for influence and control amidst the world's second largest concentration of lobbyists. In both arenas, unexpected things happen. And, as this chapter discusses, their interaction can produce surprising influences and constraints on policy-makers that destabilise constitutional structures and established policies alike.

In the case of health, devolution in the UK has come at about the same time as a largely unexpected and, from the point of view of EU member states, unintended expansion of EU powers. Moreover, this has happened over an area of policy that is crucial for devolved governments because of its size and political prominence. That is substantial enough in conventional UK politics, but is greater still in devolved polities that have a narrower range of powers.

Within the UK, devolution at the turn of the century created four distinctive, devolved, and relatively unfettered health systems — what I call elsewhere a 'fragile divergence machine'.[5] But in the EU, there is increasing erosion of the autonomy of member states to maintain their own social policy models — including their delegation of powers over health or other services to their regional governments. Insofar as developments in EU politics change the allocation of competencies between the EU and member states, they also change the constitutional settlements between states and regions.The implications for health of divergence-enhancing devolution and convergence-creating Europeanisation are only now emerging, as the European Union — its court, its legislation, and its networks — start to remake the environment of health policy-makers around the 25 member states.

---

[4] In the standard terminology for such discussions, Northern Ireland, Scotland and Wales are all regional governments. This suggests no insult and involves no comment on their national identities.

[5] S. L. Greer, 'The Fragile Divergence Machine: Citizenship, policy divergence, and intergovernmental relations,' in A. Trench (ed.), *Devolution and Power in the United Kingdom* (Manchester: Manchester University Press, forthcoming).

The tension is powerful. On one side there is the UK devolution settlement, born in large part of the desire of Scottish and Welsh leaders to defend their welfare states, and which, like others in Europe, is supported by powerful forces on the ground. Their institutional and political differences press for divergent health policies. On the other side, there is the EU, which is seeing its institutions (particularly the European Court of Justice and latterly the Commission) becoming engaged in an effort to incorporate health services into the broader, and convergent, European internal market of which they are the guardians and to a good extent progenitors.The problem for the stability of devolution begins with the fact that health policy, along with education, is the policy area in which the devolved governments have their largest commitments, greatest budgets, and most visible responsibilities. If the development of EU legislation and jurisprudence reduces member state autonomy and promotes convergence, that is a direct blow to the ability of the devolved bodies to make distinct policies. But the framework of the European Union is not one in which the devolved bodies of the UK have an easy time influencing policy-making.[6] It is at bottom, despite many layers of complexity that regions exploit, an organisation of states and the best chance of success for a region in policy-making comes from the region's ability to get 'its' state to represent it.[7] And even that might not work if the member states are having trouble establishing control over policy; the development of the EU's health policy is largely a case study in the difficulty member states have in controlling the EU institutions that they created.[8] The result can be that EU law constrains regional autonomy, and insofar as there is a political response in the EU arena, the member state is almost always the leading actor.

Health is one of the last areas to be subjected to EU policy, and for most policy areas this chapter's warning is one or two decades too late. But it is also one of the biggest policy areas for most regional governments across Europe and, with the education sector, it dominates devolved policy-making. It also has the virtue of being a policy area in which member states tried hard to control (and limit) the role of the EU institutions, and is therefore a case study not just in the extent to which regional governments are weaker than member states, but also in the extent to which even the member states find it hard to keep the EU institutions they created on a leash. If the European Court of Justice starts to reshape health services, to the surprise of the member states, and even well-networked Whitehall finds it a challenge to respond, the devolved systems — politicians, officials,

---

[6] See C. Jeffery, 'Devolution and the European Union: Trajectories and Futures' in this volume for a full discussion.

[7] C. Jeffery, 'Continental Affairs: Bringing the EU Back In', Trench (ed.), forthcoming.

[8] S. L. Greer, 'Uninvited Europeanization: Neofunctionalism and EU health policy', *Journal of European Public Policy*, 13 (1), (2006).

managers and professionals — are even less likely to know in time, understand in time, and be able to act effectively, in time, or at all. In other words,
the future of devolved autonomy in a major policy area is in play right now,
and the game is that of EU politics. In it, Northern Ireland, Scotland and
Wales are operating under a disadvantage because they are not states and
therefore have no automatic, legal, right to influence the EU — no matter
whether it is one of the most important environmental factors in their health
policy-making. Instead, they must work through and with Whitehall in
Europe. Autonomy gives way to influence, and their fate lies in the hands of
the UK's intergovernmental relations.

The rest of this chapter makes the case. The first section discusses the
unintended development of EU health policy. It explains the very limited
role that the EU has in health services under the treaties, and then follows the
interventions of first the European Court of Justice and then the European
Commission in health services policy. The point is simple: due to particular
characteristics of the EU policy arena, it has been possible for an EU role in
the formally defended area of health services to develop. The second section
discusses the consequence for devolution of this interesting development in
EU politics. It analyses both the stakes for devolved autonomy and the structures put in place to try and cope with this intervention by the EU in what has
heretofore been an internal question of division of powers.

HEALTH SERVICES AND THE DECAY OF DEVOLVED AUTONOMY

The story of EU health policy so far has been a dispiriting one not just for
advocates of regional autonomy, but even for advocates of an EU run by the
member states. Despite member states' clear decision to keep the EU out of
their health services, expressed above all in their repeated decisions not to
create an EU health competency, the machinery of integration on the EU
level has created a strong EU health services policy.[9] Public health, an area
in which member states are better disposed towards European integration,
also sees the EU institutions taking an increasingly visible role.

The Status Quo Ante

If we look at the formal bases of both devolution and the EU, the distribution
of health competencies is simple to understand.

The UK's internal allocation of powers over health services, then, looks to
be defended externally by the recognition in the EU treaties, backed up by
some statements of member states, that health services are a power for

---

[9] Tamara K Hervey, 'Mapping the Contours of European Union Health Law and Policy,' *European
Public Law*, 8 (1): 69–105, (2002). This article is also the most accessible history of the legal issues
involved.

member states and not the EU. Internally, it is the devolution legislation and the informal practices surrounding it that should sustain the division of powers within the UK.

The defence of health services against the EU is that health services are not identified anywhere in the EU treaties or constitution as an EU competency. At least in theory, this is enough to keep the EU out, and it has done so for most of the history of European integration. In addition, though, when member states have had an opportunity to pass legislation on health services, as in discussions of patient mobility, they have made it clear that they want to maximise their autonomy and minimise the EU role.[10]

There is presently a coordinating, complementary, and therefore limited EU power in public health (art. 152) with its origins in the BSE ('mad cow') scare, as well as a new European centre for infectious disease control in Stockholm, modelled on the American Centers for Disease Control. The Treaty establishing a European Constitution, in one of its few extensions of EU competencies, proposes that the EU have a blanket power for the 'protection and improvement of human health' (II–16–2). The EU's remit in public health is thereby clarified — and qualified, for it is only authorisation for 'supporting, coordinating, or complementary action'. The Constitution also, for the first time in EU treaty law, discusses the member states' view of the EU role in health services: 'Union action shall respect the responsibilities of the Member States for the definition of their health policy and for the organisation and delivery of health services and medical care' (III–278–7). Regardless of whether the Constitution takes effect, that statement of preferences is pretty clear.

It is this collection of public health powers and disease-specific programmes that the EU Health Council would traditionally discuss; while the councils were held, they were far from the most important EU policy areas, or most important thing health ministers did.[11] Health departments in most countries remained largely uninterested in the EU — public health is generally not the centre of any health department's tasks, and the EU role in even that was patchy.

If the EU activities that were directly relevant to the delivery of health services and public health protection were once minimal, there was a relatively established EU role in the purchasing and regulation of medicines and medical devices, dating back to the Thalidomide scandal and the consequent adoption of a 1965 directive that required all proprietary medicines to have

[10] V. G. Hatzopoulos, 'Do the Rules on Internal Market Affect National Health Care Systems?', in M. McKee *et al.*(eds.), *The Impact of EU Law on Health Care Systems* (Brussels: Peter Lang, 2002), 123–60; Y. Jorens, 'The Right to Health Care across Borders', in McKee *et al.*, 2002, 83–122.

[11] See the suggestive evidence in N. Fligstein and J. McNichol, 'The Institutional Terrain of the European Union', in W. Sandholtz and A. Stone Sweet (eds.), *European Integration and Supranational Governance* (Oxford: Oxford University Press, 1998), 59–91.

marketing authorisation in at least one member state in order to be sold anywhere in the EU.[12] Later legislation extended it to include all medicine, including generics.[13] The European Medicines Evaluation Agency is a consequence of this market-integrating logic; it has responsibilities for evaluating the safety of 'new' substances for which medicinal claims are made, and also offers pharmaceutical companies a way to reduce their contact with the many different member state regulators. The EU also has an intense interest in pharmaceuticals and medical devices in its international trade policy, reflecting the size and importance of the EU chemicals, pharmaceuticals, and medical devices industries.

Signally, these issues of drugs and devices were handled primarily as internal market or trade matters rather than health policy. The policy area of medicine and medical devices regulation is like public health — relatively disconnected from the core of health services policy as UK policy-makers define it, and also European for a longer time as a result of both legislation and some important ECJ decisions over time. The shock of Europeanisation in health has been the sudden, lawyer-led entry of the EU into service design — the core of devolved health policy and the preoccupation of ministers.

Health services (treatment — doctors, nurses, hospitals and the rest) are in the UK almost wholly devolved, as in the case of Scotland, or offer a great deal of autonomy, as in the cases of Northern Ireland and Wales. Indeed, the UK's intergovernmental relations and finance make Scotland one of the least constrained regions in the rich world. The intricate relationship between block finance and a basically nonexistent framework for social rights creates great latitude for political divergence in the UK.

The Impact of the EU on Health Systems: The European Court of Justice

The member states, therefore, have insulated their health services from the European Union through the simple, and on paper very effective, device of giving it no powers over health services and only limited, complementary and coordinating ones over areas of public health. If the member states then have internal constitutional arrangements that give regions autonomous health services roles, that is not an EU matter.

---

[12] Council Directive 65/65/EEC of 26 January 1965 on the approximation of provisions laid down by law, regulation or administrative action relating to proprietary medicinal products (OJ 022 , 09/02/1965, p. 369, English special edition: Series I Chapter 1965–1966, p. 24); L. Hancher, 'The Pharmaceuticals Market: Competition and Free Movement Actively Seeking Compromises' in McKee *et al.* (eds.), 2002, 235–77; E. Randall, *The European Union and Health Policy* (Basingstoke: Palgrave, 2001); and R. Goldberg and J. Lonbay (eds.), *Pharmaceutical Medicine, Biotechnology and European Law* (Cambridge: Cambridge University Press, 2001).

[13] As part of the single market programme. Directive 89/341/EEC (OJ C 142, 25/03/1989, p. 11). My thanks to Alan Trench for explaining the pharmaceuticals issues to me.

The problem is that health systems cannot truly be isolated from the internal single market that is the core of the EU's powers, policies and achievements. Everything that goes into a clinic or hospital got there via the internal market: the staff by a labour market increasingly regulated at the EU level; the patients via their rights to mobility created at the EU level; and the equipment via product markets often regulated by the EU. If the EU has a competency over the staff, patients, and objects, it as good as has a competency over health services.

It is in its powers over staff and patients that we have seen the most significant, unexpected, and, for devolution, worrisome recent changes. These changes, led by the European Court of Justice (ECJ or 'the Court'), ultimately come from the 'constitutional' principles of the EU, namely the free movement of goods, services, capital, and people. They also draw on the mass of EU legislation required to achieve the 1992 single market and legislation since then, which is increasingly likely to have some identifiable connection with health services.[14]

In the case of health, as in other fields as well, it has been the ECJ that has led the way.[15] Broadly, its technique is to use various internal market provisions to eliminate what it sees as policies that discriminate in favour of a state's own providers or patients. The more firmly a system is based on markets, the more likely it is that the Court will someday rule that it cannot discriminate against providers from elsewhere in the EU. The English NHS is particularly vulnerable to such decisions because the UK Government is determined to smudge the line between public and private. It does this most notably by trying to constitute acute trusts as purportedly autonomous 'foundation hospitals' and by steadily increasing the role of contracted 'treatment centres', specialised clinics often run by the private sector.[16] This is accompanied by much rhetoric about the virtues of private provision and competitive markets. The Department of Health, responsible for developing and implementing these policies, is at the same time attempting to argue that there is nothing about them that will make healthcare in the English NHS appear to the ECJ to be a competitive tradeable service. Not everybody is convinced of the sustainability of this combination. The UK Government is running the risk that the ECJ will take it at its word about the purpose of NHS reforms and force it to truly open the NHS to competitive provision under

---

[14] M. Wismar and R. Busse, 'Analysis of SEM Legislation and Jurisdiction', in R. Busse *et al.* (eds.), *The European Union and Health Services: The impact of the Single European Market on member states* (Amsterdam: IOS/ European Health Management Association, 2002), 41–8, here pp. 42–3.

[15] T. K. Hervey, 'The Legal Basis of European Community Public Health Policy', in McKee *et al.* (eds.), 2002, 23–56.

[16] S. Stevens, 'Reform Strategies for the English NHS', *Health Affairs*, 23 (3): 37–44, written by Blair's former personal advisor on health, is the most coherent statement of Labour's emergent strategies for the English NHS.

internal market rules — that is, make it a real market rather than the sandbox it is.

Nickless refers to this jurisprudence of nondiscrimination as 'translation into "Euro-speak"'.[17] It essentially means deleting "Scotland" or "French" and replacing them with "the EU" or "European". It means eliminating policies based on territory or citizenship within the EU and replacing them with policies whose reference group is EU citizens who happen to be in a given state. It also incorporates value judgements as to what sort of health service is and is not justifiable when it makes decisions about what ends could justify policies that discriminate or otherwise do not fit well with a single market perspective. Unfortunately, some of the value judgements of European lawyers appear to run contrary to basic mechanisms that underpin all the NHS systems.

In terms of *labour*, the main driver of European health policy has been the interaction between EU legislation on working time (the Working Time Directive, WTD) and the Court. The WTD is part of the 'European social model' if anything is. Part of the Social Chapter of the Maastricht Treaty, it sets EU-wide ceilings on the number of hours an employee may work. The initial directive[18] was filled with exemptions but subsequent legislation brought various kinds of employees in, including junior doctors. Starting with a 58–hour per week limit as of 1 August 2004, junior doctors' hours will drop to 48 per week in 2009.[19] Preparation might have been patchy, but at least member states understood that they had legislated that much. The problems arise because the ECJ developed interpretations of the WTD that few had expected. The two major cases are *Sindicato de Médicos de Asistencia Pública (SiMAP)*, decided in 2000, and *Jaeger*, decided two years later.[20] *SiMAP* established that time spent asleep while on call amounts to work for purposes of the WTD. *Jaeger* decided that the WTD's provision for immediate compensatory rest after a shift therefore applied to the shift before or after the shift spent on call.

The WTD, interpreted this way, caused serious problems around the EU when the delayed phase-in started. *SiMAP* and *Jaeger* meant that the real reduction in hours was much greater and sharper than member states expected. The problem is that regulation premised on shift work is not compatible with many traditional forms of medical rota. While staffing is extremely complex and difficult to summarise, a common pattern is that

---

[17] J. Nickless, 'The Internal Market and the Social Nature of Health Care', in McKee *et al.* (eds.), 2002, 57–82.

[18] Council Directive 93/104/EC of 23 November 1993. OJ L 307, 13/12/1993, pp. 18–24.

[19] Directive 2000/34/EC of the European Parliament and of the Council of 22 June 2000 (OJ L 195, 01/08/2000, pp. 41–5).

[20] C–303/98 *Sindicato de Médicos de Asistencia Pública (Simap) v Conselleria de Sanidad y Consumo de la Generalidad Valenciana.* [2000] ECR I–07963. Case C–151/02 *Landeshauptstadt Kiel v Norbert Jaeger.* [2003] ECR I–08389.

junior doctors and trainees would be held on call, often on hospital premises, for long periods of time during which little or no work might be required of them. Thus, for example, a junior doctor might work one shift doing scheduled procedures and appointments and then have another shift on-call, staying (and perhaps sleeping) in the hospital in case an emergency procedure was required. The effect of *SiMAP* and *Jaeger* was to make this structure impossible. In the run-up to the first implementation, different member states produced eye-popping analyses of the costs that the WTD, after the two decisions, would cause them to incur. The Netherlands estimated that it would have to spend around 100 million Euros on extra staff, Germany that it would require a fifth more doctors (at a cost of 1.75 billion Euros) and the UK that compliance would cost it the equivalent of 3700 junior doctors' labour.[21] At the time of writing, enforcement is lax (permitting all sorts of scarcely veiled noncompliance) while member states consider a package deal to reform the WTD that would undo the effects of the two decisions while tightening other, unrelated, parts of the WTD.

Professional mobility, compared to labour market policy, is an area in which member states have been supportive of a significant EU role. The basic logic of freedom of movement, combined with some individual member states' interests in poaching professionals from other jurisdictions, points to the abolition of as many restrictions as possible on the rights of professionals to practice and even establish themselves anywhere in the EU.[22] Starting with directives on mutual recognition of professional qualifications in 1975, and leading to a consolidating directive in 1993, EU legislation had promoted the development of an EU-wide labour market for most professions.[23] The problem with mutual recognition, and the reason that it has proved a very slow process, is that even good training programmes can adopt significantly different approaches and emphases across the continent and can train doctors in different specialties. Meanwhile, there are widespread suspicions that some systems (in the north) exercise tighter quality control than others (in the south). The Court has pushed mutual recognition of professional qualifications further and faster than most state authorities, given their suspicions about each other, would probably like. Applying a general jurisprudence of nondiscrimination to qualifications regimes (that,

[21] T. Sheldon, 'Pressure mounts over European Working Time Directive', *British Medical Journal*, 328: 911, (2004).

[22] Given the prominence of English and the comparatively low number of professionals and trainees in the UK, the UK has become a major beneficiary of crossborder movement — and not just from the EU, either.

[23] Reference to the consolidating directive, which is current law: Directive 93/16/EEC, (OJ L 165, 07/07/1993, p. 1–24). On the development of an EU-wide labour market for professions, see: E. Jakubowski and R. Hess, 'The Market for Physicians', in M. McKee *et al.* (eds.), *Health Policy and European Union Enlargement* (Maidenhead: Open University Press, 2004), 130–42. The exception is pharmacy.

for example, has been hard on efforts to require licensing for hairdressers), it tends to assume that a doctor is a doctor and a nurse is a nurse. For the Court, any EU member state's education, once it conforms to certain minimum standards, is good enough, as is any EU member state's licensing system.[24]

Patient mobility is, along with the WTD, the biggest creator of new challenges for health policy-makers. The patient mobility issue was created by two unexpected ECJ decisions, both dealing with challenges to Luxembourg reimbursement policy. In both cases a Luxembourger used a service outside the country and then requested reimbursement from a Luxembourg health insurance scheme, had the request denied, and sued.[25] The Court ruled in both cases that Luxembourg was not justified in denying the request. The basis of both decisions was that Luxembourg was wrong to limit its health contracting to services within its borders. It could indeed regulate the services it would provide, and the providers, but that regulation could not discriminate against providers in other EU member states.[26] Filling in the gaps in law and in policy will take time, but the principle is established: EU member states cannot limit their list of health providers to those in their territory. This principle automatically destabilises some policies (such as quality assurance based on territorial regulators) and threatens others (such as the durability of member states' decisions to cover some services and not others — the case *Geraets-Smits and Peerbooms* suggested that a 'European' rather than merely Dutch justification would be required if the Netherlands were not to pay for a treatment that Austria covers).[27] For irritated policy-makers one of the biggest problems with the Court's activities in the field of patient mobility is that its decisions are based not on interpretation of legislation but rather on direct readings of the EU treaties. Amending interpretations of legislation — as in the case of the WTD — requires only more legislation. Legislation, however, is often inadequate to undo ECJ interpretations of Treaty law.

The specific problem for the UK — and above all for Northern Ireland and Wales — is that the Court's jurisprudence runs against acceptance of waiting lists. To quote a UK Department of Health official in a July 2004 interview:

[24] J. Nickless, 'A Guarantee of Similar Standards of Medical Treatment Across the EU: Were the European Court of Justice Decisions in Kohll and Decker Right?' , *Eurohealth*, 7 (1): 16–18, (2001); Nickless, 2002.

[25] Case C–158/96. *Raymond Kohll v Union des caisses de maladie*. [1998] ECR I–01931. 28 April 1998. And Case C–120/95 *Nicolas Decker v Caisse de maladie des employés privés*. [1998] ECR I–01831. Note that these decisions are *not* about EU citizens' rights to travel and receive services; that was established by Cases C–262/82 and 26/83 *Luisi and Carbone v. Ministerio del Tesoro* [1984] ECR 377 in which the court ruled that 'it follows that the freedom to provide services includes the freedom, for the recipients of services, to go to another Member State in order to receive a service there', whether as tourists or business travellers.

[26] Nickless, 2001.

[27] Case C–157/99 *B.S.M. Geraets-Smits v Stichting Ziekenfonds VGZ and H.T.M. Peerbooms. v Stichting CZ Groep Zorgverzekeringen*. [2001] I–5473.

'The real significance of the Court's thinking is that it has no problem with people paying more or a national government restricting services. What they do have a problem with is people waiting longer than they as lawyers think people should wait.' At the time of writing, there is a case (the *Watts* case) referred from the UK courts to the ECJ which should settle, with possibly momentous effects, the issue of what constitutes the 'undue delay' after which patients may seek treatment elsewhere on their home system's tab.[28]

This is, conceptually, a major problem for NHS systems. The NHS, in order to be free and universal at the point of use (i.e. an egalitarian, highly redistributive sector in an increasingly unequal society), rations scarce health resources by controlling supply rather than by price or limitations on the medical care people can have for free. It establishes a universal citizenship right to get any and all appropriate treatment, eventually. That is why those who share the values of the NHS are right to be very suspicious of a Court that appears to dislike waiting but has no visible problem with sharply limited lists of public services or with patient payments. If this and other cases produce a jurisprudence in which it is incumbent on health systems to get patients treated within a short time, or to pay for a patient's trip and treatment elsewhere, the effects will vary with devolution. Northern Ireland, Scotland, and Wales all currently have longer waiting times than England. Scotland might be able to focus its energies enough to get its waiting lists down to European lawyers' standards if it sacrificed a lot of other policies, but Northern Ireland and Wales could find themselves in a very difficult situation.

It is possible to argue that they *should* get their waiting times down, and that is the position of several of the ministers in Whitehall who are supposed to fight the devolved corner in the EU, but that misses the point. Waiting times are a question of priorities in spending, political energy and organisation. There are many good ways to justify health policies that focus on something other than waiting times for cataract surgery. All three devolved systems, Northern Ireland largely by default, are pursuing values other than, or in addition to, short waiting times. Wales is particularly explicit about doing so. Their autonomy to do so — which amounts to their autonomy in priority-setting — could be badly damaged by the ECJ over the next couple of years. A Welsh official explained the difference between principle and pragmatism — and the challenge for devolution — in a 3 March 2005 interview:

> We need to raise issues with the DH [UK Department of Health] when there is Welsh sensitivity. Take the *Watts* case. The DH was pragmatic, since they are getting waiting times down. We alerted them to the fact that there is a principle in

[28] *The Secretary of State for Health v R (on the application of Yvonne Watts)*, 20 February 2004, LTL 23/2/04; [2004] EWCA Civ 166.

there for Wales...that it is not another part of a waiting list policy but a principle for the Welsh Assembly Government.

The Impact of the EU on Health Systems: The Commission

The analysis so far has focussed on the activities of the Court in expanding the provisions of both single market legislation and Treaty law to include health services. The Court certainly led the way in developing a EU health role, but other actors in the complex ecosystem of the EU have followed. The most important of these is the European Commission. The European Commission is a unique organisation in comparative politics: it is the EU's executive, responsible for implementation, and it is the only EU organisation with the right to initiate or change legislation. It is made up of a number of highly competitive Directorates-General (DGs) that resemble the 'ministries' of an ordinary government. Each is headed by a Commissioner, who is appointed and participates in the College of Commissioners, the Commission's collectively responsible executive. The Commission is, in Cram's words, a 'purposeful opportunist'.[29] In seeking to expand its influence and power, it expands the reach of the EU, whether through legislation, court cases, or funding that creates useful clienteles in areas such as research and public health.It is also highly fragmented. On paper, the Commission is a corporate body with collective decisions. In practice, DGs mark out turf in both policy terms and in terms of what they regard as 'their' base in the Treaties. Both DGs and their Commissioners resist any efforts by other DGs to use 'their' treaty bases. Overall status and political power within the Commission comes from a mixture of these powers, the strength of the treaty base, luck with courts, and less tangible factors such as established credibility, age, skill and manoeuver in internal Commission politics, and the strength or weakness of the Commissioner. Beyond the intra-Commission politics, much of what each DG does is devise and offer member states tools that they calculate will appeal to enough important constituencies in enough states to get adopted 'their' policy rather than that of some other DG, or perhaps no policy at all.

There are three DGs at work in health, each with its own scheme to integrate health into the EU system. The first, and to outsiders perhaps most obvious, is DG Health and Consumer Protection (aka 'Sanco'). This DG is weak in health policy precisely because it presides over the components of health policy present in the treaties, namely public health protection. This means that its opportunism is in most cases purposefully directed away from health services towards issues such as tobacco control or obesity — issues in which it can hope to use the EU's great powers over markets. It also

---

[29] L. Cram, 'Calling the tune without paying the piper? Social policy regulation: The role of the Commission in European Community Social Policy', *Policy and Politics*, 21 (2): 135–46, (1993).

organised the member states' first responses to the developing EU health policy, which were prompted by *Kohll* and *Decker* and an influential EU-funded study of the impact of the single market on health.[30] This was initially a High Level Reflection on patient mobility (which, in a sign of success, had not just high-ranking health ministers but also three commissioners present at its meetings). The outcome of the High Level Reflection, in true EU fashion, was a High Level Working Group. In this permanently-constituted group, representatives of member states try to establish firm policies on patient mobility and reimbursement, including the conditions under which patients may travel, the tariffs they will pay, the forms they must fill out, and issues such as who pays for travel. Serviced by a weak and largely Luxembourg-based DG that has no legal tools in heath services, the High Level Working Group is the most intergovernmental health services policy instrument. It was only barely started as an organisation, let alone a policy, in March 2005.

The second DG to get involved is DG Employment and Social Affairs. It has defined a right to health as part of the 'European Social Model' that it sees itself as defining and defending, and it has an advantage over DG Sanco in that it also has a useful tool with which to make policy. That tool is the Open Method of Coordination (OMC), a recent form of 'soft law' in the EU in which a committee of member state representatives organises benchmarking, peer review and comparison in a given policy area.[31] The great virtue of the OMC is that it is comparatively judge-proof; it is also a particular, relatively intergovernmentalist, balance between intergovernmentalism and a coordinating EU role. And it was also only beginning to meet and develop an agenda in March 2005.

Finally, there is a very different and much more powerful policy tool that may be wielded by a third DG. DG Internal Market (aka DG Markt) is one of the most powerful DGs due to a combination of age, strong commissioners, and a starring role in the Single Europe Act that made the EU much more of a common market and which bequeathed to Markt a large number of legal instruments grounded in the hard law of European economic integration. DG Markt has recently proposed a Services Directive, which would cover much of the EU economy, applying to services most of the principles of non-discrimination and harmonisation that already cover trade in goods. In health, this means that it would impose at a stroke the internal market

---

[30] Busse *et al.* (eds.), 2002.

[31] S.Borras and K. Jacobsson, 'The open method of coordination and new governance patterns in the EU', *Journal of European Public Policy*, 11 (2): 185–204, (2004); E. Szyszczak 'Social Policy in the Post-Nice Era' in A. Arnull and D. Wincott (eds.), *Accountability and Legitimacy in the European Union* (Oxford: Oxford University Press 2002), 329–44.

framework that the ECJ has only slowly been able to develop. This last option, most worrisome for the NHS systems, was ascendant at the start of 2005. Part of the reason is the political agenda of the new Commission, which focuses on the 'Lisbon Agenda' of competitiveness and economic growth. The President of the Commission, José Manuel Barroso, put it this way in February 2005:

> Let me say this. It is as if I have three children: the economy, our social agenda, and the environment. Like any modern father, if one of my children is sick, I am ready to drop everything and focus on him until he is back to health. That is normal and responsible. But that does not mean I love the others any less![32]

Given that the EU's powers are strongest in areas of internal market legislation and competition, advancing the Lisbon strategy is likely to mean a renewed focus on the internal market and the elimination of barriers to competition within Europe in a sort of revival of the spirit of the 1992 drive to complete the internal market. That means, in particular, that the much-attacked Services Directive is a Commission priority. Passed by the College of Commissioners in late 2004, it was hit by an avalanche of criticism of its provisions for health and got into trouble with powerful states such as France and Germany[33]. The combination of its importance to the Commission and its political troubles mean that (as of the time of writing in April 2005) health is very likely to be dropped. If the Services Directive does pass with much of a health component, the High Level Working Group and the OMC are both likely to become irrelevant until the Commission's focus on extending the internal market begins to diffuse again. If health services largely escape the Services Directive, neither the internal market nor the ECJ nor DG Markt will go away but the playing field between the three approaches and their DG advocates will be more level.

What is the representation of regions in each case? Formally, there is none. The High Level Working Group is a forum of state representatives. The Department of Health in Whitehall sends the representatives. The OMC Committee likewise is made up of member-state civil servants, with the UK representative again coming from the Department of Health. The Services Directive would slip loose of even member state control, leaving enforcement and development in the hands of DG Markt. Given the light weight of regional governments in Brussels, it is likely that Northern Ireland, Scotland and Wales would be better placed to influence the UK representative on the High Level Working Group or the OMC process than the powerful DG

---

[32] 'Working together for growth and jobs: a new start for the Lisbon Strategy', Remarks to the Conference of Presidents, European Parliament, Brussels (2 February 2005).

[33] French electricians opposed to the directive cut off the electricity to the holiday home of ex-Commissioner Frits Bolkestein, the man who had proposed it. See T. Buck and I. Bickerton, 'Changes to services directive on the cards', *Financial Times* , 14 April 2005, p. 7.

Markt. But in all three cases the future looks bleak for regional representation — unless they get their member state to represent them.

WINNING FRIENDS AND LOSING INFLUENCE

The furore over the Services Directive and health, the OMC, and the High Level Working Group are all evidence of member states' willingness and capacity to contest and try to channel the EU health policies that the Court and latterly the Commission have been creating for them. But consider the problem discussed earlier with the case of Welsh waiting lists as an example of a problem inherent in the combination of English and UK Government. The UK Department of Health might be in European matters a 'federal' department responsible for the interests of the whole UK, but in practice it has a pronounced tendency to think of itself as the English NHS. This is hardly surprising — its main responsibility is a huge, politically-salient organisation in England. The result, though, is oversights at present and potential failures of representation in the future. Having prioritised, and partly solved, its English waiting times problems, the DH was more inclined to take a relaxed view of the *Watts* case than the Welsh Assembly Government, which had decided to use its democratic legitimacy to focus on issues other than waiting times. In other words, it took some Welsh lobbying to alert the DH to the fact that one of 'its' health services had both pragmatic and principled objections to what amount to EU limits on waiting times.

What can the Welsh — and Northern Irish, and Scots — do? Hooghe and Marks, inventors of the idea of 'multi-level governance', point to the loss of powers as leading to a regional counter-mobilisation through Brussels offices, transregional associations, demands for formal channels with the EU, campaigns to play a greater role in decision-making, and demands for information.[34] Regional governments that can supply useful and timely information to the Commission at the right stage of a policy debate, or that can influence the European Parliament at the right moment, can be effective lobbyists. But they are competing for influence in one of the world's most-lobbied cities, and many focus their political activities on securing EU grants rather than watching for developments that might shape their policy options in the future. How, then, do regions in the UK negotiate this fragmented environment in which they have no structural voice?

The UK 'Model'

So far, regions in the UK work with and through their member state. There are grounds for cooperation in even the most contentious systems of

[34] L. Hooghe and G. Marks, *Multi-level Governance and European Integration* (Lanham, MD: Rowman and Littlefield, 2001), pp. 77–8.

intergovernmental relations — the alternative can be a mess for which voters might blame somebody. Also in favour of regions is that there are bound to be more laws and practices defending regions against the central state than there will be in an EU arena. Finally, there are the powerful regional social coalitions that stand behind the creation and strength of the devolved governments; Scotland's Parliament and the National Assembly for Wales rest on powerful social supports. A regional government almost certainly has many more ways to bargain with its central state than it does ways to bargain with EU institutions — it is likely to be more at home in the 'internal' (member state) arena than in an EU arena in which it has almost no *necessary* representation.

The UK has something of a template for EU affairs in spending departments, one developed through trial and error in areas much longer and more thoroughly 'Europeanised' than health. In this template, the lead in coordinating UK policy is taken by desk officers in the Cabinet Office European Secretariat and UKREP (the UK permanent representation to the EU). The unit of the spending department charged with European affairs does not generally act as a clearing house for EU policy; it focuses on the less-tractable problems and acts loosely as a gatekeeper between the UK's overall policy coordinators and the various parts of the line department.

This is the case in health. The UK Department of Health's international unit is small and spends much of its time training functional parts of the UK Department of Health to identify and cope with EU issues; the goal is to 'Europeanise' the whole department rather than concentrate expertise in a special EU unit.[35] On technical issues surrounding patient mobility or the WTD, for example, the lead will normally be in the hands of the finance and personnel experts in the old NHS management cadre based in Leeds rather than in the Department. This requires a shift in the Department's culture and in the expectations of taxpayers — it is still difficult to explain why NHS managers should be going on what are often seen as 'jollies' to Belgium or other EU capitals. Small but growing networks in the NHS of Greater London, the West Midlands and the North-West also feed information between Brussels, the Department, and NHS director-level managers. Their virtue is that they can give the Department the kind of detailed responses to policy ideas that will reduce the likelihood of policy problems.

---

[35] The Department did something similar with devolution, setting up a Constitution Unit for a short period, during which it was expected to make the Department devolution-literate and handle the transition. See A. Trench, 'Whitehall and the Process of Legislation After Devolution', in R. Hazell and R. Rawlings (eds.), *Devolution, Law Making and the Constitution* (Exeter: Imprint Academic, 2005), 193–225, especially pp. 201–6 and 209–10 for this pattern of 'mainstreaming'.

Devolution in the UK Model

There is cause to worry about the devolved systems. They have all adopted, more or less thoughtfully, a model that concentrates EU expertise in a person in the department responsible for health, who has a liason relationship with the UK Department of Health and who channels information. In each case, this is a person who also has other responsibilities; in keeping with the size of the different civil services, these other responsibilities are heaviest in Northern Ireland and lightest in Scotland. This is backed up, at least in theory, by ministerial discussions between governments. The problem with this model of an individual official contact is that it is likely to limit diffusion of information about Europe within the central services of the devolved governments, let alone ability to participate in the formulation of EU policy.

Understanding the actual impact of policies on the health services is extremely complex and depends on good upward information flows. Right now, these are to a large extent confined to Greater London. The detail and depth of the information available from the large operation of the Greater London NHS threatens to make the Department's understanding of EU issues in the NHS pronouncedly London-centric. This already worries the Whitehall officials and bothers NHS managers from the rest of England; one can only wonder how much concrete, nuanced information about conditions in devolved health systems flows up to devolved capitals and then to London for further transmission to Brussels. Not much, we should probably assume.

There is an argument that the devolved systems should be making more of an effort to engage with Europe, particularly in the broadly favourable climate presently offered by the Labour government and the stable cadre in the Department of Health. Given, for example, that Scotland's remote and rural hospitals suffer a great deal from the effects of the WTD, it could well be possible that there should be much more information flow between the managers responsible for solving the staffing problems and the policy-makers who discuss such issues and possible legislative changes with London and Brussels.

In addition to their connections with the UK Department of Health, Northern Ireland, Scotland and Wales all have Brussels offices. These are all largely focussed on economics, including inward investment and EU funding, although Wales and Scotland in 2004 added desk officers primarily charged with health policy. Their role will be to observe policy and coordinate with the UK and with health decision-makers in Edinburgh and Cardiff. This diversification of information sources should make the devolved decision-makers better informed. It also offers some prospect of being able to lobby. In interviews, officials in Scotland and Wales explained that the Brussels office did the 'horizon-scanning' and lobbying while back at home a key official or groups would receive, screen, and either respond to or pass on information sent from the UK Department of Health. There was very little direct interaction between the European affairs divisions of the Scottish Executive and the Welsh Assembly Government and the officials responsible for EU affairs in their health departments. Instead, the devolved health departments' primary connections were with the Brussels offices and the DH, which they relied upon to send them the relevant information about policy and events in the EU. The amount of time this required was low for the Welsh officials compared to the Scots — as little as a few hours a week, according to the Welsh. This probably reflected the general view that the Welsh Assembly Government needed only to intervene when Wales had a meaningful divergence from UK issues.

The offices also point up a particular pathology of relationships with the EU: there is a strong tendency among regional and local governments to think primarily of the EU as a source of funds, and not to pay much attention to its policy role. It is not difficult to find events in which an official from Whitehall or the Commission has given a presentation about major EU policy issues, only to be questioned exclusively about ways to sneak into the last of the Structural Funds or other such sources of funding.[36] The EU's relative success in using granting programmes such as structural funds or research money to develop clienteles in society and the public sector does not, it seems, automatically and smoothly translate into the development of interest in EU policy among those client groups. Blindness to everything but bidding opportunities is distressingly common.

Can it Last?

For all that it is not yet running as well as in sectors that have been more European for longer, health is still identifiably being incorporated into the UK model of European relations. The problem with the UK model is that it is founded on what might be the great comparative advantage of the UK public administration: the unity and decisiveness of action that comes from centralisation and a unified civil service. The generalists of the home civil service, responding to a unified collective government, were able to develop the fast and generally well-coordinated system now in place. The problem is that while the extent of change in the devolved civil services is unknown, the extent of change in politics is large and growing. There are arguments that the unity of the home civil service might break down over time. More to the point is the argument that the Labour Party has so far helped damp down

---

[36] 'I wouldn't apply for money from us' opined a DG Sanco official in a February 2005 event; 'there's far too much bureaucracy.' This view had no impact on the remaining half hour of questions from public health officials, which focused on perceived opportunities to improve their chances of getting structural funds by applying with lead partners from the 'south-eastern' countries on account of an obscure underspend in one of the four regional offices through which the EU accepted structural funds bids.

conflict by giving UK, Scottish and Welsh politicians shared incentives — a common interest in preserving a unified face and in resolving disputes before they are noticed.

In practice there is presently something of a standoff between scholars of intergovernmental relations (some of them in this book) and contemporary UK policy-makers. Many of the scholars argue that such partisan or bureaucratic disputes are a *normal* feature of *all* regionalised polities and that it is therefore worrying that the UK has very few formal structures to cope with any conflict that cannot be contained by civil servants or Labour amity. Not a few practitioners will point out that devolution is hardly new, that students of intergovernmental relations have been saying this for years, that disputes remain rare, and that the informal networks of the civil service and officials still appear to do the job of preventing serious conflict. The test will come when an opposition party, not Labour, enters government somewhere in the UK. Would a Conservative UK Government want to defend in the OMC committee a Welsh Labour decision not to focus on waiting lists,or lobby DG Markt to preserve Scotland's decision to avoid creating an internal market in health? Government ministers might argue instead that the Conservative electoral mandate was hardly to fight in Brussels in defence of Labour policies that they had attacked during the election.

Northern Ireland, of course, has the worst problem. It has a distinct system but no politicians able (if willing) to stand up for its autonomy and approach. Its distinct system means that it cannot simply shelter under the UK Department of Health, because the interests of the English NHS, or of Scots and Welsh who successfully lobbied Whitehall, might not be those of the system in Northern Ireland. Its general inability to articulate health policies and priorities has two distinct explanations.[37] Under direct rule when devolution is suspended, its best representatives are the junior ministers charged with running (among other things) the health service. This situation is far from ideal. Northern Ireland Office junior ministers carry little weight with big Whitehall departments such as Health, let alone with the Department of Trade and Industry (which leads on the Services Directive), the Cabinet Office's European Secretariat, or FCO, and they have little career incentive to start conflicts in Whitehall over Northern Ireland issues. Under devolution, there are Northern Ireland politicians capable of standing up for themselves, and in some areas (mostly on matters relating to funding), Northern Ireland has shown skill at European politics. The problem is that Northern Ireland's political system tends not to focus political minds on policy development at all, let alone the kind of horizon-scanning and patient politicking required to influence EU policy via Whitehall. It did not help much that the

[37] S. L. Greer, *Territorial Politics and Health Policy* (Manchester: Manchester University Press, 2004), Chapter 6.

minister responsible for health under devolution was from Sinn Féin and was not particularly interested in 'East-West' (i.e. UK) politics, preferring to focus her extra-Northern Ireland efforts on 'North-South' politics (i.e. relations with the Republic of Ireland). This focus, perfectly tenable as ideology for a Republican, hardly equipped Northern Ireland to win the support of the central UK Government. So inability to represent itself well in Europe may be added to the long list of other charges against direct rule and the structure of Northern Irish politics in general.

If the charge against Northern Ireland is that it is missing its chance to be a firm friend of Whitehall, and firm with Whitehall, that also highlights the problem facing Scotland and Wales. Their most effective strategy depends on making friends in Whitehall. That friendship in turn depends on either a coincidence of interests or on somebody bending to meet the other. Relations have been friendly so far. But it could well be that friendship in politics is a poor substitute for power.

CONCLUSION

The complexity of politics — both the politics of the UK and the politics of the EU — is such that developments in either arena are difficult to predict. The challenge is much greater when it is a question of an unexpected development in one arena reshaping politics in the other. And that is the problem for health policy-makers in the UK and any other EU state. The unexpected development of an EU health policy has reduced their ability to shield the organisation of health services from EU law. Their internal constitutional arrangements, which are often justified precisely by the desire of different areas to diverge, are now open to the convergence-inducing effects of EU policies. And that leaves the regional governments badly exposed, since the EU arena is still state-centric and not an easy one for them.

This is a constitutional issue as well as a policy issue. The powers that the peoples of Northern Ireland, Scotland and Wales voted to have assigned to their devolved bodies are in danger of being vitiated by EU institutions and by the slow transfer of power over their health systems to an EU legislative arena dominated by states. Their most successful policy solution is to work with, and through, the member states. There are wide areas of shared interest, as well as cultural similarities and networks, with member states. If nothing else, few governments want to be in flagrant violation of EU law or suffer some form of policy breakdown because the member states agreed a policy that regions cannot implement. The result is that policy should, at best, be worked out cooperatively, that information should flow in both ways, and that regions and central states should work together for better policy for their people. This is on paper not hard, but practice is more difficult — late-night negotiations and rows are not that uncommon, and it is difficult to imagine a state jeopardising its position by leaving the table to go and telephone regional governments.[38] The UK model of EU policy, with its tight integration focussed on UKREP and the Cabinet Office European Secretariat, is probably at the moment one of the quickest and most flexible influencing devices around, even if there is room to question the adequacy of devolved investment in EU health policy. But if the future of devolved autonomy depends on their ability to get member states to represent them, then these bonds of friendship and constructive interdependence will be tremendously important for the future of devolved politics — and will be under tremendous strain.

BIBLIOGRAPHY

Official Documents

Barroso, J. M., 'Working together for growth and jobs: a new start for the Lisbon Strategy', Remarks to the Conference of Presidents, European Parliament, Brussels (2 February 2005).

Secondary Sources

Borras, S. and K. Jacobsson, 'The open method of coordination and new governance patterns in the EU', *Journal of European Public Policy*, 11 (2): 185–208 (2004).
Börzel, T., *States and Regions in the European Union: Institutional adaptation in Germany and Spain* (Cambridge: Cambridge University Press, 2002).
Buck, T. and I. Bickerton, 'Changes to services directive on the cards', *Financial Times*, 17 April 2005.
Busse, R., M. Wismar, and P. C. Berman (eds.), *The European Union and Health Services: The impact of the Single European Market on member states* (Amsterdam: IOS/ European Health Management Association, 2002).
Cram, L., 'Calling the tune without paying the piper? Social policy regulation: The role of the Commission in European Community Social Policy', *Policy and Politics*, 21 (2): 135–46 (1993).
Fligstein, N. and J. McNichol, 'The Institutional Terrain of the European Union', in W. Sandholtz and A. Stone Sweet (eds.), *European Integration and Supranational Governance* (Oxford: Oxford University Press, 1998), 59–91.
Goldberg, R., and J. Lonbay (eds.), *Pharmaceutical Medicine, Biotechnology and European Law* (Cambridge: Cambridge University Press, 2001).

---

[38] For the theory of its ease (and likelihood), T. Börzel, *States and Regions in the European Union: Institutional adaptation in Germany and Spain* (Cambridge: Cambridge University Press, 2002). For the real difficulties, see C. Jeffery in this volume and C. Jeffery in Trench (ed.), forthcoming 2005.

Greer, S. L., 'The Fragile Divergence Machine: Citizenship, policy divergence, and intergovernmental relations', in A. Trench (ed.), *Devolution and Power in the United Kingdom* (Manchester: Manchester University Press, forthcoming 2005).

Greer, S. L., 'The politics of policy divergence', in S. L. Greer (ed.), *Territory, Democracy, and Justice* (Basingstoke: Palgrave Macmillan, forthcoming).

Greer, S. L., *Territorial Politics and Health Policy* (Manchester: Manchester University Press, 2004).

Greer, S. L., 'Uninvited Europeanization: Neofunctionalism and EU health policy', *Journal of European Public Policy*, 13 (1) (2006).

Grodzins, M., *The American System: A new view of government in the United States*, 2nd ed. (New Brunswick, New Jersey: Transaction, 1984[1966]).

Hancher, L., 'The Pharmaceuticals Market: Competition and Free Movement Actively Seeking Compromises', in McKee *et al.*(eds.), *The Impact of EU Law on Health Care Systems* (Brussels: Peter Lang, 2002), 235–77.

Hatzopoulos, V. G., 'Do the Rules on Internal Market Affect National Health Care Systems?', in M. McKee *et al.*(eds.), *The Impact of EU Law on Health Care Systems* (Brussels: Peter Lang, 2002), 123–60.

Hervey, T. K., 'The Legal Basis of European Community Public Health Policy', in McKee *et al.*(eds.), *The Impact of EU Law on Health Care Systems* (Brussels: Peter Lang, 2002), 23–56.

Hervey, T. K., 'Mapping the Contours of European Union Health Law and Policy', *European Public Law*, 8 (1): 69 –105 (2002).

Hooghe, L., and G. Marks, *Multi-level Governance and European Integration* (Lanham, MD: Rowman and Littlefield, 2001).

Jakubowski, E. and R. Hess, 'The Market for Physicians', in M. McKee *et al.* (eds.), *Health Policy and European Union Enlargement* (Maidenhead: Open University Press, 2004), 130–42.

Jeffery, C., 'Continental Affairs: Bringing the EU Back In', in A. Trench (ed.), *Devolution and Power in the United Kingdom* (Manchester: Manchester University Press, forthcoming).

Jorens, Y. 'The Right to Health Care across Borders', in McKee *et al.*(eds.), *The Impact of EU Law on Health Care Systems* (Brussels: Peter Lang, 2002), 83–122.

Marks, G., L. Hooghe, and K. Blank, 'European Integration from the 1980s: State-Centric v. Multi-level Governance', *Journal of Common Market Studies*, 34 (3): 341–78 (1996).

Nickless, J., 'A Guarantee of Similar Standards of Medical Treatment Across the EU: Were the European Court of Justice Decisions in Kohll and Decker Right?', *Eurohealth*, 7 (1): 16–18 (2001).

Nickless, J., 'The Internal Market and the Social Nature of Health Care', in McKee *et al.*(eds.), *The Impact of EU Law on Health Care Systems* (Brussels: Peter Lang, 2002), 57–82.

Randall, E., *The European Union and Health Policy* (Basingstoke: Palgrave, 2001).

Sheldon, T., 'Pressure mounts over European Working Time Directive', *British Medical Journal*, 328 (2004).

Stevens, S., 'Reform Strategies for the English NHS', *Health Affairs*, 23 (3): 37–44 (2004).

Szyszczak, E., 'Social Policy in the Post-Nice Era', in A. Arnull and D. Wincott (eds.), *Accountability and Legitimacy in the European Union* (Oxford: Oxford University Press, 2002), 329–44.

Trench, A., 'Whitehall and the Process of Legislation After Devolution', in R. Hazell and R. Rawlings (eds.), *Devolution, Law Making and the Constitution* (Exeter: Imprint Academic, 2005), 193–225.

Watts, R. L., 'Origins of Cooperative and Competitive Federalism', in S. Greer (ed.), *Territory, Democracy and Justice* (Basingstoke: Palgrave Macmillan, forthcoming).

Wismar, M. and R. Busse, 'Analysis of SEM Legislation and Jurisdiction', in R. Busse *et al.* (eds.), *The European Union and Health Services: The impact of the Single European Market on member states* (Amsterdam: IOS/ European Health Management Association, 2002), 41–8.

11

Regional Economic Policies in a Devolved United Kingdom

John Adams and Peter Robinson

INTRODUCTION

It has been traditionally claimed, with much justification, that the United Kingdom is one of the most centralised of developed nations. London has been the seat of parliament and government, the City of London is one of the world's leading financial centres and the majority of UK media are based in London. The economic performance of the Greater South-East of England is superior to that of the other regions of the UK.

The creation of devolved institutions following the election of a Labour Government in 1997 represented a fundamental step away from this portrait of an over-centralised polity. However, the link between political devolution and economic growth is not uncontroversial. While the UK's constitution, at least until 1997, was significantly more centralised than those of comparable nations in Europe, regional economic disparities within the UK are not worse than in other EU countries, despite the fact that many European nation states have had strong 'regional' governments for many years. Nevertheless, the creation of devolved institutions transformed the institutional landscape of economic development within the UK.

In this chapter, we shall first (briefly) discuss divergence in economic development within the UK, before then exploring the link between devolution and economic growth; that is, whether the creation of devolved or regional institutions necessarily leads to the better performance of that economy. Third, we shall discuss the 'map' of political responsibility within the UK and the geographical reach of Whitehall departments. Finally, we turn to consider the developing quasi-federal role of the UK government in a nation with devolved polities.

DIVERGENCE WITHIN THE UK

There are numerous similarities to the economic development strategies pursued in the different territories of the United Kingdom. In recent years political pundits, media commentators and influential academics have developed a popular narrative on the causes of and trends in economic growth in the UK.

This narrative starts with an emphasis on the impact of 'globalisation' on the UK economy, and an emphasis that the success of the regional economy in a devolved nation or English region depends on becoming a dynamic, 'knowledge-based economy', producing high-quality 'niche' products and services. This narrative is reflected in the economic development strategies of the UK's nations and regions, despite the fact that many of the assertions supporting this narrative are not supported by the evidence and that some of the 'facts' are myths.[1]

Although GDP or GVA per head is an imperfect measure of economic prosperity, it probably remains the best measure of the economic performance of a nation or region.[2] At the most basic level, regional differences in GVA per capita will primarily be a function of regional variations in productivity and employment. Table 11.1 uses the most up-to-date figures that were available from official sources in the spring of 2005 to examine these three economic measures together. It should be noted that we have used as a measurement of productivity output per hour worked, rather than the Government's preferred index of output per person employed. The latter does not take into account any differences in working hours between different parts of the UK, and if one part of the nation decides to forego extra economic output to voluntarily work fewer hours this should not be a cause for concern.

The figures for GVA per head will come as little surprise to most people, detailing a broad North-South divide within the United Kingdom, with a 'winners' circle' in the Greater South-East of the United Kingdom. These regional disparities emerged during the Great Depression of the 1930s, and there has been remarkably little change since then. Only Scotland has broken free from this pattern; its income per head has improved since the 1970s so that it currently stands only just below the UK average. This improvement will be due in large part to the exploitation of North Sea oilfields and associated benefits to Scotland's financial and banking industries. Wales and Northern Ireland lag significantly. England is the richest nation in the United Kingdom, but it is also by far the largest and many of its regions are larger than the devolved territories. The North East of England is one of the poorest parts of the United Kingdom.

---

[1] See, for example, Welsh Assembly Government, *A Winning Wales* (Cardiff: National Assembly for Wales, 2002); Scottish Executive, *Framework for Economic Development in Scotland*, (Edinburgh: Scottish Executive, 2000).

[2] Gross Value Added (GVA) differs from Gross Domestic Product (GDP) in that GDP is measured at a market price, while GVA excludes taxes or subsidies on products. Information on taxes and subsidies is, however, not available at a regional level — making GVA the appropriate measure of regional prosperity.

The relative importance of differences in employment and productivity in explaining these differences in GDP per head differs from region to region. The low GVA per head in North East England is explained in large part by low levels of employment; its productivity levels are similar to many regions with higher GDP per head. On the other hand, the South West has above average levels of employment, but relatively poor productivity (and a low working age population share). Employment rates in Wales have risen significantly in recent years, and both employment rates and productivity levels are noticeably low in Northern Ireland. London's prosperity is due to its high levels of productivity, although it has a high working age population share. London has had a very disappointing employment record in recent years.

Table 11.1:
Levels of Regional Prosperity, Productivity and Employment (UK=100)[3]

	Productivity (GVA per hour worked 2003)	**Employment** (seasonally adjusted as a percentage of all people of working age – Spring 2003)	**Output** (GVA per head 2003, residence-based)
Wales	91.9	97.7	79.0
Northern Ireland	84.3	93.3	81.2
Scotland	98.1	99.9	96.4
England	101.1	100.4	102.2
North East	95.1	91.3	79.7
Yorkshire & the Humber	93.7	99.2	89.0
North West	94.4	98.1	89.8
East Midlands	96.9	101.9	90.8
West Midlands	94.6	99.1	91.0
South West	95.4	105.2	94.1
East	97.1	105.1	109.2
South East	106.5	106.2	115.2
London	115.4	94.1	131.3
UK	**100**	**100**	**100**

[3] Sources: www.statistics.gov.uk/pdfdir/prod0305.pdf ; National Statistics, *Regional Trends* (London: The Stationery Office, 2004).

It is worth stressing that much of the UK Government's initial focus on regional economic disparities seemed to stem from its concern to close the difference in productivity levels between the UK and comparable countries, in particular the USA, Germany and France. The Treasury has identified five key drivers of productivity growth: the level of business and public *investment*, the *skills* of the workforce, the role of *innovation* and *enterprise*, and the importance of *competition*.[4] In itself this is a relatively uncontroversial list at the national level, but it does have limitations as a way of thinking of differences in prosperity between the nations and regions of the UK. Treasury documents, such as the *Productivity 3* report, initially seemed to struggle to make this framework fit easily with an analysis of regional disparities as these five productivity drivers miss out some of the more important drivers at a local level, for example the efficiency with which labour and housing markets operate.[5]

This might be part of the explanation for a recent change in the thrust of UK Government policy. Whether one looks at the 'five year plans' of the Department for Work and Pensions (DWP) or the Office of the Deputy Prime Minister (ODPM), the emphasis is on the Government's long-term aspiration of increasing the employment rate in the UK to 80 per cent of all adults of working age, although a time-scale for achieving this aspiration is not specified.[6] This compares with about 73 per cent of working age adults in employment in 2004, which indicates the scale of ambition. In terms of dealing with regional economic disparities, ODPM now puts the focus squarely on tackling high levels of economic inactivity amongst key groups, but especially those inactive due to sickness and disability. Because levels of economic inactivity are highest in the disadvantaged regions, including Northern Ireland and Wales, this agenda has an in-built 'bias' in favour of these regions; they simply have more to make up in terms of reducing economic inactivity. This is perhaps one of the most important ways in which gaps in regional economic prosperity can be closed.

It is within this context that the devolution settlement operates. Central government retains many of the regulatory functions at a UK level, notably competition policy. Most of the powers which could affect aggregate demand are reserved to Whitehall and Westminster — for example taxation policies, the monetary policy framework and policies in relation to the exchange rate. Furthermore, numerous active labour market policies are

---

[4] HM Treasury, *Productivity in the UK: The evidence and the government's approach* (London: HM Treasury, 2000a).

[5] HM Treasury and Department for Trade and Industry, *Productivity in the UK: 3 — The regional dimension* (London: The Stationery Office, 2001).

[6] Department for Work and Pensions, *Five Year Strategy: Opportunity and security throughout life* Cm 6447 (London: The Stationery Office, 2005); Office of the Deputy Prime Minister, *Sustainable Communities: People, places and prosperity — a five year plan from the Office of the Deputy Prime Minister* Cm 6425 (London: The Stationery Office, 2005).

reserved, such as the Jobcentre Plus network, the various New Deal programmes and the various measures to improve work incentives such as the Working Families Tax Credit. The devolved institutions do have a number of responsibilities which could help stimulate labour demand; for example, they are responsible for financial assistance to industry and for spending EU Structural Funds. The devolved institutions certainly have responsibility for a number of policy instruments which impact upon the supply-side. To a greater or lesser degree they are responsible for policies in the fields of education, training and skills, business-university links, transport, business advice and support for new firms.

Having discussed the approach of the UK Government, in the remainder of this section we will briefly discuss some of the policy developments within the devolved territories.

Scotland

In Scotland, responsibility for economic development and post–16 education and training is currently situated within the Department of Enterprise, Transport and Lifelong Learning. Compared to other parts of the United Kingdom, this is a broad range of competences to vest in a single government department, and some commentators have argued that this provides the opportunity for policy integration and 'joined up' government. The department largely operates through two institutions which predate devolution: Scottish Enterprise and Highlands and Islands Enterprise. Since the late 1980s Scottish Enterprise had also been responsible for aspects of training, delivered through a network of Local Enterprise Companies.

Prior to devolution, Scottish Enterprise had established itself as an effective institution, and, with the Scottish Office, had begun to pursue a number of quite distinct agendas several years before they were to appear on the English agenda. Cluster policy, for example was developed in Scotland in the early 1990s, several years before it was enthusiastically embraced by the Department of Trade and Industry (DTI) following the 1998 White Paper *Our Competitive Future*.[7] Clusters are geographic concentrations of interconnected companies which hold out the possibility of increasing knowledge spillovers, such as the IT cluster in Silicon Valley in the USA. While this was fashionable in the regional development literature a few years ago, and is currently embraced by numerous policy-makers, it is worth noting that cluster policy also has its critics.[8] In the 1990s Scotland also promoted entrepreneurship, and in particular focussed on new form formation whereas the rest of the UK directed support towards established rather than new firms. At

[7] Department for Trade and Industry, *Our Competitive Future: Building the knowledge driven economy* (London: The Stationery Office, 1998).

[8] See, for example, J. Adams, P. Robinson and A. Vigor, *A New Regional Policy for the UK*, (London: IPPR, 2003).

the start of the new century, policy across the UK seems to be returning to promoting new firm start-ups.[9]

Policy divergence post-devolution has in many ways been less dramatic. The Scottish Executive's first policy document in this area, the *Framework for Economic Development in Scotland* (FEDS), reaffirmed much of the UK Government's policy framework.[10] For example, the limitations to public sector intervention in relation to the strength of market forces were explicitly acknowledged and the importance of supply-side issues, such as skills and technology, were stressed. Initiatives such as the Business Birthrate Strategy and the Scottish Science Strategy effectively continued divergent paths begun under the pre-devolution Scottish Office regime. Furthermore, Scotland appears not to have been particularly innovative in its use of the powers of industrial intervention, particularly Regional Selective Assistance.[11] On the other hand, social inclusion — also known as 'extending economic opportunities' — has perhaps a higher profile in Scottish economic development debates than it generally does in Whitehall.[12] And the 'Fresh Talent Initiative', which aims to attract newcomers to Scotland and encourage overseas students to stay in the country after graduation, seems to be based less on an analysis of migration or demographic trends than on a desire to create a more entrepreneurial and innovative culture by attracting what it is hoped will be 'creative individuals'.[13] While some themes of the 'Fresh Talent Initiative' will resonate with institutions across the UK, this is clearly a significant divergence from policy pursued in other parts of the United Kingdom.

Wales

Whereas FEDS focussed very much on productivity issues, in its economic development strategy — *A Winning Wales* — the Welsh Assembly Government (WAG) gave a much greater emphasis to increasing levels of employment and to reducing economic inactivity.[14] The issue of economic inactivity is of crucial importance to poorer regions, as a far larger number of people claim state benefits related to sickness or incapacity than claim Jobseeker's Allowance. However, it is not yet clear how actual policy instruments will be altered to reflect this divergent analysis and rhetorical commitment. As

---

[9] HM Treasury and Small Business Service *Enterprise Britain: A modern approach to meeting the enterprise challenge* (London: HM Treasury, 2002).

[10] Scottish Executive, 2000.

[11] A. Gillespie and P. Benneworth, 'Industrial and Regional Policy in a devolved United Kingdom', in J. Adams and P. Robinson (eds.), *Devolution in Practice* (London: IPPR, 2002).

[12] M. Keating, *The Government of Scotland: Public policy making after devolution* (Edinburgh: Edinburgh University Press, 2005).

[13] Scottish Executive, *New Scots — Attracting fresh talent to meet the challenge of growth* (Edinburgh: Scottish Executive, 2004).

[14] Welsh Assembly Government, *A Winning Wales* (Cardiff: Welsh Assembly Government, 2002).

already emphasised, the situation is complicated by the fact that what are probably the most important policy instruments are reserved matters, particularly the Jobcentre Plus network and the tax and benefit system. However, there will be a large number of local initiatives in this policy area, often run by local authorities and funded by EU Structural Funds. As discussed above, it does seem that some parts of Whitehall have come to the same conclusion as WAG in appreciating the importance of an emphasis on employment rates.

In *A Winning Wales,* the Welsh Assembly Government committed to a target of raising Welsh GDP per head from about 80 per cent of the UK average to 90 per cent of the UK average by 2012. This target has been widely criticised as being wildly over-optimistic, and indeed the standard of the analysis contained in *A Winning Wales* and associated documents is noticeably weaker than that in comparable documents in Scotland or Whitehall. This situation is perhaps unsurprising in light of Wales's traditionally weaker policy communities.[15]

While the Welsh Assembly Government does place a greater emphasis on levels of employment, it also brings forward a plethora of initiatives which aim to improve levels of productivity. Cluster policy, science parks, the knowledge economy *et al.* form much of the bedrock of economic development strategy in Wales.

However, the institutional structure of economic governance in Wales is diverging substantially from the rest of the United Kingdom. The Welsh Assembly Government has separate divisions for Economic Development and for Education and Lifelong Learning. A number of institutional reforms were set in motion by the Welsh Office in the period between the Labour victory at the 1997 UK general election and the creation of the National Assembly for Wales in 1999. Specifically, a number of economic development agencies — the Development Board for Rural Wales, the Land Authority for Wales and the existing Welsh Development Agency — were merged into a new-style Welsh Development Agency, and a new agency — Education and Learning Wales (ELWa) — was made responsible for all post–16 education and skills, with both organisations to operate through four coterminous sub-regions (as does the Assembly). However, in a controversial move the Welsh Assembly Government has announced that by April 2006 the WDA and ELWa will be merged with their sponsor department in the Welsh Assembly Government, reflecting the wish to increase political control of economic development.

[15] M. Keating., 'Devolution and Public Policy in the United Kingdom: divergence or convergence?' in J. Adams and P. Robinson (eds.), *Devolution in Practice* (London: IPPR, 2002).

Northern Ireland

In Northern Ireland, the two Departments with lead responsibility in the field of economic development are the Department for Enterprise, Trade and Investment and the Department for Employment and Learning. These structures were fixed in the Good Friday Agreement. There have been two significant post-devolution institutional changes to economic governance in Northern Ireland. First, a new economic development agency — Invest Northern Ireland — was created in April 2002 with the merger of three economic development agencies. Second, post–16 education and training has moved from a 'Next Steps Agency' into the Northern Ireland civil service.

One of the key economic problems facing the Northern Ireland Executive during its all-too-brief existence was the widely-acknowledged deficiency in infrastructure investment. In a significant change to the devolution settlement, the UK Chancellor of the Exchequer and the Prime Minister visited Belfast in May 2002 to announce that a 'prudential' system for capital spending would be introduced to allow the Northern Ireland Executive to undertake borrowing to spend on infrastructure. The fact that Northern Ireland does not have the same system of local government as the rest of the UK would undoubtedly have influenced this decision.

Conclusion

As this brief overview indicates, most divergence in economic development has been institutional, reforming the structures of the devolved administrations and the public bodies within their remit. However, such reforms are time-consuming and expensive and often divert staff attention from fulfilling their responsibility to deliver front-line services. Structural reform also takes time to bed down, so it is too early to judge the impact of this institutional reform on the performance of the public sector, and certainly too early to judge its impact on actual policy outcomes. Nevertheless, as time goes by we might expect such structural differences to begin to impact on the provision of front-line services.

While there have been significant differences in the way economic development policies have evolved since the creation of the devolved institutions, the roots of this policy divergence can often be traced back to initiatives that emerged over the last 20 years or so. That is, during a period of administrative devolution. This has led some to argue that the initial step of administrative devolution has been more significant than the political follow-up.[16] Interestingly, the policy divergence that developed in Scotland and Wales

---

[16] Gillespie and Benneworth, 2002.

during administrative devolution has proved to be influential for regional and industrial policy in the English regions.

DEVOLUTION AND ECONOMIC PERFORMANCE

Devolution should not been seen as simply a means to improving democracy or a straightforward constitutional reform — there was always an expectation that it would result in different public policy outcomes. For example, the Scottish Referendum Survey (a detailed survey of the Scottish electorate immediately following the devolution referendum) indicated that support for devolution was strongly related to people's expectations that it would improve the quality of their lives in terms of policy outcomes.[17] For many, devolution was a means, rather than an end in itself.

However, the link between devolution and economic performance has been one of the most hotly-debated topics in the field of territorial politics. Increased capacity at the regional level is one of the key principles upon which Labour's new regional economic policy has been built. Building regional institutions and enhancing the autonomy of those regional institutions is, it is claimed, what distinguishes current regional policy from its predecessors. In the words of Ed Balls, former Chief Economic Advisor to the Chancellor of the Exchequer:

> Our new regional policy is based on two principles — it aims to strengthen the essential building blocks of growth — innovation, skills, the development of enterprise — by exploiting the indigenous strengths in each region and city. And it is bottom-up not top-down, with national government enabling powerful regional and local initiatives to work by providing the necessary flexibility and resources.[18]

This commitment to bottom-up policies is informed by a fairly wide-spread academic consensus that regional institutional capacity matters to economic performance.[19] However, Scotland, Wales and Northern Ireland had strong institutions of administrative devolution for many years prior to the creation of the devolved institutions.

By contrast, the English regions lacked strong institutions and for some years the less prosperous regions of England had envied the advantage granted to the Celtic nations by this greater institutional capacity,

[17] P. Surridge and D. McCrone, 'The 1997 Scottish referendum vote', in B. Taylor and K. Thomson (eds.), *Scotland and Wales: Nations again?* (Cardiff: University of Wales Press, 1999).

[18] E. Balls, 'Britain's New Regional Policy: sustainable growth and full employment for Britain regions', in E. Balls and J. Healey (eds.) *Towards a New Regional Policy: Delivering growth and full employment* (London: The Smith Institute, 2000), pp. 12–13.

[19] A. Harding *et al.*, *Regional government in Britain: An economic solution?* (Bristol: The Policy Press, 1996); W. Russell Barter, *Regional Government in England: A preliminary review of literature and research findings* (London: Department of the Environment, Transport and the Regions, 2000).

particularly in the form of the development agencies launched 23 years before Regional Development Agencies (RDAs) in England. The creation of the RDAs and Regional Chambers following the Regional Development Agencies Act 1998 was a decentralising reform, which helped to improve the weak institutional capacity in the English regions.[20]

However, the role of elected devolved or regional governments in achieving economic growth is more contested. One stream of academic opinion is that the link between elected devolved government and improved economic performance 'remains unproven and underexplored' and that while democracy may be an intrinsically good thing 'its implications for economic development are more ambiguous than we may care to admit'.[21]

Other academics stress the importance of elected assemblies in delivering policies matched to the diversity of regional conditions and their role in providing strong political leadership and regional consensus building.[22] This stream of thought argues that if the assemblies, for example, can mobilise resources which were hitherto untapped and ill-organised, then they could be said to play a clear and positive role in regional economic renewal. This approach has resonance with the Government and others supportive of regional devolution, for example Peter Mandelson MP:

> We cannot achieve economic revitalisation in the North East without modernising the means of delivering our economic policies, and this means renewing the region's political institutions.[23]

The decision by the electorate of North East England on 4 November 2004 not to back an elected regional assembly would seem to put an end to the prospect of regional devolution in England for the foreseeable future.[24] However, it is still useful to reflect on some conclusions that can be drawn from these discussions.

It seems to be accepted, first, that *administrative* devolution to strong regional institutions is important for regional economic growth; the UK Government is right to recognise that regional economic policy cannot be run from the centre. Second, that *democratic* devolution is probably not a

[20] J. Tomaney, 'Reshaping the English Regions' in A. Trench (ed.) *The State of the Nations 2001: The second year of devolution in the United Kingdom* (Exeter: Imprint Academic, 2001).

[21] Harding *et al.*, 1996, p. 75; K. Morgan and G. Rees, 'Learning by Doing: devolution and the governance of economic development in Wales', in P. Chaney, T. Hall and A. Pithouse (eds.), *New Governance — New Democracy* (Cardiff: University of Wales Press, 2001).

[22] Office of the Deputy Prime Minister Select Committee, *Reducing Regional Disparities in Prosperity* (Session 2002–03, 9th Report, Volume 3: oral and written evidence) (London: The Stationery Office, 2003), Memorandum by Professor John Tomaney, Dr Andy Pike, Dr Paul Benneworth, Centre for Urban and Regional Development Studies, University of Newcastle-upon-Tyne.

[23] P. Mandelson, Keynote Address at 'The State of the English Regions Seminar', University of Newcastle-upon-Tyne, 21 June 2001.

[24] For a fuller discussion of this, see M. Sandford and P. Hetherington in Chapter 5 of this volume.

necessary precondition for any reduction in regional economic disparities. The case for devolution to elected institutions may be stronger on democratic and public service delivery grounds. Third, that the impetus for regional devolution is likely to have come from dissatisfaction with the way recent UK Governments have treated the lagging regions, politically as well as economically. While the impact of devolution in the UK upon economic performance will not be capable of being independently assessed for some years, it is quite clear that the record of Whitehall in reducing regional economic disparities is far from distinguished.

While important, the debate over whether or not there is an 'economic dividend' to devolution is not the only issue of economic governance of interest to those who follow territorial politics. For many years there have been vigorous debates within the academic and policy-making communities about the relative importance of industrial policy and regional policy. Industrial policy is traditionally concerned with *efficiency* and raising national output; while regional policy is traditionally about *equity*, as reducing disparities in prosperity across the UK can be regarded as crucially important for improving an individual's life chances. It is also argued that reducing regional economic disparities buttresses the UK's *solidarity* as a nation, since sharp disparities undermine the sense of citizenship and cohesion that create a national polity. In practice, the divide is never quite that simple, as regional policy considerations have often been rationalised in efficiency terms, while industrial policy has always been vulnerable to political decisions and special pleading from business and employment concerns.

However, regional policy has in the past been an essentially 'top-down' exercise, as it depends on notions of fairness, equity and social justice within a single national polity. This has led some to conclude that 'devolution itself seems to weaken the basis and motives for spatially redistributive regional policies, indeed in some respects to be an alternative to these as a strategy of political management'.[25] Furthermore, 'devolution inevitably involves a promotion of bottom-up forms of territorial competition'.[26] These concerns do not yet appear to be borne out, but it does pose new challenges for the centre to on the one hand facilitate 'bottom-up' development while at the same time taking a strategic approach to addressing unjust social and economic disparities, particularly those inequalities in outcomes that could undermine the Union.

Those who believe in the unity of the UK must articulate a role for the centre in tempering inter-regional disparities and achieving social and economic justice between the various nations and regions of the UK. Clearly

[25] I, Gordon, 'Industrial and Regional Policy: a London perspective', in J. Adams and P. Robinson (eds.) *Devolution in Practice* (London: IPPR, 2002), pp. 87–8.
[26] Gordon, 2002, p. 88.

this must be achieved in a way compatible with the principles of devolution, and is what Professor Kevin Morgan has eloquently described as:

> The biggest challenge in post-devolution Britain: how to strike a judicious balance between subsidiarity and solidarity or more specifically how to secure the holy grail of a devolved polity, namely equality-in-diversity.[27]

To the traditional tension between industrial and regional policy must be added a new tension, which arises from HM Treasury's productivity agenda. The Treasury has been the driving force behind the renaissance in regional policy in recent years, and their motivation has been explicitly to ensure the regions play their part in improving the UK's productivity record as measured against other nations, particularly France, Germany and the USA. However, it is not at all clear that this reflects the concerns of lagging regions themselves, as evidenced by the decision of the Welsh Assembly Government to prioritise employment over productivity. Nor is it clear that this analysis is fully shared by some other Whitehall Departments, particularly ODPM and DWP. While the Treasury's approach could best be described, to paraphrase former US President Kennedy, as 'ask not what your country can do for your region, but what your region can do for your country', the productivity agenda does seem to have been somewhat de-emphasised in government policy.

THE TERRITORIAL DIMENSION IN WHITEHALL

In a post-devolution world, the governance of economic development is a complicated matter, with a mix of reserved, devolved and concurrent powers varying between Whitehall, Scotland, Wales, Northern Ireland and London. There can even be significant variation in policy between the eight RDAs accountable to the Secretary of State for Trade and Industry.

Modern government does not work on the basis of watertight divisions of functions and competencies. This is a fact of life that has to be accepted by politicians and policy-makers, and is a real challenge that needs to be met to ensure that the public sector is effective in its interventions. Policy-makers will need to be clear about the objectives of policy, clear about which policy tools are most appropriate, clear about the spatial scale at which these policy tools should be designed and administered, and clear about how they will interact in practice 'on the ground'. It is the people who most rely on government action and strong public services that suffer most from such failures of coordination.

---

[27] K. Morgan, 'The English Question: Regional Perspectives on a Fractured Nation', *Regional Studies*, 36 (7), (2002).

Unfortunately, Whitehall is struggling to rise to these challenges, and departments are still unclear about when they operate on an English basis, when they are performing UK-wide functions and when they are performing a quasi-federal responsibility. Despite this confusion there is actually a little-known but straightforward guide to the geographical extent of Whitehall's spending programmes.

Every two years, as part of the UK Government's Spending Review process, HM Treasury publishes *A Statement of Funding Policy*. This document sets out some of the arrangements that apply in deciding the budgets of the devolved institutions, and details the extent to which the public sector services delivered by UK government departments correspond to services within the budgets of the devolved administrations. If we can use public expenditure as an indicator of whether or not a programme is devolved, at least as defined by the Departmental Expenditure Limits (DELs), it is relatively simple to determine whether a Whitehall departmental programme extends to England, England and Wales, Great Britain or the United Kingdom.

The term the Treasury use to describe this is 'comparability'. Officially defined, comparability is 'the extent to which services delivered by Departments of the United Kingdom Government correspond to the services within the assigned budgets of the devolved administrations'.[28] If a programme is devolved, the mechanisms that finance the devolved institutions provide monies that would allow the devolved institutions to fund a comparable programme (of course, the devolved institutions are free to use that money in any way they think fit). Therefore, if a programme is devolved there could be a comparable devolved programme, so the comparability percentage is 100 per cent. If the programme is not devolved, the comparability percentage is zero.

This is clearly not a perfect proxy. First, not all public policy issues involve public expenditure: trade rules or regulation, for example. Second, the Treasury regard a small number of exceptional sub-programmes as unique at the United Kingdom level, such as the Channel Tunnel Rail Link. Third, the DELs do not include some agency-type functions, such as some expenditure under the Common Agriculture Policy. However, the devolved administrations have almost no discretion in this field. Fourth, DELs do not include the revenue-raising sources under the control of the devolved administrations, namely Non-Domestic Rates revenue, Local Authority Self-Financed Expenditure and the proceeds of the 'tartan tax' in Scotland (if it is ever used).

---

[28] HM Treasury, 2004a.

Table 11.2: Comparability Percentages for 2004 Spending Review[29]

	Scotland	Wales	Northern Ireland
Forestry	100.0	100.0	100.0
Education & Skills	99.8	93.5	99.8
Office of the Deputy Prime Minister (not local government)	99.6	99.6	99.7
Health	99.5	99.5	99.5
Culture, Media and Sport	95.4	89.1	99.0
Local Government	65.7	100.0	49.3
Environment & Rural Affairs	85.2	80.4	85.2
Transport	71.3	63.8	94.7
Trade & Industry	18.6	18.6	27.6
Home Office	99.6	1.5	3.5
Work & Pensions	6.4	6.4	100.0
Legal Departments	96.1	0.0	1.3
Chancellor's Departments	0.9	0.9	4.0
Cabinet Office	2.0	2.0	18.7

Table 11.2 lists the Treasury's 'comparability percentages' for each Whitehall Department in the 2004 Spending Review. It should be noted that while there are numerous different comparability percentages at the departmental level, public expenditure at the programme level is either devolved or not, and the percentages are either 100 per cent or 0 per cent. It is also worth noting that the National Assembly for Wales has limited control over the non-domestic rating system, but in Scotland and Northern Ireland this falls within the DEL. This technicality means that the comparability percentages for local government in Scotland and Northern Ireland are misleading, and in fact the comparability percentage for Wales of 100 per cent should be taken as indicative for all three territories.

[29] Source: HM Treasury, *Funding the Scottish Parliament, National Assembly for Wales and Northern Ireland Assembly — A statement of funding policy, fourth edition* (London: HM Treasury, 2004a).

Table 11.3: Classification of Whitehall Departments

'Mostly English'	'Hybrid'	'Mostly UK'	International
Health Education and Skills Office of the Deputy Prime Minister	Culture, Media and Sport Environment, Food and Rural Affairs Home Office Legal Departments Transport	HM Treasury Work and Pensions Cabinet Office Trade and Industry	Defence Foreign Office International Development

Notes:

A 'mostly English' department has only very modest reserved powers.

A 'hybrid' department exercises functions on behalf of England (or England and Wales) that are carried out on a devolved basis in the territories, with Departments explicitly covering these functions in Cardiff, Edinburgh and Belfast but they also exercise significant reserved powers.

A 'mostly UK' Department carries out mostly reserved functions but with some English Functions too.

Table 11.3 then goes on to classify Whitehall Departments into rough territorial groupings. We can classify three Whitehall Departments as 'Mostly English' in the sense that they exercise only very modest reserved powers on behalf of the UK: Health, Education and Skills and the Office of the Deputy Prime Minister (which has responsibility for local government, planning and housing functions). There are five 'Hybrid' Departments that have counterparts in one or more of the devolved territories but do exercise some significant reserved powers. There are four 'Mostly UK' Departments that carry out mostly reserved functions, but also exercise some specifically 'English' functions too.[30] Finally we have three Departments that deal with international issues.

Whitehall, its Geographical Reach and Economic Development

Being clear about the exact geographical reach of Whitehall is not a dry issue of importance only to constitutional anoraks, as a lack of clarity could lead to tensions between the UK Government and the devolved administrations. Even despite regional economic disparities, England is the most prosperous

---

[30] We have decided to classify the DTI as a 'mostly UK' department because it has a low comparability score, four out of five of its main policy responsibilities are exercised at the UK level and many of the functions it exercises at the UK level do not involve large amounts of public expenditure.

part of the United Kingdom, and the Greater South-East of England is one of the most prosperous parts of Europe. Therefore, an England-only policy will in all likelihood be skewed towards affluence and affluent areas. On the other hand, a UK-wide policy might take a very different approach. An England-only policy might well have adverse consequences for the poorer nations of the United Kingdom, such as Wales and Northern Ireland.

Certainly the degree of public expenditure associated with economic development is not insignificant. In 2004–5 the planned level of central government's own expenditure on 'Enterprise and Economic Development' was £5.7 billion, while the equivalent sum for the DTI's role in 'Science and Technology' was £2.2 billion. Within the Department of Trade and Industry, a number of regional economic programmes are England-only initiatives, each of which will have some form of equivalent in the devolved territories. These include such programmes as the Regional Development Agencies, the Regional Innovation Fund, Regional Selective Assistance (now entitled 'Selective Finance for Investment in England'), the Higher Education Innovation Fund, and the Small Business Service. It also delivers some quite straightforward economic development programmes on behalf of the UK as a whole, including inward investment programmes, trade development programmes and the Enterprise Fund/Small Firms Loan Guarantee Scheme.

The large amount of money spent by the DTI on science policy is regarded as a UK-wide policy — this includes spending on the Research Councils, the Office of Science and Technology, the Cambridge MIT Institute and numerous other science programmes. Clearly some of the Research Council expenditure will be spent in devolved territories, but only as part of a UK-wide research strategy that will need to be ratified by Whitehall Ministers. By contrast, the spending on the Higher Education Funding Council for England by the Department for Education and Skills (DfES) is, as its name implies, for England only.

The DTI also has a number of important functions that do not entail significant amounts of public expenditure. While financial assistance to industry is a devolved matter, the designation of Assisted Areas is a reserved function. Where the boundaries for the Assisted Areas are drawn will have a significant influence on the relative ability of the different nations and regions of the UK to attract mobile investment projects, and is therefore a possible source of tension between the UK government and the devolved administrations. The issue of regulating mobile investment is discussed further below in the section on the role of the centre.

Tables 11.2 and 11.3 indicate that DWP is a UK department, which mostly carries out reserved functions. DWP's remit does not extend to Northern Ireland, and the Northern Ireland social security system is separate for historical reasons. However, the Northern Ireland Act 1998 provides for 'parity' in social security and it is extremely difficult, if not practically impossible, for Northern Ireland to depart from UK standards and the UK framework. Therefore, we have classified DWP as a 'Mostly UK' department. The few programmes which DWP runs that are comparable to programmes within Scotland and Wales mostly relate to programmes funded by the European Union through the European Social Fund and the European Regional Development Fund.

There is no direct equivalent to DWP in Northern Ireland — the main responsibilities are shared between the Department for Social Development and the Department for Education and Learning. As part of its 'Welfare Reform and Modernisation Programme' Northern Ireland policy converged with that in Great Britain, when Jobs and Benefits Offices were created as a mirror image to the British Jobcentre Plus network.

Interestingly, a highly significant change to the devolution settlement occurred following the introduction of the Child Tax Credit in Britain, which resulted in Northern Ireland Government Departments losing responsibility for child benefit. When the Child Tax Credit was introduced on the mainland, the UK Government decided that only one agency should be responsible for support for children and that this agency should be the Inland Revenue. However, the Inland Revenue is a UK-wide agency and is responsible to UK Government ministers. Prior to this reform central government had no responsibility for child benefit in Northern Ireland, but in November 2001 the Northern Ireland Assembly agreed to cede responsibility for child benefit to the Inland Revenue.[31] A reform introduced by Whitehall on the basis of administrative convenience, with little or no public debate on the merits of situating this policy responsibility in Whitehall or Stormont, significantly altered the devolution settlement, transferring a public policy responsibility which involved a large amount of public expenditure. It is an excellent example of the ad hoc manner in which the boundaries of devolution are drawn in the UK.

Tables 11.2 and 11.3 indicate that the DfES is an England-only department. However, higher education occupies a somewhat ambiguous position in relation to the devolved administrations. While the research councils responsible to the DTI are UK-wide bodies, there are four devolved Higher Education Funding Councils. However, each of the devolved Higher Education Funding Councils subscribes to a common UK-wide system for quality assessment and the ranking of disciplines and departments — the Research Assessment Exercise (RAE).[32] While the devolved funding councils can choose to allocate a different degree of funding to each RAE ranking — for

[31] Department for Work and Pensions, *Departmental Report 2003*, Cm 5921 (London: The Stationery Office, 2003).

[32] G. Rees, 'Devolution and the restructuring of post–16 education and training', in J. Adams and P. Robinson (eds.), *Devolution in Practice* (London: IPPR, 2002).

example, unlike the rest of the UK, Scotland does not allocate higher levels of funding for a department ranked 5* than one ranked 5 — the RAE exercise does imply that the devolved administrations are expected to 'match' resources provided to departments elsewhere in the UK with similar RAE rankings. In practice, they accommodate funding levels for higher education on assessments that are largely outside their control.

However, the link between basic research and economic growth is not straightforward, and perhaps of more importance for economic development is the learning and skills sector. Again, policy in this field is almost completely devolved. One exception is the Sector Skills Development Agency (SSDA). The SSDA and the Sector Skills Councils (SSCs) are UK-wide agencies charged with improving levels of qualifications in numerous industry or business sectors, for example for the automotive industry or the hospitality sector. SSCs are licensed by the DfES Secretary of State, but in consultation with the Lifelong Learning ministers of the devolved administrations.

The SSDA and the SSCs have the tricky task of pursuing this UK-wide agenda while simultaneously responding to the institutional and policy contexts of Scotland, Wales and Northern Ireland. Interestingly, the DfES agreed to fund the Sector Skills Development Agency in its entirety, and the devolved administrations do not contribute to the SSDA's core costs. However, many 'on the ground' programmes of the SSDA and the SSCs will be funded by local agencies: the Local Learning and Skills Councils in England, ELWa in Wales, the Local Enterprise Companies in Scotland and the Department for Employment and Learning in Northern Ireland. It should be noted that even prior to the creation of the SSDA, Northern Ireland already had a network of thirteen Sector Training Councils.

THE ROLE OF THE CENTRE: REGULATING THE NEW LANDSCAPE

A nation state with devolved polities is still a nation state (albeit in the case of the UK, one consisting of four stateless nations). Westminster and White-hall do retain a responsibility for all parts of the United Kingdom, and such 'quasi-federal' responsibilities must be exercised in a way that is compatible with the devolution settlement. Far from 'hollowing out' Whitehall, devolu-tion means that it must develop important new roles, not least to manage territorial rivalries and try to ensure some degree of territorial justice.

Regional economic policy is undergoing something of a renaissance at the moment, with a specific commitment in the Spending Review of 2004 to 'make sustainable improvements in the economic performance of all English regions and over the long term reduce the persistent gap in growth rates between the regions'.[33] HM Treasury, the DTI and ODPM jointly own this target. This PSA target can be criticised for a lack of ambition, as it simply aims to reduce the rate at which the South gets richer and the North gets poorer, rather than aiming to reverse regional disparities. Nevertheless, we do have an explicit UK Government commitment that focuses on regional economic disparities — at least in England.

Interestingly, the equivalent target in the 2000 Spending Review appeared to apply to the whole of the UK. dhis target was less ambitious in its scope, aiming only to 'improve the economic performance of all regions measured by the trend in growth of each region's GDP per capita'.[34] However, in this case the term 'regions' appears to apply to all 12 of the UK's nations and regions (Scotland, Wales, Northern Ireland, and the nine English regions). Of the three Departments that own the PSA 2004 target, both HM Treasury and the DTI exercise significant reserved powers on behalf of the UK. As a commitment to equity seems to be at the heart of the Government's approach, it is not clear what the basis is for the exclusion of the national territories.

The 2000 regional economic PSA target was jointly owned by the DTI and the Department for the Environment, Transport and the Regions (which subsequently became the Office of the Deputy Prime Minister). In a sign of the rising interest of HM Treasury in regional economic policy, it became a joint signatory to the PSA target during the 2002 Spending Review process, when the commitment to reduce 'the persistent gap in growth rates between the regions' was added.

There are two other areas that it is traditionally thought have the potential to ignite territorial rivalries: regulating financial assistance to industry, and distributing public expenditure.

The DTI is responsible for regulating financial assistance in industry in order to prevent zero-sum competition. Inward investors could seek to play off different devolved or regional agencies against each other with the objective of maximising financial subsidies. There is clearly an argument that policies designed to capture mobile investment are ineffective and wasteful, and that regional and local agencies should concentrate on nurturing the successful firms already present and promoting enterprise. Although this is a powerful argument, there will still be occasions when devolved, regional and local agencies pursue policies that may have a positive economic impact when viewed from the perspective of the territory, but which are zero-sum when viewed from a wider perspective. This situation is most likely to occur in the pursuit of mobile investment. There is therefore a powerful case for a

[33] HM Treasury, *2004 Spending Review: Public Service Agreements 2005–2008*, Cm 6238 (London: The Stationery Office, 2004b), p. 18.

[34] HM Treasury, *2000 Spending Review: Public Service Agreements July 2000*, Cm 4808 (London: The Stationery Office, 2000b).

strong framework at the UK (and European) level for regulating territorial competition.

It is worth noting that the devolution White Papers produced in the summer of 1997 specifically said that while financial assistance to industry would be devolved to the Scottish Parliament and the National Assembly for Wales, it would 'remain subject to common UK guidelines and consultation arrangements, to be set out in a published concordat'.[35] Subsequently, one of the supplementary agreements incorporated with the Memorandum of Understanding first produced in July 2000 concerned financial assistance to industry.[36] The political importance given to this form of regulation at this time may well have reflected the concerns of the then Secretary of State for Trade and Industry, Margaret Beckett.

At the beginning of 2005 levels of foreign direct investment were lower than in previous years, and are disproportionately concentrated in the Greater South-East of England. Therefore, there were few major inter-regional tensions concerning incentives to attract mobile investment. The importance of incentives such as Regional Selective Assistance in relation to inward investment is continually being re-appraised, and some recent research indicates that expenditure on government subsidies has little correlation to levels of inward investment. Partly as a result, there seems less of a desire to pursue such investment by devolved, regional and local decision-makers. Nevertheless, such tensions will not disappear entirely — for example, a National Audit Office report in 2003 referred to a grant being paid to retain an American-owned plant in the West Midlands in the face of enticements from Northern France *and* the National Assembly for Wales and the Welsh Development Agency.[37] The DTI has been criticised for failing to regulate this form of pointless zero-sum competition with sufficient urgency.[38]

The potential for conflicts of interest is written into the structure of the DTI. It is supposed to protect the interests of consumers and safeguard the rights of the workforce, yet it also sees itself as the voice of business in Whitehall and provides various forms of support for industry. At the same time it has difficulty in separating its 'English' responsibilities (for example, relating to innovation, business support or the English RDAs) from its 'UK' responsibilities (for example, relating to competition and trade policy,

---

[35] Welsh Office, *A Voice for Wales: The Government's proposals*, Cm 3718 (London: The Stationery Office, 1997) paragraph 2.24.

[36] *Memorandum of Understanding and Supplementary Agreements between the United Kingdom Government, Scottish Ministers, the Cabinet of the National Assembly for Wales and the Northern Ireland Executive Committee*, Cm 4444 (London: The Stationery Office, 1999).

[37] National Audit Office, 'The Department for Trade and Industry: regional grants in England', *Report by the Comptroller and Auditor General* (London: The Stationery Office, 2003).

[38] Adams, Robinson and Vigor, 2003.

consumer protection and employment relations).[39] There is a strong case for a fundamental rethink of the DTI's role and structure in the light of devolution and in the light of the potential conflicts of interest in its roles.[40]

The other issue that runs a particular risk of territorial rivalry concerns the distribution of public expenditure — the so-called Barnett debate. All advanced industrial countries consciously redistribute resources across regions and localities to achieve more equitable outcomes in terms of public spending. In some countries with federal constitutions the processes that achieve this are very formalised. As befits a country without a codified constitution, the UK's system of fiscal equalisation has evolved over time in response to particular political pressures and requirements. This does not, however, *necessarily* mean that it is any the less effective at achieving a desirable distribution of resources when compared with other countries.[41]

When the Treasury publishes its figures in April of each year, in the *Public Expenditure: Statistical Analysis* (PESA) publication, they are invariably the subject of much comment in the Scottish, Welsh and English regional newspapers. The Treasury figures indicate that the difference in public spending between the different nations of the United Kingdom have changed little since the devolution took place. In *theory*, the Barnett formula ought to produce a convergence in per capita spending; the so-called 'Barnett squeeze'. As the Barnett mechanisms distribute equal per capita increments to each country, smaller percentage spending increases are automatically delivered to those territories with the highest spending levels. As far as Scotland and Wales are concerned, the 'Barnett squeeze' is not yet in operation and concerns on this score would seem to be unfounded. Levels of spending in Northern Ireland, however, may be converging towards the UK average. This might be partly explained by lower security costs due to the peace process, expenditure on which falls to the Northern Ireland Office.

In the North East of England these Treasury figures have had a high profile for some years. *The Journal* newspaper has run a campaign against the Barnett formula and headlines such as 'On the wrong side of the £1 billion border' were commonplace.[42] However, the publication of the Treasury's public expenditure figure in April 2004 proved to be a shock to

[39] J. Adams and P. Robinson, 'Divergence and the Centre', in J. Adams and P. Robinson (eds.), *Devolution in Practice* (London: ippr, 2001).

[40] P. Robinson, 'Comment', in *New Economy*, 8 (3), (2001).

[41] See also D. Bell and A. Christie in Chapter 8 of this volume; D. Bell and A. Christie, 'Finance — The Barnett Formula: Nobody's Child?', in A. Trench (ed.), *The State of the Nations 2001: The second year of devolution in the United Kingdom* (Exeter : Imprint, 2001); and D. Heald , 'Beyond Barnett? Financing Devolution', in J. Adams and P. Robinson (eds.), *Devolution in Practice* (London: IPPR, 2001).

[42] *The Journal*, 'On the wrong side of the £1 billion border' (20 April 2002).

campaigners in the North.[43] First, the methodology for compiling the PESA was changed so that the figures published in PESA 2004 were not comparable to the numbers published in previous years — this new methodology had the effect of increasing what was thought to be the level of public expenditure in the North-East.[44] Second, the PESA figures indicate a year-on-year increase in the North-East's share of public expenditure. In short, not only did the North-East have higher levels of spending than was previously thought; the share was growing. Therefore, by the time the 2004 figures came out there was actually very little difference in the per capita spending in the North-East and Scotland and Wales. As a result, the Barnett formula had a much lower profile in northern England than in previous years.

A wide array of individuals and organisations has argued that the Barnett formula should be abolished: Ken Livingstone in London, the SNP in Scotland, Plaid Cymru in Wales and the North East Assembly in England. However, the 2004 PESA figures have taken the steam out of North-East complaints. And in any case, it was always very hard to see how reform of the Barnett formula could be achieved in the near future, given the reluctance of the UK Government to open up a politically- divisive issue when the achievable public expenditure savings are likely to be limited. In particular, one would assume that as a Scottish MP the current Chancellor of the Exchequer will be understandably concerned that levels of spending in Scotland are not disadvantaged. Nevertheless, this it is still the issue most likely to ignite divisive territorial rivalries in the UK.

The Role of the Treasury

However, the Treasury's post-devolution role has not been limited to public expenditure issues. One of the unexpected consequences of devolution has been the strengthening of the role of HM Treasury. Because of its responsibility for allocating public expenditure to the various territories of the United Kingdom, the Treasury was always going to be an important institution after devolution. This is, after all, perhaps the issue whose handling is most important for ensuring that the UK does not fall into divisive territorial rivalry.[45] However, the Treasury has developed an interesting post-devolution role in an unanticipated way.

It is the Treasury, not the DTI, which has been the driving force behind the current renaissance of debates over the 'North-South divide' and Labour's

---

[43] HM Treasury, *Public Expenditure Statistical Analyses 2004* (London: The Stationery Office, 2004c).

[44] I. McLean, *Identifying the Flow of Domestic and European Expenditure into the English Regions* (Oxford: Nuffield College, 2003).

[45] Morgan, 2002.

'New Regional Policy'.[46] The explicit commitment to narrow regional economic disparities — to 'reduce the persistent gap between regions' — is perhaps the closest the UK government has come to admitting a responsibility for promoting territorial justice.[47]

The Treasury has also been active in developing UK-wide policies in areas that are almost completely devolved to Scotland, Wales and Northern Ireland. For example, in 2003 the Treasury and ODPM commissioned Kate Barker to 'conduct a review of issues underlying the lack of supply and responsiveness of housing in the UK'.[48] The review was established with a clear UK remit, and numerous consultation meetings were held with the Scottish and Welsh devolved administrations, and with local authorities, quangos and NGO bodies based in Scotland and Wales. Similarly HM Treasury, DTI and DfES commissioned the Lambert Review in 2002 to explore the links between business and industry. Again this review had a UK wide remit.[49] Even the Wanless Review into health spending had a UK remit.[50] In this case, the Treasury commissioned Wanless and subsequently invited the participation of the devolved administrations — the idea of the four constituent parts of the UK jointly commissioning the work was apparently not considered.

While a number of these reviews were commissioned jointly with other Whitehall departments, it seems clear that the Treasury was the driving force behind these public policy reviews. There are a number of reasons that might explain the rise of the Treasury in these 'quasi-federal' policy matters. Clearly the intellectual appetite and political authority of the current Chancellor of the Exchequer, Gordon Brown, will partly explain the current dominance of the Treasury. The failure of other Whitehall departments to develop their post-devolution role compounds the matter. Certainly the DTI could have become the locus for UK-wide regional economic policy, but handed that role by default to HM Treasury. Similarly, the DWP could well have been the logical place to coordinate important elements of social policy post-devolution.

Nevertheless, the Treasury has been the most effective department in thinking through the implications of devolution and the concept of territorial justice in relation to the policy areas on which devolution has impacted.

[46] E. Balls and J. Healey, *Towards a New Regional Policy: Delivering growth and full employment* (London: The Smith Institute, 2000).

[47] HM Treasury and the Department for Trade and Industry, *Productivity in the UK: 3 — The regional dimension* (London: HM Treasury, 2001), p. 55.

[48] K. Barker, *Review of Housing Supply — Delivering Stability: Securing our future housing needs — final report* (London: The Stationery Office, 2004), p. 3.

[49] R. Lambert, *Lambert Review of Business-University Collaboration: Final report* (London: The Stationery Office, 2003).

[50] D. Wanless, *Securing Our Future Health: Taking a long-term view* (London: HM Treasury, 2002).

Interestingly, it now seems as if the Treasury was one of the more important Whitehall Departments in dealing with the elected government of Northern Ireland at Stormont, prior to the imposition of direct rule in the early 1970s.[51] However, more recently ODPM and DWP have been more pro-active than in the past, and have somewhat taken the initiative with their appreciation of the importance of the issue of employment in driving economic prosperity.

CONCLUSION

It is not inevitable that the poorer parts of the United Kingdom will automatically prefer devolution. In other European countries poor regions have often preferred centralisation, especially when this is accompanied by good lines of access to the central state.[52] For example, Italy is the European country with the most severe and persistent regional economic disparities, yet it is noticeable that the southern regions of Italy — the Mezzogiorno — have failed to generate autonomist movements. This is in large part because of their dependence on the centre.

Within the UK there has been a traditional unease on the left of British politics with the notion of devolution. The process does highlight the historic tensions between subsidiarity and solidarity and many have argued that what matters is class or group identity, not territory. Bevan famously said 'there is no Welsh problem' and thirty years later the future Labour leader Neil Kinnock led the charge against the Welsh devolution proposals in similar terms.[53] This is compounded by the fact that devolution and decentralisation are more popular when political parties are in opposition, and enthusiasm tends to wane when parties get closer to a return to power at the centre.

The rise of territorial politics from 1960 onwards seems to have been accompanied (possibly fuelled) by a growing lack of confidence in the ability of Whitehall to deal with territorial inequalities within the United Kingdom. Pressure for decentralisation and devolution has been greatest in the stateless nations and historical communities of Scotland, Wales and Northern Ireland. In the regions of England, on the other hand, regional identity is much weaker — yet some of the English regions are, and have persistently been, amongst the poorest areas in the United Kingdom.

There is a broad consensus that strong economic development institutions are necessary at the regional level in order to promote balanced economic growth. However, this does not mean that either regional elites or the general public believe that regional devolution will provide an economic dividend.

---

[51] J. Mitchell, *Understanding Stormont-London Relations*, (2004), available at: www.strath.ac.uk/Departments/Government/staff_pages/jm/pdf/understanding_stormont-london_relations.pdf

[52] M. Keating, *The New Regionalism in Western Europe — Territorial restructuring and political change* (Cheltenham: Edward Elgar, 1998).

[53] A. Bevan, HC Deb, 10 October 1944, col 2312; N. Kinnock, HC Deb, 3 February 1975, col 1031.

The 'North-South' regional economic divide did not have a significant impact on the North East Assembly referendum in November 2004. In contrast to Scotland, where support for devolution was closely linked to policy expectations, support in the North East (such as there was) seemed to be based on quite straightforward political grounds and antipathy to 'far-away London'. In conclusion, it seems that the demand for self-government is less likely to be caused by the level of regional economic disparities, and more likely to emerge if regional needs are perceived to be ignored or if regional policy demands are resisted. Such a situation could very easily arise in regional economic policy, but it could also arise in numerous other policy areas.

BIBLIOGRAPHY

Official Documents

Barker, K., *Review of Housing Supply — Delivering Stability: Securing our future housing needs — final report* (London: The Stationery Office, 2004).

Department for Trade and Industry, *Our Competitive Future: Building the knowledge driven economy* (London: The Stationery Office, 1998).

Department for Work and Pensions, *Departmental Report 2003*, Cm 5921 (London: The Stationery Office, 2003).

Department for Work and Pensions, *Five Year Strategy: Opportunity and security throughout life*, Cm 6447 (London: The Stationery Office, 2005).

HM Treasury, *Productivity in the UK: The evidence and the Government's approach* (London: HM Treasury, 2000a).

HM Treasury, *2000 Spending Review: Public Service Agreements July 2000*, Cm 4808 (London: The Stationery Office, 2000b).

HM Treasury, *2002 Spending Review: Public Service Agreements 2003–2006* Cm 5571 (London: The Stationery Office, 2002).

HM Treasury, *Funding the Scottish Parliament, National Assembly for Wales and Northern Ireland Assembly — A statement of funding policy, fourth edition* (London: HM Treasury, 2004a).

HM Treasury, *2004 Spending Review: Public Service Agreements 2005–2008*, Cm 6238 (London: The Stationery Office, 2004b).

HM Treasury, *Public Expenditure Statistical Analyses 2004* (London: The Stationery Office, 2004c).

HM Treasury and the Department for Trade and Industry, *Productivity in the UK: 3 — The regional dimension* (London: HM Treasury, 2001).

HM Treasury and Small Business Service, *Enterprise Britain: A modern approach to meeting the enterprise challenge* (London: HM Treasury, 2002).

House of Commons Office of the Deputy Prime Minister Select Committee, *Reducing Regional Disparities in Prosperity* (Session 2002–3, 9th Report, Volume 3: oral and written evidence) (London: The Stationery Office, 2003).

Lambert, R., *Lambert Review of Business–University Collaboration: Final report* (London: The Stationery Office, 2003).

Memorandum of Understanding and Supplementary Agreements Between the United Kingdom Government, Scottish Ministers, the Cabinet of the National Assembly for Wales and the Northern Ireland Executive Committee, Cm 4806 (London: The Stationery Office, 2000).

National Audit Office, 'The Department for Trade and Industry: regional grants in England', *Report by the Comptroller and Auditor General* (London: The Stationery Office, 2003).

National Statistics, *Regional Trends 38* (London: The Stationery Office, 2004).

Office of the Deputy Prime Minister, *Sustainable Communities: People, places and prosperity — a five year plan from the Office of the Deputy Prime Minister*, Cm 6425 (London: The Stationery Office, 2005).

Scottish Executive, *Framework for Economic Development in Scotland* (Edinburgh: Scottish Executive, 2000).

Scottish Office, *Scotland's Parliament*, Cm 3658 (London: The Stationery Office, 1997).

Wanless, D., *Securing Our Future Health: Taking a long-term view* (London: HM Treasury, 2002).

Welsh Assembly Government, *A Winning Wales* (Cardiff: National Assembly for Wales, 2002).

Welsh Office, *A Voice for Wales: The Government's proposals*, Cm 3718 (London: The Stationery Office, 1997).

Secondary Sources

Adams, J. and P. Robinson, 'Divergence and the Centre', in J. Adams and P. Robinson (eds.), *Devolution in Practice* (London: IPPR, 2001).

Adams, J., P. Robinson and A. Vigor, *A New Regional Policy for the UK*, (London: IPPR, 2003).

Balls, E., 'Britain's New Regional Policy: sustainable growth and full employment for Britain regions', in E. Balls and J. Healey (eds.) *Towards a New Regional Policy: Delivering growth and full employment* (London: The Smith Institute, 2000).

Balls, E. and J. Healey, *Towards a New Regional Policy: Delivering growth and full employment* (London: The Smith Institute, 2000).

Bell, D. and A. Christie, 'Finance — The Barnett Formula: Nobody's Child?', in A. Trench (ed.), *The State of the Nations 2001: The second year of devolution in the United Kingdom* (Exeter: Imprint Academic, 2001).

Gillespie, A. and P. Benneworth, 'Industrial and Regional Policy in a devolved United Kingdom', in J. Adams and P. Robinson (eds.), *Devolution in Practice* (London: IPPR, 2002).

Gordon, I., 'Industrial and Regional Policy: a London perspective', in J. Adams and P. Robinson (eds.) *Devolution in Practice* (London: IPPR, 2002).

Harding, A., R. Evans, M. Parkinson and P. Garside, *Regional Government in Britain: An economic solution?* (Bristol: The Policy Press, 1996).

Heald D., 'Beyond Barnett? Financing Devolution', in J. Adams and P. Robinson (eds.), *Devolution in Practice* (London: IPPR, 2001).

Keating, M., *The Government of Scotland: Public policy making after devolution* (Edinburgh: Edinburgh University Press, 2005).

Keating, M., 'Devolution and Public Policy in the United Kingdom: divergence or convergence?' in J. Adams and P. Robinson (eds.), *Devolution in Practice* (London: IPPR, 2002).

Keating, M., *The New Regionalism in Western Europe — Territorial restructuring and political change* (Cheltenham: Edward Elgar, 1998).

McLean, I., *Identifying the Flow of Domestic and European Expenditure into the English Regions* (Oxford: Nuffield College, 2003).

Mitchell, J., *Understanding Stormont-London Relations*, (2004), available at: www.strath.ac.uk/Departments/Government/staff_pages/jm/pdf/understanding_stormont-london_relations.pdf

Morgan, K., 'The English Question: Regional Perspectives on a Fractured Nation', *Regional Studies*, 36 (7), (2002).

Morgan, K. and G. Rees, 'Learning by Doing: devolution and the governance of economic development in Wales', in P. Chaney, T. Hall and A. Pithouse (eds.), *New Governance — New Democracy* (Cardiff: University of Wales Press, 2001).

Rees, G., 'Devolution and the restructuring of post–16 education and training', in J. Adams and P. Robinson (eds.), *Devolution in Practice* (London: IPPR, 2002).

Robinson, P., 'Comment', in *New Economy*, 8 (3), (2001).

Russell Barter, W., *Regional Government in England: A preliminary review of literature and research findings* (London: Department for the Environment, Transport and the Regions, 2000).

Surridge, P. and D. McCrone, 'The 1997 Scottish referendum vote', in B. Taylor and K. Thomson (eds.), *Scotland and Wales: Nations again?* (Cardiff: University of Wales Press, 1999).

Tomaney, J., 'Reshaping the English Regions' in A. Trench (ed.) *The State of the Nations 2001: The second year of devolution in the United Kingdom* (Exeter: Imprint Academic, 2001).

12

Conclusion: The Future of Devolution

Alan Trench

This book has sought to identify what the main currents of the future of devolution are likely to be, and to set out some of the pressures which will shape that future. This conclusion will briefly discuss the results of the 2005 UK general election (which occurred during the final editing of the book), seek to bring together the various themes and pressures discussed in earlier chapters, and set out a framework for thinking about how the UK's territorial politics are likely to develop over the next two decades. It will look at two sets of scenarios for the development of devolution, as a way of seeking to identify how the various pressures for change (and those resisting change) may operate. Any attempt to predict the future is a risky, even foolhardy undertaking, of course, but it is worth thinking about how that future will look (and over what sort of timescale) if we are to get a full sense of the forces at play.

THE 2005 UK ELECTION

The UK general election, held on 5 May 2005, may have had major implications for UK politics generally, but less so for devolution. This is partly because the results affected only Westminster and Whitehall, but more because they say relatively little about devolution, neither markedly developing or reversing trends already in force. Perhaps the most important implications are the obvious ones: that Labour remains in office across the UK, and will do until 2009 or 2010; that Tony Blair remains, but with his authority ebbing away in favour of Gordon Brown; and that a smaller Parliamentary majority, the Government's policy commitments and external political factors mean that life in Labour's third term is likely to get more difficult.

The overall result of the UK election is well known (see Figure 12.1). Labour experienced a significant decline in votes and a lesser decline in Westminster seats (losing 47 seats and 5.5 per cent of the vote), the Tories experienced an appreciable increase in seats (up 33) if a small increase in their share of the vote and the Liberal Democrats increased their number of seats by 10 and their share of the vote by 4.3 per cent (from 18.3 per cent to

Figure 12.1: May 2005 UK General Election Results

	Labour		Conservative		Lib Dem		SNP		Plaid Cymru		Others		Total	
	% Votes	Seats Won	% Votes	Seats Won	% Votes	Seats Won	% Votes	Seats Won	% Votes	Seats Won	% Votes	Seats Won	% Votes	Seats Won
England	35.4	286	35.7	193	22.9	47	0.0	0	0.0	0	5.9	2	100	528
Scotland	39.5	41	15.8	1	22.6	11	17.7	6	0.0	0	4.4	0	100	59
Wales	42.7	29	21.4	3	18.4	4	0.0	0	12.6	3	5.0	1	100	40
GB	**36.2**	**356**	**33.2**	**197**	**22.6**	**62**	**1.6**	**6**	**0.7**	**3**	**5.8**	**3**	**100**	**627**
UK	**35.2**	**356**	**32.3**	**197**	**22.0**	**62**	**1.5**	**6**	**0.6**	**3**	**8.2**	**21**	**100**	**645**

Notes: (1) These figures treat the Speaker, Michael Martin, as a Labour candidate.
(2) 645 seats were contested on 5 May. The 646th, Staffordshire South, was not, due to the death of a candidate

22.6). However, looked at from a territorial point of view, the picture is rather different.

For Wales, the election was treated as a serious setback for Plaid Cymru. The Party of Wales lost one of the seats it held in the previous Parliament (Simon Thomas's in Ceredigion) and failed to win Ynys Mon (Anglesey), contrary to widespread expectations and its own hopes. Both results were narrow (Labour's majority in Ynys Mon was 1242, and the Liberal Democrats' in Ceredigion only 211 votes), however. The erosion of Plaid Cymru's share of the vote was limited, declining from 14.3 per cent in 2001 to 12.6 per cent (a loss of 1.7 per cent). While plainly a disappointing performance, this was not so serious a setback as initial reaction may have suggested. The Liberal Democrats gained two more seats, with their share of the vote increasing by 5.6 per cent, and the Tories won three but with an increase in vote of only 0.4 per cent. Labour lost five seats (including the spectacular win of Peter Law as an independent in Blaenau Gwent) and 5.9 per cent of the vote. Thus the best view is that Labour did poorly from a high base and that Plaid Cymru failed to do well, but that the real winners were the Conservatives and Liberal Democrats. However, both parties' gains were nonetheless pretty limited, with the Tories benefiting from targeting of seats rather than an improved overall vote, and the Liberal Democrats suffering from the disproportionality of the first-past-the-post electoral system.

In Scotland, there was a similar pattern of clear Labour decline, with the benefits being distributed among the opposition parties. It is hard to track how that has translated into the number of Westminster seats, as new constituency boundaries were in use following the reduction in the number of Scottish seats from 72 to 59. Labour still won 39.5 per cent of the vote, down by 4.4 per cent, and won 41 seats – down by 15 from its former representation, but constituting 69 per cent of the Scottish seats compared with 77 per cent in the old Parliament. The Conservatives stood nearly pat in share of vote (up by 0.2 per cent) and won one seat. The Liberal Democrats increased their share of the vote by 6.2 per cent to 22.6 per cent and won 11 seats (1 more than in 2001). The most intriguing result was for the SNP, who gained an extra seat while their share of the vote declined to 17.7 per cent, from 20.1 per cent in 2001. Clearly the SNP successfully and aggressively targeted their vote in winnable seats at the expense of votes in unwinnable ones – effective in Westminster representation, but less so if their goal were to maintain their position as the main challengers to Labour, as they came third in the popular vote behind Labour and the Liberal Democrats.

And in England, although Labour retained a clear and substantial majority of seats (a lead of 93 over the Conservatives), it was narrowly behind the

Tories in the popular vote, trailing by 0.3 per cent. A more proportional system would increase the reliance of Labour on Scottish and Welsh votes, raising the West Lothian question once again.

One relatively minor consequence of the election was the re-emergence of the dual mandate in Great Britain – representatives elected to both Westminster and a devolved body. This was admittedly on a small scale; both of those with dual mandates following the election were from Wales, where David Davies (a Conservative Assembly Member) and a former Labour Party member (Peter Law, standing as an independent) were elected to Westminster. Given that Peter Law's election was largely a personal response to internal Labour party matters, and that many in the Welsh Conservatives have found the Assembly a secondary body, it is hard to read any broader lesson into these results – especially as there were no similar results from Scotland, where party discipline is perhaps stronger. If there is a lesson to be drawn, it is that the proliferation of elected assemblies and parliaments – the European Parliament as well as the Scottish Parliament and National Assembly for Wales – increases the number of possible political platforms for those aspiring to Westminster.[1]

Perhaps more important were some of the changes announced following the UK election. In the ministerial reshuffle immediately following it, Peter Hain was moved from the post of Leader of the Commons, and became Secretary of State for Northern Ireland with a mandate to seek to restart the peace process. At the same time he retained the post of Secretary of State for Wales. That may be politically convenient, but it will strain the amount of time he is able to spend on matters relating to Wales. As he also loses the chair of the Legislative Programme (LP) Cabinet committee, it may also make it harder for him to secure access to Westminster time for legislation sought by the Assembly. In a restructuring of Cabinet committees announced later in May, the overall number was reduced from 61 to 44, and among the casualties was the DP (Devolution Policy) committee, whose functions were absorbed into those of the main Constitutional Affairs (CA) committee, chaired by the Deputy Prime Minister. (DP committee had been chaired by Lord Falconer, Lord Chancellor and Secretary of State for Constitutional Affairs.) The Prime Minister chairs 15 of the new committees himself, and John Prescott only five, which suggests that the CA committee is one of the less important ones within the new system. This is a very clear

---

[1] Thus Ben Wallace, a former MSP, was elected for the Tories in Lancaster and Wyre. The same applies to the European Parliament, with serving MEP Robert Kilroy-Silk standing as a Westminster candidate for Erewash, and former MEPs Nick Clegg and Chris Huhne being elected for the Liberal Democrats for Sheffield Hallam and Eastleigh respectively. The dual mandate has of course never died in Northern Ireland, with elected politicians commonly sitting in two legislatures plus a local council. Until the 2004 European elections, Ian Paisley sat as an MP and MEP as well as in the Northern Ireland Assembly.

signal that, so far as the UK Government is concerned, devolution is largely accomplished, and requires only a limited commitment of ministerial time or Cabinet resources. However, the establishment of a Local and Regional Government Committee (LRG) at the same time suggests that regional government for England in some form remains on the Government's agenda.

The 2005 election therefore sets the scene for four or five years in which the UK Government will largely resist further change. It may have to respond to pressures from outside (including those discussed elsewhere in this book), but the election and the decisions taken immediately after it suggest little desire actively to lead the process.

THE TIMING OF THE NEXT STEPS

In the early days of devolution, a former senior civil servant addressing an academic conference said '2007 is the key. That is when the Scots will decide whether to renegotiate the Treaty of Union or tear it up'. For some time that has seemed an improbable deadline – one that may have made sense in the late 1990s, when 2007 seemed a long way off, but less credible since the turn of the century and especially since the 2003 elections in Scotland and Wales largely repeated the outcomes of 1999. The pressures for change appear to be building up rather more quickly than one might have thought, however. To understand how these pressures may play out, it is worth setting out some of the key dates that may affect devolution that will arise in the nearer future, and why they are significant:

Figure 12.2: Key Dates in Devolution, 2005-2015

Date	Event	Significance
May 2005	UK general election and cabinet reshuffle	
October 2005	3rd anniversary of last meeting of Joint Ministerial Committee	Demonstrates a continued reluctance to use formal machinery for intergovernmental relations
Spring 2006	UK Spending Review	Likely to constrain growth in public spending – and so to produce modest increases in funding for devolved administrations
2006 or 2007	Blair stands down as UK Prime Minister, to be succeeded by Gordon Brown	

May 2007	Elections to Scottish Parliament and National Assembly for Wales	Will take place in a different political context to 1999 or 2003 elections – with funding under pressure, and perhaps a less confident UK Labour Party
2007	Expiry of EU Objective 1 funding for West Wales & Valleys	
Spring 2008	UK Spending Review	
May 2009	UK General election?	
May 2011	Elections to Scottish Parliament and National Assembly for Wales	

This table deliberately omits events relating to the English regions or to Northern Ireland, where there are no clear dates at which key decisions will have to be made. What is apparent from this table is that, even within a short time, the climate in which the devolved institutions operate is likely to change. Two factors underlie this. One is the changed UK political environment. The 2005 UK general election showed (if proof were needed) that the Labour Party is far from invincible. With hindsight, it is possible to view the 2001 election as a less enthusiastic repeat of the 1997 one. That plainly does not apply to the significant erosions of the Labour vote in 2005. Similarly, the Scottish Parliament and National Assembly for Wales elections in 2003 can be viewed as echoing the 1999 results, with similar outcomes even if the parties' votes changed (with all the established parties performing less well in Scotland and Labour improving on its performance in Wales). Expectations that the electorate is willing to 'bear with' Labour and its coalition allies have to be qualified, however; the electorate's patience would appear to be finite, and to be approaching its limit. That in turn indicates that Labour is under pressure – pressure to identify what the electors in Scotland and Wales want, and pressure to produce tangible results that deliver those desires. To the extent that Labour has been able to rely on not being the Conservatives to win elections, it cannot do so for much longer.

The second factor at work here is finance. The benign climate for public spending that has lasted since the 1998 Comprehensive Spending Review is coming to an end. At best, public spending will grow much more slowly in the 2006 and 2008 Spending Reviews. For Labour at UK level (meaning in England, for practical purposes), the political implications of this may not be hugely serious. It has yet to draw the political benefit from the sustained growth and investment in public spending seen during the first years of the new century. Such benefit inevitably takes time to manifest itself. The UK Government is also counting on being able to extract significant extra value from existing levels of spending, by increasing productivity and reducing costs and overheads – witness the Gershon review of spending generally, and related work such as the Lyons review on the location of government offices. (Whether these reviews will in fact produce the expected gains remains to be seen, of course.)

The situation is rather different for the devolved administrations. All feel something of a financial squeeze, even generously-funded Scotland. Wales has a particular problem, with its low personal incomes, high levels of need (by any measure) and low allocation of spending through the Treasury's formula. Each territory is therefore keen to secure as much funding as possible – especially as their policy performance has been widely criticised in some areas (NHS waiting lists in Wales being a notable example). Moreover, their embrace of the 'reform' agenda, notably the Gershon efficiency programme, has been limited.[2] The effect will mean that only limited increases in public spending will have disproportionately severe effects on Scotland and Wales (and Northern Ireland too).

That has two political consequences: it puts the devolved administrations under political pressure, and it means that they have a declining incentive to embrace or support the UK Government. The effect will be particularly hard for under-funded Wales, especially as the EU's Objective 1 funding for West Wales and the Valleys comes to an end in 2007, and with it the Treasury's enhanced funding to the National Assembly. If the Treasury wishes to supplement the Assembly's funding to compensate for its harsh financial treatment, it will have to find another (and probably more open) rationale for it. However, the political ramifications of declining spending growth may be particularly severe in Scotland, assuming Gordon Brown is by this point the UK Prime Minister. He will face increasing demands from his political base to deliver extra funding but will have his hands tied in doing so. That will be a political gift to the Nationalists – vivid evidence of the inability of the UK system to deliver for Scotland, even when Scots are so prominent in the UK Government. Quite apart from any personal embarrassment, this creates the risk of electoral losses, perhaps even defeat, for Scottish Labour under a Brown premiership.

These two factors alone suggest that the devolved landscape of the UK may change rather sooner than has been widely expected. Even if Labour or

---

2 Although Gordon Brown included figures for savings from Scotland and Wales when he presented the Gershon Review figures to Parliament, these were only indicative. The Scottish Executive's own figures suggest it is seeking around 50 per cent of the level of savings that are being required of UK Government departments.

Labour-dominated administrations return to office in Scotland or Wales after 2007, they will owe little to the UK Government for their election, as this will have happened despite rather than because of the financial settlement in the 2006 Spending Review. This will highlight the extent to which their political and electoral interests and those of the UK Government are becoming different. Parties holding office in Scotland or Wales will need to show that they can 'deal with' the UK Government, either by securing good deals from it or by standing up to it. Labour administrations that cannot secure good deals and are precluded by party ties from standing up to London are at a severe disadvantage. The political choices for Scotland and Wales increasingly appear to be to elect Labour governments committed to the Union and hoping to play on ties to Westminster to deliver special deals or at least minimise confrontation, or nationalist governments prepared to take a more confrontational approach.

Looking to a broader timescale, the range of changes increases. One source is general divergence in policy; the longer devolved governments exist, the more scope there is for them to do things differently, and in doing things differently they increasingly build on their inheritance from a devolved administration rather than the UK Government. The overall level of change therefore cumulates. Thus policy is likely to form a pattern of increasingly divergent lines from a UK standard over time.[3]

There are other factors at work as well. Various chapters in this book have highlighted longer-term pressures for change. The EU is likely to prove to be a major source of this. Regardless of whether the EU Constitution comes into force, Charlie Jeffery shows in Chapter 9 that the impact of the EU on Scotland and Wales will be significant. Scott Greer shows how that is all the more the case as the EU expands into new areas of competence which are already devolved functions. That will not be changed by the decision to put ratification of the Constitution on hold (though it might if the EU is more generally affected by the political consequences of the Constitution's rejection). That development is likely to spell the definitive end of belief in the practicability of a 'Europe of the regions' and to divide sub-national and supra-national interests that had coincided to a notable degree in the late 1980s and early 1990s. It will also put increasing pressure on the means by which devolved governments make themselves heard in Brussels. Charlie Jeffery has emphasised the differences in approach between the UK Government (minimal formal rights but a high level of informal and bureaucratic liaison and involvement) with other decentralised EU member states such as Belgium and Germany (where the rights are formal, and in some cases supersede

---

[3] The extent to which policy programmes are inherited and therefore give only limited discretion to governments at any one point in time is clearly shown in R. Rose and P. L. Davies, *Inheritance in Public Policy: Change without choice in Britain* (New Haven: Yale University Press, 1994).

those of the national government to represent the member state). Whether informal access to the Council of Ministers will be adequate or effective may be doubtful if the devolved administrations are seen to threaten the UK Government, and all the more so if a Eurosceptic UK Government (possibly a Tory one after the 2009 or 2013 elections) holds office.

Another factor is the question of finance. The developing debate in Scotland about 'fiscal autonomy', an idea that is discussed across the political spectrum if seldom clearly defined, suggests a broader willingness to rethink the relationship between Scotland and the UK than has been apparent hitherto. This is all the clearer given the interest shown by Wendy Alexander from Holyrood's backbenches.[4] Alexander is likely to be a strong contender to replace Jack McConnell, if or when he chooses to stand down, suggesting that at least one current of debate within the Labour Party is to embrace a more markedly 'Scottish' position than it has so far. At the same time, some within the SNP such as Kenny MacAskill MSP also appear to be rethinking what 'independence' might mean, and to reconsider the need wholly to sever Scottish institutions from those of the UK in order to secure their goals.[5] However, institutional changes (whether in the devolved territories or in London) are likely to have only a limited impact. As John Curtice showed, there is solid public support across the UK for the present arrangements – not just from Scotland and Wales, but also in England for devolution for Scotland and Wales as well. Existing arrangements for Scotland are likely to be quite adequate. The key questions relate more to party politics – whether the SNP or Plaid Cymru comes to hold office, and how it acts when it does so, whether Labour in Scotland or Wales becomes more 'national' and less bound up with the UK party, and the ongoing significance of the UK Government in intergovernmental matters. If the UK Government were to seek to pull intergovernmental strings so as to direct what a Scottish government can do, it runs a serious risk of its intervention becoming a matter of public controversy. Either it needs to exercise the minimum of influence, or to work covertly and in such a way that the Scottish Executive has no incentive to publicise what happens.

Wales is a somewhat different story. The key issue for Wales (and increasingly in Wales) is the question of whether the Assembly has primary legislative powers or not. The shaky foundation of liaison between Westminster and Cardiff Bay has long been clear, and during the 2005 UK general

[4] For example, by contributing an introduction to a paper considering the appropriateness of 'fiscal federalism' in the Scottish context; R. MacDonald and P. Hallwood, *The Economic Case for Fiscal Federalism in Scotland* (Fraser of Allander Institute: Glasgow, 2004).

[5] K. MacAskill, *Building a Nation: Post devolution Nationalism in Scotland* (Edinburgh: Luath Press, 2004).

election campaign was made apparent to all by the First Minister and the Secretary of State for Wales when they wrote:

> A Tory victory would end the strong partnership we have been able to forge between Governments at Westminster and the Assembly. An Assembly Labour Government and a Tory UK Government at constant loggerheads, with megaphone diplomacy conducted through the media, would be a paradise for headline writers and journalists, but it would be a disaster for our schools, hospitals and hard-working communities.[6]

By assuming that different parties in office would necessarily be at 'constant loggerheads' so as to make devolution unworkable, the ministers have contradicted an argument often made by officials. What is said is that the present system is sustainable because it would be in the interests of no devolved government, whatever its party basis, to create difficulties with the UK Government. Devolved governments have too much to lose to upset the applecart. This argument has always smacked of being a rationalisation of the status quo, but it has some merit. But even if the ministers are right, that is because they have not taken the opportunity to establish both institutions and ways of working within those institutions that would minimise the risks of such behaviour. The lack of change in the formal structure of devolution since 1999 (despite massive informal change within the Assembly) indicates the importance of both arena and party in Welsh politics. As noted in the Introduction, Rhodri Morgan's decision not to press for primary powers was taken in the interest of Labour Party unity within Wales, rather than building on broader support for devolution within Wales and so seeking to secure Labour's long-term electoral base.

The only alternative to primary powers will be to accept the pre-eminent role of Westminster in Wales's affairs.[7] Given the existence of the National Assembly, that would involve developing explicit conventions allowing for some sort of 'co-governance' between Westminster and the National Assembly. Such conventions would have the effect of enabling the Assembly to get measures through Westminster even if they were contrary to the policy of the UK Government of the day. However that would imply a significant sacrifice of power by the UK Government, significantly limiting its power to govern once it had been elected to office and placing a heavy burden on its goodwill and commitment to devolution in this particular form. This would also raise serious concerns about the authority of Parliament and government's accountability to it if effectively the Assembly could submit bills to a

---

[6] P. Hain and R. Morgan, 'Our strategy for taking devolution to a new level', *Western Mail*, 9 April 2005.

[7] At the time of writing, a White Paper on devolution for Wales in response to the Richard Commission report was expected to be published in June 2005. It had not yet been published, however.

Parliament for sanction which Parliament could neither amend nor scrutinise in operation. And the credibility of such conventions would always be open to question, with a high likelihood that they would fail at exactly the time when political differences between London and Cardiff meant that they were most under strain and most needed. Relying on intergovernmental goodwill to shore up rickety institutional structures has been a long-standing refrain of the UK Government, but may not be a sustainable position for very long.

For the UK institutions, devolution has so far been a damp squib. There has been little change in how either Westminster or Whitehall work. As contributions by Alan Trench and by Guy Lodge, Meg Russell and Oonagh Gay to *Has Devolution Made a Difference?* made clear (and John Adams and Peter Robinson discuss in this volume), such change as there has been is minimal and incremental. Whitehall has avoided any sort of systematic restructuring of departments, all departments continue to deal with devolution matters (even if some have more devolution business than others), intergovernmental relations are largely conducted bilaterally, the West Lothian question has not been answered but is seldom asked, and Westminster scrutiny of legislation affecting devolved matters is very limited. Civil servants, ministers and Parliamentarians have all succeeding in avoiding having to deal with the broader implications of the constitutional changes of devolution. They have been helped in this by the fact that most of those involved have pragmatic concerns rather than a concern with constitutional principle, or constitutional matters at all. Coupled with this have been a lack of interest on the part of the broader public, and the relatively limited significance of Scotland or Wales from a central government point of view. (Taken together, they account for less than 15 per cent of the UK's population and 14.1 per cent of public spending.) In return, however, devolution has added significantly to the complexity of policy-making and administration, a burden falling most heavily on those officials (in both government and Parliament) who have to make this machinery work.

Is there any reason why this situation cannot continue? Despite the pressures and tensions created by devolution, the ability of central institutions to resist major change by making a variety of minor adaptations in response has been impressive to date. Further fundamental change would only be needed if there were some sort of systemic shock that overwhelmed the present arrangements, or if the complexity of the present system developed to such a degree that it collapsed under its own weight. It is hard to see either happening.

The only respect in which institutional change would be both realistic and simplifying from a UK point of view would concern Wales. One attraction of granting such increased powers to Wales is that, in effect, it enables the UK Government and Parliament to stop having to worry about Welsh issues.

Every bill at present is indeed a devolution bill – causing much discussion between governments (if little debate or scrutiny in Parliament), and complex drafting and implementation arrangements. There is a significant 'nuisance factor' to Welsh devolution, which would be avoided if greater autonomy were ceded to Wales. This is unlikely to have much of a political dimension, however, as the only votes in it are those of civil servants themselves.

STARING INTO THE CRYSTAL BALL:
TWO SCENARIOS FOR THE FUTURE OF DEVOLUTION

On this basis we can start to construct some sorts of scenarios about the development of devolution in Scotland and Wales, and across the UK. These scenarios are intended to demonstrate ways in which devolution might develop, and to set out some criteria by which we might judge how far devolution has gone and how it has affected the UK state come 2020 or thereabouts. They are emphatically *not* predictions (see Figure 12.3).

The 'mini' scenario can largely be regarded as a continuation of the status quo, assuming that the forces presently at work continue to dominate but that what appear to irresistible factors nonetheless play out. It therefore resembles to a striking degree the situation in 2005. By contrast, the 'maxi' scenario assumes that the pressures for change prove much harder to resist, and that the forces that have so far resisted it lose their present strength. Curiously, both of these closely resemble the mini and maxi scenarios set out in *Constitutional Futures* (see pp. 4–5 in the Introduction) – what has changed is more the timescale than the nature of the changes themselves.

How does Northern Ireland relate to these developments? That is hard to say. As Robin Wilson and Rick Wilford showed in Chapter 4, the politics of Northern Ireland are driven by a set of factors largely internal to the six counties, but also shaped by London and Dublin. Whatever happens in Scotland or Wales is unlikely to affect to any perceptible degree what happens in the province, and likewise developments in Northern Ireland are unlikely to affect Scotland or Wales. EU policy-making will affect Northern Ireland in the same way as Scotland or Wales, but this may raise less concern.

Figure 12.3: 'Mini' and 'Maxi' scenarios for devolution in 2020

	The 'Mini' scenario	The 'Maxi' scenario
Scotland	Labour dominated governments continue. Declining Labour strength means either an increasing broad coalition or Labour becomes increasingly 'Scottish' and less aligned to the UK party.	Government with substantial SNP involvement, seeking to maximise its autonomy if not actively delivering independence.
Wales	Labour has to accommodate itself to other parties – either by coalition government or by becoming increasingly 'Welsh'. Assembly Government legally and formally separate from the Assembly as legislative and deliberative body. Still no formal primary legislative powers; arguments about Westminster legislation frequent, despite flexibility in much legislation to achieve Welsh Assembly Government policies.	Plaid Cymru in government, and Labour restructures itself to emphasise its Welsh character. Extensive primary legislative powers, despite Labour's resistance.
UK institutions	Minimal change at Westminster; no mechanism to deal with West Lothian question. Departmental organisation remains confused, with England, GB and UK functions overlapping and no department with clear responsibility for managing relations with the devolved administrations.	Reformulation of UK Parliament's function, distinguishing between 'England' and 'Great Britain' and 'UK' legislation. Departmental organisation clarified. Overlaps in functions managed both within and between departments, and a department responsible for overall management of relations.

Finance	Barnett formula survives, despite increasing criticism and various supplementations and add-ons that distort its working and reduce its transparency.	Needs assessment carried out and used as basis for block grants to devolved administrations. Restructuring of finance to include different formula for annual uplift than comparable spending for England, and possibly handover of discretion and revenue from one or more tax bases to devolved administrations.
Policy development	UK policy treated as the norm, and devolved policy as a departure from it that is practically difficult and politically contentious. Concerns about 'postcode lotteries' when levels of benefit or services vary.	Policy variations common and increasing. Restructuring of finance makes this easier practically and attempts to clarify what attaches to UK social citizenship reduces political difficulties.
Intergovern-mental relations	Still predominantly bilateral, both between UK Government and one devolved administration, and between one UK department and its devolved counterparts. Constitutional issues a regular theme. Meetings of plenary JMC remain ad hoc and accompanied by air of crisis. Other ministerial meetings use a variety of settings. Transparency seriously lacking.	Significantly, if not predominantly, multilateral. Largely concerned with coordination of policy matters (both regarding 'devolved' functions, and the relationship between devolved functions and those reserved to the UK level. Plenary JMC meetings a regular and routine event. Other ministerial meetings use JMC framework and are well-publicised.

However, what happens in Northern Ireland may have an effect on the broader UK context – even if it is hard to say what that might be. Devolution will only be restored if there is some sort of deal between the Democratic Unionists and Sinn Féin. That presumes some sort of power sharing, possibly taking a more 'consociational' form than in the Belfast Agreement. It also presumes some greater step toward arms decommissioning than happened between 1998 and 2004. A DUP-dominated administration is likely to want to minimise ties with the Republic of Ireland, and to exercise devolved power within a clearly United Kingdom context, while seeking to avoid any UK Government action that compromises Northern Ireland's 'Britishness'. Sinn Féin can be expected to resist those features. The question is the extent to which the restoration of some form of devolved government impels or encourages the UK Government to conduct territorial management on a multilateral basis. Conducting both territorial finance and intergovernmental relations may be easier to manage in such a setting if they are conducted multilaterally – particularly because that will make it easier for the UK Government to be demonstrably even-handed in its approach. The restoration of devolution to Northern Ireland therefore gives a small nudge toward some parts of the 'maxi' scenario rather than the 'mini' one.

Similarly, the English regions are now out of the picture. As Mark Sandford and Peter Hetherington showed in Chapter 5, elected regional government for England is off the agenda for at least seven years and probably longer. Moreover, as Sandford and Hetherington show, halting moves toward elected regional government does not halt the use of regional structures for a wide range of administrative purposes. England will get regional government whether it votes for it or not – the question is whether that government is elected or not. The drive toward a more symmetric structure for the UK as a whole, including regional government for England, was a factor underlying many of the predictions in *Constitutional Futures*, but clearly is no longer driving constitutional change.

What is remarkable is that these pressures for change in Wales, and questions about Scotland, remain, regardless of what happens or does not in England or Northern Ireland. In other words, asymmetry is not a driver of change, and is not in itself a cause of instability or dynamism. Rather, the dynamic nature of devolution lies more in the political pressures it unleashes in a specific sphere or territory, not in creating pressure to have some sort of rough similarity across the UK. What happens in Wales and Scotland reflects politics in Wales and Scotland. That may affect, and be affected by, UK politics, but what is involved in each is unique to each territory, and only to a limited degree affects the UK state as a whole. Devolution is first and foremost concerned with bilateral issues, not multilateral ones.

This means that the value of the categories used in the introduction – public attitudes and society, parties, policy and institutions – are more useful analytically than as a guide to the future. We can identify dynamic forces affecting Scotland, Wales, Northern Ireland or England in these terms – but although developments in health policy in one territory, for example, may affect public opinion there, neither factor appears to have much apparent spillover into other parts of the UK. Health in Wales affects public opinion in Wales, but not public opinion in Scotland or (except, perhaps, as a bad example) health in England. So far there is little sign of developments in one part having large-scale effects on the whole. The pattern devolution creates is more a mosaic than a watercolour – little, distinct blocks of colour, which collectively add up to a larger picture but in which each block has little bearing on other blocks. Whether that changes, and how, will be an interesting question for the future.

Yet the largest element at work over the next 15 or 20 years consists of imponderables. How will the Labour Party behave when its instinctive responses, hitherto at work, cease to be viable? Will its behaviour change on a change of leader and Prime Minister? What will the outcome of the next general election in 2009 or 2010 be, and if an opposition party takes office how will it regard both the formal arrangements and the informal understandings that underpin devolution? While we can identify some of the key issues and decisions that lie in wait, and some of the questions of timing relating to those issues and decisions, we cannot know what the outcomes of the many and varied factors in play will be. The future will be interesting indeed.

Index

The **Constitution** Unit

Robert Hazell and
Richard Rawlings (ed.)
Devolution, Law Making and the Constitution

350 pp. £35.00/$69.90 1-84540-037-2 (cloth) 2005

This book represents the fruits of a four-year collaboration between top constitutional lawyers from Scotland, Wales and Northern Ireland and leading researchers in UCL's Constitution Unit. The book opens with detailed studies of law making in the period 1999–2004 in the Scottish Parliament and the Assemblies in Wales and Northern Ireland, and how they interact with Westminster. Later contributions look at aspects of legislative partnership in the light of the UK's strongly asymmetric devolutionary development, and also explain the unexpected impact of devolution on the courts. Individual chapters focus on various constitutional aspects of law making, examining the interplay of continuity and change in political, legal and administrative practice, and the competing pressures for convergence and divergence between the different parliaments and assemblies.

This book is essential reading for academics and students in law and in politics, and for anyone interested in the constitutional and legal aspects of UK devolution, not least the practitioners and policymakers in London, Edinburgh, Cardiff and Belfast.

Table of Contents

Alan Page, *A Parliament that is Different? Law Making in the Scottish Parliament;* **Barry Winetrobe**, *A Partnership of Parliaments? Scottish Law Making under the Sewel Convention at Westminster; and Holyrood;* **Richard Rawlings**, *Law Making in a Virtual Parliament: the Welsh Experience;* **Keith Patchett**, *Principle or Pragmatism? Legislating for Wales by Westminster and Whitehall;* **Gordon Anthony** and **John Morison**, *Here, There, and (Maybe) Here Again: The Story of Law Making for Post–1998 Northern Ireland;* **Alan Trench**, *Whitehall and the Process of Legislation after Devolution;* **Robert Hazell**, *Westminster as a 'Three-In-One' Legislature for the UK and its Devolved Territories;* **Graham Gee**, *Devolution and the Courts;* **Robert Hazell**, *Devolution as a Legislative Partnership.*

full details, sample chapter etc: **imprint-academic.com/hazell**

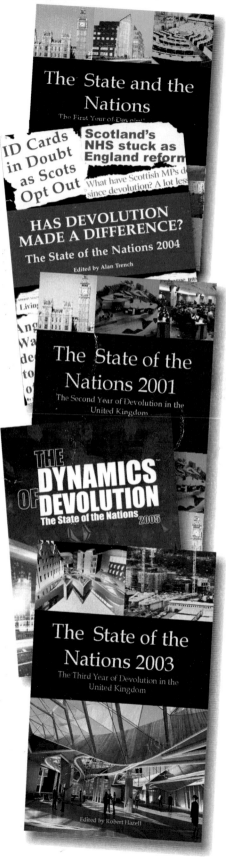